Counseling and Family Therapy with Latino Populations

THE FAMILY THERAPY AND COUNSELING SERIES

Consulting Editor

Jon Carlson, Psy.D., Ed.D.

Counseling and Family Therapy with Latino Populations

Strategies that Work

Edited by
Robert L. Smith and R. Esteban Montilla

Routledge
Taylor & Francis Group
New York London

Published in 2006 by
Routledge
Taylor & Francis Group
270 Madison Avenue
New York, NY 10016

Published in Great Britain by
Routledge
Taylor & Francis Group
2 Park Square
Milton Park, Abingdon
Oxon OX14 4RN

Printed in the United States of America on acid-free paper
10 9 8 7 6 5 4 3 2 1

International Standard Book Number-10: 0-415-95109-7 (Hardcover)
International Standard Book Number-13: 978-0-415-95109-8 (Hardcover)
Library of Congress Card Number 2005017221

Library of Congress Cataloging-in-Publication Data

Counseling and family therapy with Latino populations : strategies that work / Robert L. Smith, R. Esteban Montilla, editors.
    p. cm. -- (The family therapy and counseling series)
  Includes bibliographical references and index.
  ISBN 0-415-95109-7 (hardbound : alk. paper)
  1. Family psychotherapy. 2. Hispanic Americans--Mental health services. 3. Hispanic Americans--Counseling of. 4. Minorities--Mental health services. I. Smith, Robert L. (Robert Leonard), 1943- II. Montilla, R. Esteban. III. Series.

RC451.5.A2C685 2005
616.89'156'08968073--dc22   2005017221

Taylor & Francis Group
is the Academic Division of Informa plc.

Visit the Taylor & Francis Web site at
http://www.taylorandfrancis.com

and the Routledge Web site at
http://www.routledge-ny.com

Table of Contents

About the Editors

Robert L. Smith, Ph.D., is a professor and the department chair of counseling and educational psychology at Texas A&M University–Corpus Christi. He completed his doctoral degree at the University of Michigan. He is the author of over sixty referred articles and six textbooks. As coordinator of the doctoral program in counselor education he has mentored a large number of Latino graduates currently working in professorships across the country. He was the first president of the International Association of Marriage and Family Counselors and serves as its executive director. Dr. Smith is a lecturer and consultant to several programs in Latin America. He has been the recipient of numerous research, teaching, and service awards. In addition to current scholarly writings in family therapy and culture, he conducts research and writes in the areas of psychopharmacology, chemical dependency, and psychotherapy efficacy. He is a Fellow in the Prescribing Psychologist's Register (FPPR).

Rev. R. Esteban Montilla D. Min., BCPC, is the director of the graduate level program in Pastoral Care and Counseling for Driscoll Children's Hospital, Corpus Christi, and the Ecumenical Center for Religion and Health, San Antonio. He is also the president of the board of trustees of the Escuela de Postgrado en Teologia y Consejeria Profesional, located in Caracas, Venezuela. He is completing his Ph.D. in Counselor Education at Texas A&M University–Corpus Christi, where he is developing a Latino theory of human development. He is a diplomate of the College of Pastoral Supervision and Psychotherapy (CPSP) and a professional member of the American Counseling Association (ACA). He is the author of *Viviendo la Tercera Edad* (2005) and is considered one of the pioneers in establishing the counseling profession in Venezuela.

Contributors

Patricia Arredondo, Ph.D., is a professor, associate vice-president and senior advisor at Arizona State University, and leading researcher and author in the areas of multicultural counseling and diversity. She served as president of the American Counseling Association (2004–2005) and has significantly contributed to the development and implementation of the multicultural counseling competencies.

Rev. Homer A. Bain, Ph.D. (University of Chicago, 1971), is emeritus director of education of the Ecumenical Center for Religion and Health. He is a diplomate in the American Association of Pastoral Counselors (AAPC) and a recipient of their 2003 Outstanding Service Award, which recognized among other things, "his…training of Spanish-speaking pastoral caregivers…and his leadership in social action efforts in the state of Texas."

Nadia Bakir has extensive experience working with culturally diverse populations. She is multilingual, having lived and worked in wide-ranging cultural settings, including Canada, Mexico, Lebanon, Côte D'Ivoire, and the United States. She is a proficient researcher in the areas of psychology and family counseling, and continues to implement her understanding of culturally diverse populations in these domains.

Catherine Cueva, M.Ed., M.S., LPCI, has worked extensively with young, minority children in the education system for over ten years. She is currently conducting research on achievement motivation with elementary-age, Hispanic children.

Celia Jaes Falicov, Ph.D., is associate clinical professor of psychiatry at the University of California, San Diego. Dr. Falicov is the author of numerous publications on cultural perspectives in family therapy and on the process of change during family transitions. Her text, *Latino Families in Therapy*, set the standard for books about culture and therapy.

Norma S. Guerra, Ph.D., is an assistant professor at the University of Texas at San Antonio and adjunct instructor with the Ecumenical Center. She completed her doctoral degree at Texas A&M University — College Station. Her professional philosophy is founded on the value of equitable opportunity to all students. Her personal commitment is to be a servant leader. Dr. Guerra teaches both graduate and undergraduate students. In the classroom, she enjoys engaging students in scholarly inquiry toward unimagined aspirations.

Salvador Minuchin, M.D., is an international leader in family psychotherapy who is renowned for his work with structural family therapy. He has served as a research professor at the New York University Medical School. He is the author of numerous articles and texts including *Families & Family Therapy, Family Kaleidoscope*, and *Family Therapy Techniques*.

Richard J. Ricard, Ph.D., is a professor in the department of counseling and educational psychology at Texas A&M University–Corpus Christi. He completed his doctoral degree at Harvard University. His research interests lie primarily in the application of psychology to educational settings, including program evaluation and measures of achievement. He is chair of the research committee of the International Association of Marriage and Family Counselors.

Stephen Southern, Ed.D., is an associate professor in the department of counseling and educational psychology at Texas A&M University–Corpus Christi. Dr. Southern completed postdoctoral studies at Masters and Johnson Institute. In his 30 years of professional experience, he has integrated his roles as a clinician, supervisor, consultant, administrator, and educator. Dr. Southern is a member of the editorial board of the *Journal of Addictions and Offender Counseling*. He is the chair of the International Association of Marriage and Family Counselors Ethics Committee and associate editor of *The Family Journal*.

Mario Zumaya, M.D., graduated from the Medical School of the Universidad Nacional Autónoma de México, DF (UNAM), and completed his residence in psychiatry with the Instituto Nacional de Ciencias Médicas y Nutrición Salvador Zubirán (INCMNSZ). He has a master's degree in psychotherapy from UNAM and a specialty in counseling couples from the Asociación Mexicana de Psicoterapia de Pareja. He has served as professor of psychiatric medicine at the Universidad Autónoma de Guadalajara, the Universidad la Salle, and the Universidad Iberoamericana. He is the author of the book *La Infidelidad. Ese Visitante Frecuente*, and has written several chapters for textbooks on human sexuality and family counseling.

Series Editor's Foreword

> [Latinos emphasize] their personal desire to continue being distinct.
>
> **Octavio Paz, *The Labyrinth of Solitude***

Western ideas have been imposed upon much of the world through colonization and now globalization. In psychology, people were declared mentally healthy or mentally ill according to how well they accepted and adapted to these ideas. In recent years, the fields of counseling and psychology have understood their oppressive approaches and developed multicultural guidelines for practice. To implement these guidelines requires a complete overhaul of our existing standards of practice.

The United States is becoming a Latino nation. By the year 2125, there will be more Latino than non-Latino Whites in the United States (Ramos, 2005). This demographic revolution will change the landscape of the nation because Latinos are not one cultural group, but many. Their history, customs, language, and beliefs are diverse. How will counselors and psychologists be able to be effective?

Robert Smith, R. Esteban Montilla, and their collaborators have provided a new paradigm that will allow mental health workers to work in a sensitive and effective fashion within the Latino culture. This book clearly shows that being Latino means having an experience unlike that of any other group in the United States.

The chapters provide a general understanding of the culture and many specific strategies that can be used in working with families. I wish this book had been available 25 years ago as I have struggled to work with Latino clients and their families in my community in southern Wisconsin. I have only recently learned that I need to work with a bilingual co-therapist in order to be helpful. The co-therapist not only translates but also rephrases my words so that they are useful.

I urge that you read this book very carefully. The contributors are seasoned professionals and their suggestions can increase your ability to work in today's multicultural world. I leave you with a thought paraphrased from P. Parker:

> The first thing to do is to forget I am Latino. Second, you must never forget I am Latino.

Jon Carlson
Lake Geneva, Wisconsin

REFERENCE

Ramos, J. (2005) *The Latino wave: How Hispanics are transforming politics in America.* New York: Rayo/Harper Collins.

Preface

Part I of this text provides an overview of important factors to consider when working with Latino families. Chapter 1 by Smith, Bakir, and Montilla presents a scholarly review of what the literature indicates as salient factors in counseling and family therapy, particularly as related to Latino families. This chapter concludes by asking Hispanic families about their preferences in a counselor or family therapist. Chapter 2 by Montilla and Smith presents background and historical perspectives concerning Latinos and their cultures. A case is presented to emphasize important considerations when working with Latino families. The importance of the family, including extended family members within the Latino culture, is further emphasized in chapter 3 by Celia Jaes Falicov. Chapter 4, "The Family in Therapy" by Salvador Minuchin, concludes part I of this text. Minuchin uses several cases to emphasize how a variety of concepts, many of them associated with structural family therapy, can be applied universally.

Part II emphasizes counseling and family therapy strategies when working with Latino populations. Many of the chapters include cases for discussion purposes. In chapter 5 on strategies when working with Latino populations, Patricia Arredondo begins by discussing the multicultural competencies, emphasizing their importance when working with families. She follows this by presenting a case and discussing many of the essentials of family therapy when working with Latino families. In chapter 6, through a detailed case approach, Catherine Cueva provides the reader with an in-depth view of counseling Latino children. In chapter 7, Stephen Southern presents a scholarly review of counseling Latino adolescents. He identifies interventions for working with problem areas, including academic and vocational adjustment, delinquency and substance abuse, pregnancy and sexually transmitted diseases, and violence.

Mario Zumaya (chapter 8) looks at reasons for couple counseling from a constructivist viewpoint. He concludes with a case on how to work with Latino couples. In chapter 9, Norma Guerra presents a case in which group counseling may be appropriate, discussing models of group counseling and illustrating the LIBRE group approach. Homer A. Bain begins and concludes chapter 10 with a case focusing on parenting in Latino families. Many examples and suggestions are presented for Latino parenting. In chapter 11, Stephen Southern presents an integrative sex therapy model, including concepts from the Masters and Johnson Institute. He concludes this chapter with a sexual counseling case involving a Latino couple.

Part III completes this text by examining current and future issues and research needs. In chapter 12, Smith, Bakir, and Ricard discuss contemporary issues and research needs in regard to counseling and family therapy with Latino populations.

Robert L. Smith

PART I

An Overview

CHAPTER 1

Counseling and Therapy With Latino Families

ROBERT L. SMITH, NADIA BAKIR, AND R. ESTEBAN MONTILLA

INTRODUCTION

The Latino population has grown from 12 million in 1980 to 39.2 million or 13.5% of the total population (U.S. Census Bureau, 2003). Therefore, the need for competent multicultural counselors and family therapists is very much in evidence. An overview of what is known from current literature when counseling Latinos is included in this chapter. Within this chapter, several writers (Corey, 2005; Gladding, 2002; Ivey, D'Andrea, Ivey, & Simek-Morgan, 2002) suggest that certain counselor characteristics are necessary for effective counseling and therapy, including those professionals working with Latino families. The relevance of these characteristics when counseling Latino families is discussed. As a major theme in Part I of this text, the authors agree with D'Andrea and Daniels (2005), Fukuyama (1990), and McFadden (1999), who support the notion of a transcultural universality. This suggests that certain factors, conditions, and therapist characteristics are important regardless of culture. Preferred family therapist characteristics as identified by four Latino families conclude this chapter.

OVERVIEW: COUNSELING AND FAMILY THERAPY WITH LATINOS, INCLUDING THE VALUES OF MULTICULTURAL COMPETENCY

Multicultural competence, its relevance, and need for it in the field of mental health were recognized in the mid-1960s. However a definition of competence was not developed until Division 17 (Counseling Psychology) of the American Psychological Association (APA) put forth a catalytic position paper in 1981 (Atkinson, Bui, & Mori, 2001). Developed by the Education and Training Committee of Division 17, this manuscript identified 11 multicultural competencies considered essential for counselors working with ethnic/racial minority clients.

Multicultural counseling competencies have largely focused on three areas: (1) awareness of the counselor's worldview and how he or she is the product of cultural conditioning; (2) knowledge of the worldviews of culturally diverse clients; and (3) the skills required for working with a culturally diverse clientele (Corvin & Wiggins, 1989; D'Andrea, Daniels, & Heck, 1992; Holcomb-McCoy & Myers, 1999). Many assumed that counselors and family therapists who were competent in these three areas possessed the characteristics and strategies necessary for effectively working with culturally different clients (Holcomb-McCoy & Myers, 1999; Ponterotto, Rieger, Barrett, & Sparks, 1994; Sabnani, Ponterotto, & Borodovsky, 1991). Perhaps this assumption is simplistic because related research has yielded mixed results.

Underutilization of mental health services by Mexican Americans has been documented (Atkinson, Casas, & Abreu, 1992) despite this population's often being in more stress than European Americans. Atkinson et al. (1992) offered three explanations for this scenario:

- Mexican Americans prefer ethnically similar counselors, which the field currently lacks (García & Zea, 1997).
- Mainstream counseling and psychotherapy values held by White therapists conflict with those of many Mexican Americans.
- Mexican Americans believe counselors and family therapists will not provide them with culturally sensitive treatment.

These three issues are discussed next.

Preference for Ethnically Similar Counselors

Research on the effects of ethnic similarity between counselors and clients has produced mixed results. Many multicultural researchers and scholars believe that matching counselor–client characteristics by ethnicity is favorable (Malgady & Constantino, 1998; Ponce & Atkinson, 1989; Sanchez & Atkinson, 1983; Santiago-Rivera, Arredondo & Gallardo-Cooper, 2002). Yet, such counselor–client matching may prove to be difficult considering the diversity within the Latino population, including race, language preference, culture, and country of origin (Santiago-Rivera et al., 2002). Moreover, the proportion of Latino professionals in mental health agencies in the United States is less than the proportion of Latinos in the general population. A review of rosters of professional organizations conducted in 1971 revealed that less than 2% of APA members had Latino surnames (Ruiz, 1971). More recently, Hess and Street (1991) found that Hispanics were among the most underrepresented minorities in counselor education programs, consisting of 3.4% of the student body and 2.1% of the faculty. Although these figures are outdated, similar percentages are believed to exist today.

The current research on preference of counselor ethnicity and counselor–client match must be interpreted with caution because many use a form of stimulus that does not adequately resemble counselor–client interaction in the natural environment (Hess & Street, 1991). Generalization of these studies to the Latino population is limited for several reasons. First, studies that used college students as subjects are not reflective of the larger and more diverse Latino population, which may differ on a range of factors including age, education, language, life experience, and coping skills (Kouyoumdjian, Zamboanga, & Hansen, 2003). Second, studies tend to rely on methods such as self-report surveys and interviews and to use the findings to evaluate outcome variables.

It is concluded that some Latino clients prefer to work with a Latino counselor, but others may not. Empirical evidence has suggested not only that ethnic matching of client and counselor has no influence on clients' perceptions of counselor credibility, but also that it is not always preferred by ethnically diverse clients (Kouyoumdjian et al., 2003). Atkinson and Lowe (1995) found that many ethnoculturally diverse individuals report a preference for counselors with similar attitudes and values over those of a similar ethnicity. Sue's (1988) review of research findings on psychotherapeutic services revealed that treatment of ethnoculturally diverse clients from culturally similar and dissimilar therapists resulted in similar outcomes.

Inherent Values of Latinos Conflicting With Those of White Therapists

To explain the underutilization of mental health services by Latinos, Kouyoumdjian et al. (2003) believe that Latino perceptions of mental health providers play a role. Many Latinos may feel that non-Latino therapists may not sensitively attend to their psychosocial needs. In addition, Latinos who do seek therapy may receive treatment that does not adequately address their specific needs (Ibrahim & Arredondo, 1986). As illustrated by Casas, Pavelski, Furlong, and Zanglis (2001), an unfortunate truth in the field is that traditional training of mental health professionals has been based largely on European American, middle-class culture. When this framework is applied to clients who are not European American and/or are not of middle-class status, problems arise.

Despite a lack of clinical support on the efficacy of cross-cultural counseling and family therapy practice, it is nevertheless safe to believe that multiculturally sensitive practitioners need to provide services in a manner congruent with the culture of the client. Religion and spirituality, for example, are central issues in the lives of most Latinos (Falicov, 1998; Santiago-Rivera et al., 2002). Despite their importance, these issues are often ignored in psychology (Koss-Chioino & Vargas, 1999).

Social bonds in the Latino culture should never be minimized. Latinos generally value relationships over the individuation from parents and family that is characteristic of the dominant culture (Gloria & Rodriguez, 2000). Mainstream psychological theory emphasizes individuation from family as a healthy counseling goal; however, failing to acknowledge the particular importance of family may actually lead a Latino client towards resistance or even premature termination of therapy (Gloria & Rodriguez, 2000). Understanding the values and influences of family and spirituality for Latinos is therefore central to the effectiveness of therapy.

Failure to Provide Culturally Responsive Treatment

Demographic studies of Latinos have demonstrated a susceptibility to mental health problems. They are often younger, less educated, and more likely located within the lower end of the socioeconomic spectrum. Their minority status alone causes them to encounter different experiences from those of their White counterparts, which include factors such as intolerance, discrimination, and socioeconomic challenges (Gloria & Rodriguez, 2000). Atkinson and Lowe (1995) suggest that culturally responsive helpers should acknowledge a client's ethnicity and culture and recognize the way in which this client's problem fits into a context of culture. Atkinson et al. (1992) have shown that Mexican American clients rate culturally responsive helpers as more credible and culturally competent than unresponsive helpers, regardless of the clients' levels of acculturation.

The literature often clusters Latinos into a general category when in fact this population is heterogeneous in nature. Numerous differences exist among Latinos, including age, gender, social class, sexual orientation, country of origin, level of acculturation, and more. Even Latinos who have certain characteristics in common differ in their individual life experiences. Several studies have attempted to link Latinos to a particular counseling style (Kouyoumdjian et al., 2003; Santiago-Rivera et al., 2002) or inferred that a counselor of the same ethnicity would best suit this population (Malgady & Constantino, 1998; Ponce & Atkinson, 1989; Sanchez & Atkinson, 1983; Santiago-Rivera et al.). However, it is important to remember that preference of a therapeutic approach or ethnicity has yet to be linked solidly to counseling outcome (Ponce & Atkinson, 1989).

KNOWING ONESELF

The rapidly changing technological society and multicultural movement amplify the need to understand the role that values play as expressed by the therapist and client (Axelson, 1999). Most multicultural theorists emphasize the importance of counselors and family therapists possessing cultural self-awareness and adhere to the expression "counselor, know thyself" (Fuertes & Gretchen, 2001; Santiago-Rivera et al., 2002; Sue, Arredondo, & McDavis, 1992). Family therapists must recognize their worldviews, how they are affected by their cultural surroundings, and how this may influence their therapy with ethnic minorities. The therapist's self-awareness can be achieved through self-exploration efforts such as experiential and didactic exercises, supervision, consultation, and therapy (Constantine & Ladany, 2001).

Most family therapists have only the best intentions when working with ethnoculturally diverse clients. Nonetheless, as Falicov (1998) asserts, "By emphasizing adaptation to normative structures of their own ecological niches in the dominant culture, therapists may come to believe that they're favoring the objective truth rather than personal cultural biases, and may unwittingly commit a form of cultural imperialism."

The truth is that some therapists are prejudiced against certain ethnically diverse clients (Wampold, Casas, & Atkinson, 1981). Although many practitioners may not consciously feel this way, they should nevertheless examine the way in which their cultural beliefs may affect their perceptions of Latinos and the therapeutic practices that they implement with Latino clients (Kouyoumdjian et al., 2003). Therapists who hold negative views of their clients have been shown to impede counseling progress by unintentionally using words and displaying behaviors that reflect these negative perceptions (Kouyoumdjian et al.). Some professionals may subtly discriminate against clients who do not conform to expected cultural stereotypes (Falicov, 1998). Also, for mental health professionals who have not sufficiently learned their own culture, the differences encountered in another culture can quickly become frustrating rather than understandable differences to which they can adjust (Vace, DeVaney, & Wittmer, 1995).

Therapists have two cultures: one is personal and the other professional. The experiences in both cultures have an impact on the thoughts, feelings, and behaviors of the therapist (Axelson, 1999). The combination of one's cultural values and theoretical orientation creates a counseling worldview that influences how one observes, evaluates, defines, and approaches client issues (Sanchez, 2001). Recognition of this enables the helping professional to be authentic, which is a necessary trait for competent therapy (Vace et al., 1995).

The field of counseling psychology has generally encouraged counselors to focus on assisting clients in developing new insights and strategies to help them overcome disabling states of depression, insecurity, phobia, dysfunctional interpersonal styles, etc. (D'Andrea et al., 2001). Although such treatment strategies may be helpful in assisting individuals of some ethnic or racial groups, they may conflict with culturally constructed meanings of coping ingrained in the values and traditions of clients from other cultural backgrounds (D'Andrea, 2000). Because within-group diversity exists among Latinos, certain interventions may be more successful with some clients than with others.

THE IMPORTANCE OF DEVELOPING A WORKING RELATIONSHIP

No single counseling or therapy model has yet been proven to have successful outcomes with all Latinos. Falicov (1998), a Latina therapist, states that no Latino way of doing therapy exists. She refutes the notion that only Latinos can adequately counsel other Latinos. Falicov and numerous others report that core conditions, such as empathic listening and a strong therapeutic alliance, transcend cultural identity of counselor and client in delivering effective treatment. Santiago-Rivera et al. (2002) agree that "the Rogerian core elements of the therapeutic alliance are fundamental to counseling practice regardless of cultural differences."

Another strategy considered helpful in working with Latino families that has been reported by several theorists (Falicov, 1998; Santiago-Rivera et al., 2002; Smart & Smart, 1994) is the "humble expert" approach. This implies approaching the family with curiosity and taking a "not knowing" stance to prevent stereotyping. Though the therapist is presumed to be an expert in his or her field, this humble approach reflects a limitation in knowledge of the individual client's culture and a genuine respect for the client and the client's family (Santiago-Rivera et al.).

When first joining with client families (often discussed by Minuchin), it is important to allow an initial social phase, rather than diving directly into impersonal procedures such as referral sheets or appointment schedules (Falicov, 1998). Showing interest in the client through small gestures is helpful (e.g., welcoming the family in Spanish and offering a handshake in certain situations). Altarriba and Bauer (1998) maintain that mastering a few Spanish words, even when one is not proficient in the language, can have a powerful effect on the counselor–client relationship. Developing a trusting relationship is especially important in enabling clients to feel secure enough to honestly express their perceptions of the counseling process and the therapist, as well as any dissatisfaction that they may be experiencing with regard to the treatment process (Santiago-Rivera et al., 2002).

The willingness of ethnoculturally diverse clients to discuss culturally sensitive issues with counselors and family therapists depends largely on the strength of this working alliance. Whatever type of intervention used by the family therapist, he or she should invite feedback from family members. Encouraging family members to express positive and negative reactions to the therapist's opinions or techniques allows for a tone of honesty and equality in the therapeutic setting (Falicov, 1998).

EVERY CLIENT SHOULD BE SEEN AS UNIQUE

In a sense, the lack of research on multicultural counseling outcomes may be a blessing in disguise. Consider the possibility that teaching counselors and family therapists specific information about minority groups may actually lead to an increase in the probability of stereotyping their ethnoculturally diverse clients based on what they have been taught about particular groups (Sue & Zane, 1987). The assumption that more knowledge about the Latino culture will allow therapists to provide more effective interventions for Latino families does seem very logical.

However, therapists must be reminded to regard their clients as unique individuals, as opposed to relying solely on their knowledge of the Latino culture (Kouyoumdjian et al., 2003). Moreover, Sue (2001) warns that "victims of pervasive stereotyping may come to believe in them." Latino clients may differ in many ways, such as cultural background or symptom expression. To tailor a framework for working with each client, an assessment of the client's worldview and other important aspects, such as cultural and family values, can be useful (Altarriba & Bauer, 1998).

Multicultural counseling researchers and professionals stress the assessment of worldview as a necessary step in understanding the client's frame of reference at the beginning of the therapeutic process (Ibrahim, Roysircar-Sodowsky, & Ohnishi, 2001; Sue & Zane, 1987). Worldview will not only provide information on the subjective realities of counselor and client, but will also help expand the knowledge base of the professional in general (Ibrahim et al., 2001). A shared frame of reference between the therapist and client will also lead to enhanced effectiveness and successful engagement in therapy (Ibrahim et al.).

DEVELOPING A CULTURALLY CONCORDANT TREATMENT WITH LATINO FAMILIES

Without stereotyping Latino clients, certain cultural considerations should still be taken into account during assessment and treatment (Altarriba & Bauer, 1998). In an objective manner, a mental health practitioner may examine where a client stands in terms of factors such as family bonds, close interpersonal relationships, language, and acculturation (Altarriba & Bauer; Falicov, 1998; Santiago-Rivera et al., 2002).

As Gloria and Rodriguez (2000) point out, numerous scales and surveys are available to assess aspects of the Latino client's worldview. To name a few:

- Cultural Awareness and Ethnic Loyalty Survey
- Multigroup Ethnic Identity Measure
- Acculturation Rating Scale for Mexican Americans
- Social, Attitudinal, Familial, and Environmental (SAFE) Acculturation Stress Scale
- Perceived Social Support—Family and Friends

However, beginning a therapeutic relationship with a paper-and-pencil survey may not be conducive to establishing trust or a caring relationship with

Latino family members. Conversely, asking a client casual questions about his or her background, culture, family and social relationships, language preference, etc. is a relatively easy and more personal way for a therapist to assess the client's worldview in a short amount of time. Asking such questions can also help the therapist understand how certain beliefs and values may influence the client's problem (Altarriba & Bauer, 1998; Kouyoumdjian et al., 2003).

Therapists may want to discuss their designed interventions with the family. The intent is to ensure that family members are comfortable with the process and that therapeutic goals are appropriate for the situation (Altarriba & Bauer, 1998). Understanding what the family wishes to gain from the therapeutic experience is a major challenge in developing an effective treatment plan (Santiago-Rivera et al., 2002). If the family therapist takes proper measures toward establishing the core conditions central to the therapeutic alliance, family members should feel free to voice any feelings of discomfort with the designed treatment plan (Santiago-Rivera et al.). A client's expectations of counseling, as well as the particular issues that he or she wishes to address in session, merit special attention because successful cross-cultural counseling implies that both the counselor and the client set the clinical agenda (Tat Tsang, Bogo, & George, 2003).

COUNSELOR/FAMILY THERAPIST CHARACTERISTICS

Satir (1987) recognized that the personal characteristics of the therapist were an integral part of family therapy that should be used consciously for treatment purposes. It has been suggested (Bugental, 1987; Combs, Avila, & Purkey, 1971) that the basic tool that counselors and therapists have at their disposal is, in fact, themselves. Most of the early writings on preferred counselor and family therapist characteristics were identified by Anglo authors (Corey, 2005; Gladding, 2002; Peterson & Nisenholz, 1999; Carkhuff, 1977; Rogers, 1957). However, counselor/family therapist characteristics found in the literature have application when working with Latino families.

Important Counselor/Family Therapist Characteristics: Rogers

In his seminal article, "The Necessary and Sufficient Conditions of Therapeutic Personality Change," Rogers (1957) was the first to research, discuss, and publish what was believed to be essential helper traits that facilitate change with individuals and families. Therapist characteristics of congruence, positive regard, and empathy have been extensively researched and findings support Rogers' claim regarding their significance in therapy (Carkhuff & Alexik, 1967; Holder, Carkhuff, & Berenson, 1967; Piaget, Carkhuff, & Berenson, 1968; Strupp, 1980; Lambert & Bergin, 1994; Miller, Duncan, & Hubble, 2002).

The alliance or relationship (viewed as one of the necessary characteristics defined by Rogers) has more recently been recognized and acknowledged within family therapy. Increasing evidence suggests that the therapist's warmth, support, and general caring are necessary ingredients affecting the outcome in family therapy (Nichols & Schwartz, 2001). Research in family therapy (Bischoff & McBride, 1996; Christensen, Russell, Miller, & Peterson, 1998; Greenberg, James, & Conry, 1988; Sells, Smith, & Moon, 1996; Waldron, Turner, Barton, Alexander, & Cline, 1997) supports the importance of relationship skills, often similar to those identified by Rogers and others, in determining successful family therapy outcomes. Although most of the research has been conducted with Anglo populations, it is believed that these characteristics are also important when working with Latino families.

Only a limited number of qualitative studies have been completed examining these variables among Latino families. However, there is some agreement (D'Andrea & Arredondo, 1998; D'Andrea & Daniels, 2005; Fukuyama, 1990; McFadden, 1999) in a transcultural universality that applies to Latino families and includes Rogers' original characteristics of congruence, positive regard, and empathy.

Counselor/Family Therapist Characteristics: Peterson and Nisenholz

Peterson and Nisenholz (1999) state that a common theme affecting the outcome in counseling and family therapy is the bond between the therapist and the family. Their position is supported by Herman (1993), who indicates that the counselor's empathy and concern for the client determine the quality of the therapeutic bond. Interpersonal skills such as empathy, congruence, and positive regard (identified earlier) are again mentioned as necessary counselor/therapist characteristics. In addition, Peterson and Nisenholz reference Combs (1986), who states that the helper's belief system is significantly related to counseling outcome and whether individuals or families will pursue or stay in therapy. Five beliefs that Combs viewed as important include:

- being sensitive and empathic by recognizing the personal meaning of others
- seeing others in a positive light as dependable, able, and trustworthy
- having a positive belief in oneself, including a good self-concept
- having strong beliefs about purposes and priorities, including wanting to help others
- having a strong belief about appropriate methods for helping

The literature supports the importance of these concepts when working with Latino families. Also, O'Neill and Smith (personal communication, 2005) found these beliefs to be salient when interviewing Hispanic families.

The following characteristics are seen as important according to Peterson and Nisenholz (1999):

- cultural sensitivity—grasping the personal meanings of another, including meanings that are cultural in nature
- a self-actualization interest and desire—monitoring and evaluating one's self-actualization efforts in order to better help others pursue self-actualization
- a level of personal energy—having a high level of energy to listen actively, attend to others, and problem solve
- risk-taking ability—challenging and at times confronting
- a tolerance of ambiguity—tolerating uncertainty and realizing the importance of process
- capacity for intimacy—communicating acceptance, caring, and understanding

These six characteristics have not been researched to determine their importance for Latino families. However, it is believed that most of them are salient when working with Latino families.

Important Counselor/Family Therapist Characteristics: Gladding

Counselors and family therapists should possess personal qualities of maturity, empathy, and warmth. They should be altruistic in spirit and not easily upset or frustrated (Gladding, 2002). Gladding cites the following desired counselor characteristics as identified by Foster (1996) and Guy (1987):

- curiosity and inquisitiveness—having a natural interest in people
- ability to listen—finding listening stimulating
- comfort with conversation—enjoying verbal exchanges
- empathy and understanding—putting oneself in another's place
- emotional insightfulness—comfortably dealing with a wide range of feelings
- introspection—seeing or feeling from within
- capacity for self-denial—setting aside personal needs and attending to others
- tolerance of intimacy—sustaining emotional closeness
- comfort with power—accepting power with a certain degree of detachment
- ability to laugh—seeing the bittersweet in life events and the humor in them

Again, although not supported by research, it is believed that most of these characteristics are important to Latino families. Those considered most relevant include empathy, comfort with conversation, humor, ability to listen, and curiosity, particularly as related to the Latino culture. Stability, harmony, constancy, and purposefulness are additional desired qualities of counselors as stated by Gladding.

Counselor/Family Therapist Characteristics: Corey

Part of the process of becoming an effective counselor involves learning how to recognize diversity issues (Corey, 2005). Corey states that it is the counselor's ethical obligation to develop sensitivity to cultural differences. The authors and most professionals agree with this counselor/family therapist characteristic; it is a salient characteristic desired by most Latino family members seeking or participating in counseling or family therapy. A consistent statement made by Latino family members is "the counselor or family therapist must understand or, at the very least, respect our culture, our beliefs, values, our way of life" (O'Neill & Smith, personal communication, 2005).

Corey (2005) provides a list of what he believes to be important characteristics when selecting a counselor or family therapist:

- should have an identity—know who one is
- respect and appreciate oneself and others
- open to change—be flexible
- have a sense of humor—put events of life in perspective
- generally live in the present—be present with others in the "now"
- appreciate the influence of culture—be aware of how one's culture affects one and be sensitive to diversity

Although counselor and family therapist characteristics cited previously (Corey, 2005, Gladding, 2005, Peterson & Nisenholz, 1999) have been for the most part identified by Anglo writers, these authors and a number of other professionals (Arredondo et. al., 1996; D'Andrea et. al., 1992; Sue et. al., 1992) agree on their universal nature as applied to diverse cultures.

ASSESSING THE WORLDVIEW OF LATINO FAMILIES

What do Latino individuals and families look for when selecting a counselor or family therapist? What are their preferences and how strong are their beliefs about the desired characteristics of a counselor or family therapist whom they might consider? Unfortunately, very little data on this subject have been reported in the literature. Research of Latino mental health worker characteristics (Manoleas, Organista, Negron-Velasquez, & McCormick, 2000) emphasized the clinician's personal and professional roles. However, very little outside of conjecture is known about the Latino individual and his or her family's preference concerning characteristics such as gender of the therapist, age, language (importance of being bilingual), religion (spirituality), or family status (married, divorced, single).

At the same time, it should be emphasized that there will never be a common generalized Latino view of the characteristics that they do prefer in a counselor or family therapist. Multiple views and viewpoints are affected by numerous variables within the culture and subcultures, including degree of acculturation, socioeconomic status, education, family history, and geographic location. However, some qualitative data exist. In an attempt to find common themes of Latino preferences, O'Neill & Smith (2005) queried four Hispanic/Latino families representing low-income and upper middle-income levels.

Genograms (see Figure 1.1 through Figure 1.4) provide a brief picture of families interviewed and their socioeconomic status. Two members of each family were queried. Five specific questions were initially asked by the interviewer. These then led to open-ended responses and discussion that enhanced the interviews and provided more in-depth understanding of characteristics important to these families when they were selecting a counselor or family therapist.

As for age preference by Latino families, a common theme (see Table 1.1) revealed a preference for middle-aged to older therapists. Age is associated with wisdom in many cultures, including the Latino culture. It is believed that younger therapists (under 40) can work with Latino families, but it may take longer to earn their trust and confidence and to overcome an initial reaction of "how can someone so young actually be wise enough to help our family." It is suggested that therapists of all ages should knowingly listen, understand their own cultural background, be aware and sensitive to the culture of their clients, and possess excellent joining skills. Some indications are that Latino families might be more traditional and prefer an elderly male with whom to talk and discuss family problems. This characteristic might fit the image of a priest, someone to whom Latino families have previously talked about family difficulties.

The therapist's gender was not as important to most families interviewed. It is believed that acculturation and changing female roles will affect therapist gender preference among Latino families, with a trend toward selecting female therapists. Marital status produced findings similar to those of age preference. Hispanic parents preferred someone who was married at some time in his or her life. This preference is understandable for individuals seeking family therapy. However, as seen in Table 1.1, younger members of these families, a son and a daughter, viewed marital status as less important. Perhaps the views of younger Latino family members interviewed will shift as they marry and begin to raise children.

All families and family members in this study preferred a bilingual therapist. It was important that the therapist understand the family's worldview from their cultural perspective, which in large part meant understanding their language. Understanding their worldview for many Latino families means in large part understanding and speaking Spanish. For family therapists who are not bilingual (Spanish/English), it is important to learn Spanish when working with a large number of Latino families. The literature has indicated that even a few words and phrases can help to develop a trusting relationship with Spanish-speaking families.

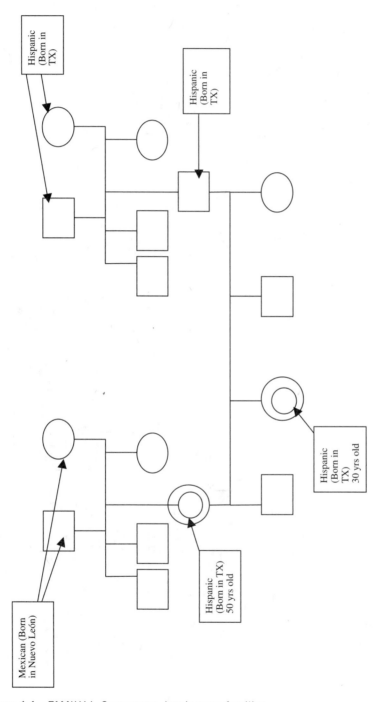

Figure 1.1 FAMILY I: Genograms, low-income families.

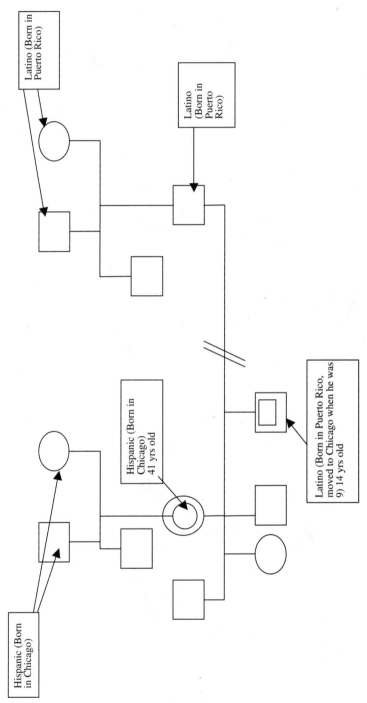

Figure 1.2 FAMILY II: Genogram: low-income family.

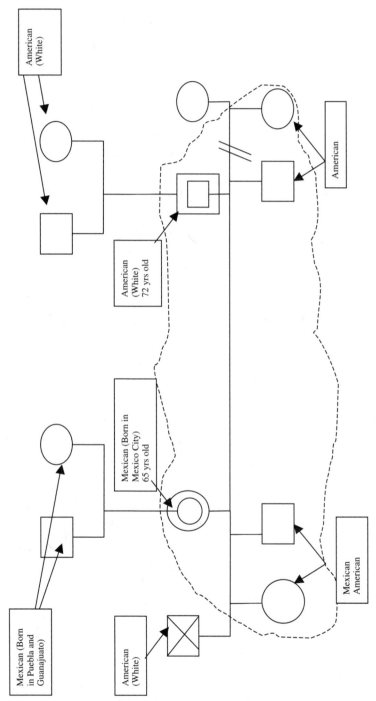

Figure 1.3 FAMILY III: Upper middle class.

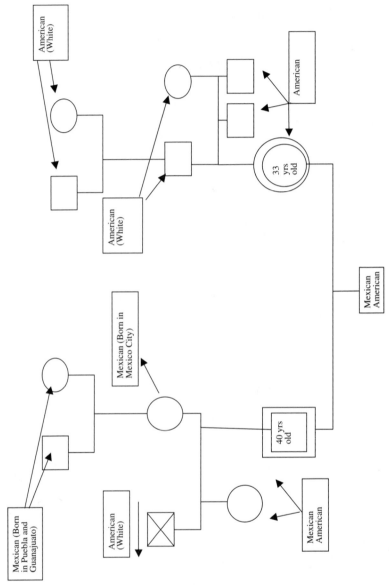

Figure 1.4   FAMILY IV: Upper middle class.

Religion has played a major role in most societies and is of great significance for Latino families. Whether defined as Catholic, religious, or spiritual,
the concept of a belief or religion was important to all families interviewed
(O'Neill & Smith, 2005). Latino family members agreed that it would be
difficult for a family therapist to understand them or their worldview if he or
she did not have a set of beliefs that were spiritual or religious in nature. The

Table 1.1 Preferences in a Family Therapist by Hispanic Family Members

Characteristic	Spanish	Family 1		Family 2		Family 3		Family 4	
		Mother (Hispanic with Mexican parents)	Daughter (Hispanic)	Mother (Hispanic with Hispanic parents)	Son Latino (born/raised in Puerto Rico)	Husband (American)	Wife (Latina; Mexican)	Husband (Latino; Mexican)	Wife (American)
1. Age	Edad	40+	30–40	45+	Does not care	40+	40+	40+	40+
2. Sex	Sexo	Not important	Woman	Not important	Not important	Woman	Man	Not important	Not important
3. Civil status	Estado civil	Married	Not important	Married or divorced	Not important	Not important	Married or divorced	Married	Married or stable
4. Language	Idioma	Bilingual	Bilingual	Bilingual	Bilingual	Bilingual	Bilingual	Bilingual	Bilingual
5. Religion	Religion	Catholic	Catholic	Religious	Does not care	Spiritual	Spiritual	Spiritual	Spiritual
6. Strong family values	Valores familiares sólidos	XXXX	XXXX	XXXX		XXXX	XXXX	XXXX	XXXX
7. Respectful	Respetuoso	XXXX	XXXX	XXXX	XXXX	XXXX	XXXX	XXXX	
8. Authenticity	Auténtico	XXXX	XXXX	XXXX		XXXX	XXXX	XXXX	XXXX
9. Understanding of culture	Comprensión de la cultura	XXXX	XXXX			XXXX	XXXX	XXXX	XXXX
10. Trustworthy	Digno de confianza	XXXX	XXXX	XXXX	XXXX	XXXX	XXXX	XXXX	XXXX
11. Nice	Agradable	XXXX	XXXX	XXXX	XXXX				
12. Caring	Se interesa en otros	XXXX		XXXX		XXXX	XXXX	XXXX	
13. Honest	Honesto	XXXX				XXXX	XXXX	XXXX	XXXX
14. Open minded	Mentalidad abierta	XXXX				XXXX	XXXX	XXXX	XXXX

particular religion seemed to be less important, giving way to a broader sense of spirituality.

A number of other desirable characteristics for a counselor/family therapist were mentioned during open-ended interviews. Common preferences discovered were

- Strong family values—The therapist should have strong family values.
- Authenticity—The therapist needs to be genuine, real, and have no facades.
- Trustworthy—Family members need to trust the therapist.
- Honest—Family members need to feel that the therapist is honest and sincere.
- Respect—The family and individuals need to be respected.
- Well educated—The therapist should be an expert in his field.
- Nationality—The therapist should be American or Mexican.
- Respects other cultures—This is important with all family members.
- Respects the family structure—This is important with older family members.
- Friendly—The therapist likes people and Hispanics.
- Attitude—The therapist has a positive attitude and smiles.
- Not prejudiced or biased—The therapist has no cultural or racial prejudices.
- Nice and caring—The therapist is able to express care and is a nice human being.

Family members provided more detailed definitions concerning several themes:

- nice—someone that makes eye contact, greets you with a smile, has a nice attitude, loves life, laughs, treats all members of the family with respect and affection
- respects family structure—understands the role of the elderly in the family, the role of the father; does not make comments that make them look inferior to the other members of the family.
- spiritual—has a belief in the possibility of experiences and dimensions that may go beyond or outside scientific proof and day-to-day experiences; a person who is aware that there is no dichotomy between science and spirit; spiritual not as a missionary but as a sensitive, humble person who would listen with his heart and soul (not only with intellect)
- open minded—has knowledge of other cultures, of mixed marriages (families), understands different lifestyles and values

Generalizations from the preceding should not be made to Latino families across the world or even within the United States. However, it is believed that therapists can learn much from Hispanic/Latino families by asking them about their wants, needs, beliefs, values, hopes, and preferences. It is hoped that by asking salient questions of Latino families, family therapists can better understand their diverse needs and cultures.

CONCLUSIONS

This chapter discusses the literature about Latinos and their interests and preferences as related to counseling and family therapy. Multicultural competencies were briefly reviewed because they are a significant force when working with diverse cultures. With a dramatic increase in the Latino population and with the possibility of more Latino families seeking assistance from helping professionals, it becomes the ethical responsibility of counselors and family therapists to expand their level of awareness and competency when working with Latinos.

Helping professionals should possess personal characteristics deemed important by their clients. A number of counselor and family therapist characteristics have been termed "essential" (Rogers, 1957). A wide range of other counselor and family therapist characteristics have been identified and described in the literature (Corey, 2005; Gladding, 2005; Peterson & Nisenholz, 1999). Despite a lack of research supporting the salience of these characteristics across cultures, it is believed that a majority of these personal characteristics do transcend culture and are meaningful for Latino families. This concept, a belief in a transcultural universality, is viewed as having merit by the authors and seems to be accepted by many in the field today.

Finally, if someone wants to know what kind of counselor or family therapist Latino family members prefer, it is suggested that the individual ask them. This is exactly what the authors did, with interesting results reported at the conclusion of this chapter. Chapters 2 and 3 take a more personal in-depth look at the history of Latinos and their cultures with an emphasis on the important role played by the family. Chapter 4 concludes part I of this text as Minuchin discusses the application of structural family therapy with several couple and family cases.

REFERENCES

Altarriba, J., & Bauer, L. M. (1998). Counseling the Hispanic client: Cuban Americans, Mexican Americans, and Puerto Ricans. *Journal of Counseling and Development, 76,* 389–396.

Arredondo, P., Toporek, R., Brown, S. P., Jones, J., Locke, D. C., Sanchez, J., & Stadler, H. (1996). Operationalization of the multicultural counseling competencies. *Journal of Multicultural Counseling and Development, 24,* 189–194.

Atkinson, D. R., Bui, U., & Mori, S. (2001). Multiculturally sensitive empirically supported treatments. An oxymoron? In J. Ponterotto, J. M. Casas, L. Suzuki, & C. Alexander (Eds.), *Handbook of multicultural counseling* (2nd ed.) (542–574). Thousand Oaks, CA: Sage.

Atkinson, D. R., Casas, A., & Abreu, J. (1992). Mexican-American acculturation, counselor ethnicity and cultural sensitivity, and perceived counselor competence. *Journal of Counseling Psychology, 39*, 515–520.

Atkinson, D. R., & Lowe, S. M. (1995). The role of ethnicity, cultural knowledge, and conventional techniques in counseling and psychotherapy. In J. G. Ponterotto, J. M. Casas, L. A. Suzuki, & C. M. Alexander (Eds.), *Handbook of multicultural counseling* (387–414). Thousand Oaks, CA: Sage.

Axelson, J. A. (1999). Counseling and development in a multicultural society. (3rd ed.). Pacific Grove, CA: Brooks/Cole.

Bischoff, R., & McBride, A. (1996). Client perceptions of couples and family therapy. *American Journal of Family Therapy, 24*, 117–128.

Bugental, J. (1987). *The art of the psychotherapist.* New York: Norton.

Carkhuff, R. (1977) *How to help yourself: the art of program development.* Amherst, MA: Human Resource Development Press, c. 1974, 1977 printing.

Carkhuff, R. & Alexik, M. (1967). Effects of client depth of self-exploration upon high- and low-functioning counselors, *Journal of Counseling Psychology, 14*(4), 350–355.

Casas, J. M., Pavelski, R., Furlong, M. J., & Zanglis, I. (2001). Advent of systems of care: practice and research perspectives and policy implications. In J. Ponterotto, J. M. Casas, L. Suzuki & C. Alexander (Eds.), *Handbook of multicultural counseling* (2nd ed.) (189–221). Thousand Oaks, CA: Sage.

Christensen, L., Russell, C., Miller, R., & Peterson, C. (1998). The process of change in couples therapy: A qualitative investigation. *Journal of Marital and Family Therapy, 24*, 177–188.

Combs, A., Avila, D., & Purkey, W. (1971). Helping relationships: Basic concepts for the helping professionals. Boston: Allyn & Bacon.

Constantine, M. G., & Ladany, N. (2001). New visions for defining and assessing multicultural counseling competence. In J. Ponterotto, J. M. Casas, L. Suzuki & C. Alexander (Eds.), *Handbook of multicultural counseling* (2nd ed., pp. 482–498). Thousand Oaks, CA: Sage.

Corey, G. (2005). *Theory and practice of counseling and psychotherapy.* (7th ed.). Belmont, CA: Brooks/Cole–Thomson Learning.

Corvin, S. A., & Wiggins, F. (1989). An antiracism training model for White professionals. *Journal of Multicultural Counseling and Development, 17*, 105–114.

D'Andrea, M. (2000). Postmodernism, constructivism, and multiculturalism: Three forces reshaping and expanding our thoughts about counseling. *Journal of Mental Health Counseling, 22*, 1–16.

D'Andrea, M., & Arredondo, P. (1998). Defining the term "multicultural counseling." *Counseling Today,* April, 40.

D'Andrea, M., & Daniels, J. (2005). *Multicultural counseling: Empowerment strategies for a diverse society.* Pacific Grove, CA: Brooks/Cole.

D'Andrea, M., Daniels, J., Arredondo, P., Ivey, M. B., Ivey, A. E, Locke, D. C., O'Bryant, B., Parham, T. A., Sue, D. W. (2001). Fostering organizational changes to realize the revolutionary potential of the multicultural movement. In J. Ponterotto, J. M. Casas, L. Suzuki & C. Alexander (Eds.), *Handbook of multicultural counseling* (2nd ed., 222–253). Thousand Oaks, CA: Sage.

D'Andrea, M., Daniels, S., & Heck, R. (1992). Evaluating the impact of multicultural counseling training. *Journal of Counseling Training and Development, 70*, 143–150.

Falicov, C. J. (1998). *Latino families: A guide to multicultural practice.* New York: Guilford.

Fuertes, J. N, & Gretchen, D. (2001) Emerging theories of multicultural counseling. In J. Ponterotto, J. M. Casas, L. Suzuki & C. Alexander (Eds.), *Handbook of multicultural counseling* (2nd ed.) (509–541). Thousand Oaks, CA: Sage.

Fukuyama, M. (1990). Taking a universal approach to multicultural counseling. *Counselor Education & Supervision, 30,* 6–17.

García, J. G., & Zea, M. C. (Eds.) (1997). *Psychological interventions and research with Latino populations.* Needham Heights, MA: Allyn & Bacon.

Gladding, S. T. (2002). *Family therapy: History, theory, and practice* (3rd ed.). Upper Saddle River, NJ: Merrill/Prentice-Hall.

Gloria, A. L., & Rodriguez, E. R. (2000). Counseling Latino university students: Psychosociocultural issues for consideration. *Journal of Counseling and Development, 78,* 145–155.

Greenberg, L., James, P., & Conry, R. (1988). Perceived change processes in emotionally focused couples therapy. *Journal of Family Psychology, 2,* 5–23.

Guy, J. D. (1987). *The personal life of the psychotherapist,* New York: Wiley.

Herman, K. (1993). Reassessing predictors of therapist competence. *Journal of Counseling and Development, 71*(4), 29–32.

Hess, R. S., & Street, E. M. (1991). The effect of acculturation on the relationship of counselor ethnicity and client ratings. *Journal of Counseling Psychology, 38,* 71–75.

Holcomb-McCoy, C. C., & Myers, J. E. (1999). Multicultural competence and counselor training: A national survey. *Journal of Counseling and Development, 77,* 294–302.

Holder, T., Carkhuff, R., & Berenson, B. (1967). The differential effects of the manipulation of therapeutic conditions upon high low functioning clients. *Journal of Counseling Psychology, 14,* 63–66.

Ibrahim, F. A., & Arredondo, P. M. (1986). Ethical standards for cross-cultural counseling: Counselor preparation, practice, assessment, and research. *Journal of Counseling and Development, 64,* 349–352.

Ibrahim, F. A., Roysircar-Sodowsky, G., & Ohnishi, H. (2001). Worldview: Recent developments and needed directions. In J. Ponterotto, J. M. Casas, L. Suzuki & C. Alexander (Eds.), *Handbook of multicultural counseling* (2nd ed., pp. 425–456). Thousand Oaks, CA: Sage.

Ivey, A., D'Andrea, M., Ivey, M., & Simek-Morgan, L. (2002). *Theories of counseling and psychotherapy: A multicultural perspective* (5th ed.). Boston: Allyn & Bacon.

Koss-Chioino, J. D., & Vargas, L. A. (1999). *Working with Latino youth.* San Francisco: Joey–Bass.

Kouyoumdjian, H., Zamboanga, B. L., & Hansen, D. J. (2003). Barriers to community mental health services for Latinos: Treatment considerations. *Clinical Psychology: Science and Practice, 10,* 394–422.

Lambert, M.J., & Bergin, A. E. (1994). The effectiveness of psychotherapy. In A. E. Bergin & S. L. Garfield (Eds.), *Handbook of psychotherapy and behavior change* (4th ed., pp. 143–189). New York: Wiley.

Malgady, R. G., & Constantino, G. (1998). Symptom severity in bilingual Hispanics as a function of clinician and language of interview. *Psychological Assessment, 10,* 120–127.

Manoleas, P., Organista, K., Negron-Velasquez, G., & McCormick, K. (2000). Characteristics of Latino mental health clinicians: A preliminary examination. *Community Mental Health Journal, 36*(4), 383–394.

McFadden, J. (Ed.). (1999). *Transcultural counseling* (2nd ed.). Alexandria, VA: American Counseling Association.

Miller, S., Duncan, B., Hubble, M. (2002). Client-directed, outcome-informed clinical work. In F. W. Kaslow & J. Lebow (Eds.), *Comprehensive handbook of psychotherapy*. Vol 4: Integrative/eclectic (pp. 185–212).

Nichols, M.P., & Schwartz, R. C. (2001). *Family therapy: Concepts and methods* (5th ed.) Boston: Allyn & Bacon

O'Neill, E., & Smith, R. (2005). [Interviews with Hispanic families, Corpus Christi, Texas]. Unpublished raw data.

Peterson, J., & Nisenholz, B. (1999). *Orientation to counseling.* (4th ed.). Boston, MA: Allyn & Bacon.

Piaget, G., Carkhuff, R., & Berenson, B. (1968). The development of skills in interpersonal functioning. *Counselor Education & Supervision, 2*, 102–106.

Ponce, F. Q. & Atkinson, D. R. (1989). Mexican-American acculturation, counselor ethnicity, counselor style, and perceived counselor credibility. *Journal of Counseling Psychology, 36*, 203–208.

Ponterotto, J. G., Rieger, B.P., Barrett, A., & Sparks, R. (1994). Assessing multicultural counseling competence: A review of instrumentation. *Journal of Counseling and Development, 71*, 316–322.

Rogers, C. (1957). The necessary and sufficient conditions of therapeutic personality change. *Journal of Consulting Psychology, 21*, 95–103.

Ruiz, R. A. (1971). Relative frequency of Americans with Spanish surnames in associations of psychology, psychiatry, and sociology. *American Psychologist, 26*, 1022–1024.

Sabnani, H. B., Ponterotto, J. G., & Borodovsky, L. G. (1991). White racial identity development and cross-cultural counselor training: A stage model. *The Counseling Psychologist, 19*, 76–102.

Sanchez, A. R. (2001). Multicultural family counseling: Toward cultural sensibility. In J. Ponterotto, J. M. Casas, L. Suzuki & C. Alexander (Eds.), *Handbook of multicultural counseling* (2nd ed., pp. 672–700). Thousand Oaks, CA: Sage.

Sanchez, A. R., & Atkinson, D. R. (1983). Mexican-American cultural commitment, preference for counselor ethnicity, and willingness to use counseling. *Journal of Counseling Psychology, 30*, 215–220.

Santiago-Rivera, A. L., Arredondo, P., & Gallardo-Cooper, M. (2002). *Counseling Latinos and la familia: A practical guide.* Thousand Oaks, CA: Sage.

Satir, V. (1987). The therapist story. In M. Baldwin & V. Satir (Eds.), *The use of self* (pp. 17–25). New York: Haworth.

Sells, S., Smith, T., & Moon, S. (1996). An ethnographic study of client and therapist perceptions of therapy effectiveness in a university-based training clinic. *Journal of Marital and Family Therapy, 22*, 321–342.

Smart, J. F., & Smart, D. W. (1994). The rehabilitation of Hispanics experiencing acculturative stress: Implications for practice. *The Journal of Rehabilitation, 60*, 8–12.

Strupp, H. (1980). Humanism and psychotherapy: A personal statement of the therapist's essential values. *Psychotherapy: Theory, Research, and Practice, 17*(4), 396–400.

Sue, D. W. (1988). Psychotherapeutic services for ethnic minorities: Two decades of research findings. *American Psychologist, 43*, 301–308.

Sue, D. W. (2001). Surviving monoculturalism and racism: A personal and professional journey. In J. Ponterotto, J. M. Casas, L. Suzuki & C. Alexander (Eds.), *Handbook of multicultural counseling* (2nd ed., pp. 45–54). Thousand Oaks, CA: Sage.

Sue, D.W., Arredondo, P., & McDavis, R. J. (1992). Multicultural counseling competencies and standards: A call to the profession. *Journal of Multicultural Counseling and Development, 20,* 64–87.

Sue, S., & Zane, N. (1987). The role of culture and cultural techniques in psychotherapy: A critique and reformulation. *American Psychologist, 42,* 37–45.

Tat Tsang, A., Bogo, M., & George, U. (2003). Critical issues in cross-cultural counseling research: Case example of an ongoing project. *Journal of Multicultural Counseling and Development, 31,* 63–78.

U.S. Census Bureau (2003). General demographic characteristics: 2003. American community survey summary tables. Retrieved March 24, 2005, from http://factfinder.census.gov/servlet/.

Vace, N. A., DeVaney, S. B., & Wittmer, J. (1995). *Experiencing and counseling multicultural and diverse populations* (3rd ed.). Bristol, PA: Taylor & Francis.

Waldron, H., Turner, C., Barton, C., Alexander, J., & Cline, V. (1997). Therapist defensiveness and marital therapy process and outcome. *American Journal of Family Therapy, 25,* 233–243.

Wampold, B. E., Casas, J. M., & Atkinson, D. R. (1981). Ethnic bias in counseling: An information processing approach. *Journal of Counseling Psychology, 28,* 498–503.

CHAPTER 2

Working With Latino Populations
Background and Historical Perspectives

R. ESTEBAN MONTILLA AND ROBERT L. SMITH

Maria is a 38-year-old Hispanic female married to Pedro. From their 14-year marriage, they have three children: Pete (12), Ana Maria (10), and Carlos (7). Maria was born in Texas and Pedro is from Nicaragua. She began her work as a science teacher after earning her B.A. at Boston University. Pedro has worked for Dell Computer Corporation since 1995 when he completed his graduate training at MIT. Maria is bilingual (English and Spanish) but, because of her profession and friends, is more comfortable speaking English. Pedro is bilingual as well. He speaks Spanish at home with the intention of teaching his children his mother tongue.

Maria's father was born in Cuzco, a southern city of Peru rich in tradition and culture. He enjoys teaching his grandchildren the Quechua language, Inca's tales, and about the Inca Empire and the Inca culture. Grandpa Alejandro sees himself as a Roman Catholic who embraces many indigenous beliefs and religious customs. Maria's mother was born in Ohio to Mexican migrant workers and considers herself a devoted Roman Catholic. Pedro's parents are from Nicaragua and practice the Protestant faith (Moravian). Pedro's father is very proud of his Amerindian Miskito origin and takes time to share stories about his Native American and African ancestors with his grandchildren. Pedro's mother was born in Managua, where they are still living. Both families see each other at least once a year.

Maria and Pedro met in Boston while attending college and married right after completing their degrees. Until 8 months ago, everything was going well for this family. They had good jobs; their children were excelling in school, had great expanded family support, were very active in their community, and were faithful in their attendance at a Roman Catholic church. All of this was shaken and challenged when Maria was diagnosed with breast cancer. Surgical, radiation, and chemical treatment did not prevent the carcinomas from metastasizing to several parts of her body. Her family doctor and oncologist recommended that Maria seek hospice care because they believed that she had less than 6 months to live. Pedro gathered the family (about 43 people) and told them about Maria's health situation. Maria decided to begin hospice services and prepare her children to face the reality of her death.

Maria suggested that Pedro call a family counselor whom they had seen about 5 years ago to help them and their children cope with her upcoming death. Now, visualize being that family counselor. What does one need to know about their backgrounds? What are the emotional, cognitive, and spiritual issues to which one must pay special attention? Which language would seem best when communicating with this family? What is the role of the "extended" family in this counseling process? Who are the consultees or clients? What are the multicultural factors one ought to consider before approaching this diverse family? What members of the community might be involved in helping this Hispanic family? How does one work with three grieving Latino children? This chapter and the remaining text provides related basic information about Latinos and Latinas to consider in practice.

HISPANICS OR LATINOS/LATINAS

Latinos and Latinas are a multicolor and multiethnic group of human beings with an array of cultures, beliefs, and traditions that defy simplistic explanations and categorization. They are seen as a policulture representing more than 20 countries and more than 500 million people living in South America, Central America, North America, the Caribbean, Europe, Asia, Africa, and Australia (Brea, 2003).

The majority of people of Latino heritage live in Latin America (520 million), which in this context is referred to as nations of Spanish, Portuguese (Brazil), and indigenous languages located in South America, Central America, North America, and the Caribbean (Brea, 2003). Another 50 million live in the Iberian Peninsula. The U.S. Census Bureau (2004) reports that, as of July 1, 2003, 39.9 million Hispanics were in the United States, representing 13.5% of the entire population of the country. (This is without including the 3.9 million Puerto Ricans living on that island.) Two thirds (66.9%) are of Mexican origin, 14.3% are Central and South American, 8.6% are Puerto Rican, 3.7% are Cuban, and the remaining 6.5% are of other Hispanic origins. The

Pew Hispanic Center (2002) indicates that 46% of the Latino population residing in the United States is bilingual (Spanish and English), 40% speak only Spanish, and 14% are largely monolingual (English). The Latino or Hispanic people living in the United States are as multiethnic and pluricultural as those living in Latin America.

This diversity invites clinicians to practice humility and recognize that the pathways to emotional, cognitive, relational, and spiritual development among Hispanics are many because *cada persona es un mundo* (each person is a world in his or her own right). Thus, to suggest a single trail for every person of Latino heritage is illusionary in nature and deceiving in intent. Although Latinos and Latinas have many worldviews and cultural factors in common, they remain a policulture composed of men and women who believe that life is best lived when it is lived in togetherness and in community. Latinos are genetically 99.9% similar to the rest of brothers and sisters across the planet, but that 0.1% makes a big difference. It is in the best interest of culturally sensitive and competent clinicians and researchers to consider that "little" difference carefully.

THE HISPANIC ROOTS

A good place to begin answering the question of who Hispanics are is by looking at their roots: America. In the 15th century, Christopher Columbus and his partners found many civilized societies that were well developed and highly structured, with clear sociopolitical and technological practices revealing their wisdom and entrepreneurial spirits (Fernandez-Armesto, 2003; Lockhart & Schwartz, 1984). The inhabitants of these lands, who perhaps immigrated from Africa, Asia, and Australia about 10,000 years ago, were strategically established throughout South, Central, and North America as independent and autonomous societies with diverse cultural, religious, social, and family values. Many of these societies had great and well-developed cities, pyramids, empires, long-distance trade, roads, advanced agricultural techniques, and written codes. Although certain cultural similarities were present within the many inhabitants of these lands, these civilizations were diverse and independent of each other (Lockhart & Schwartz).

Christopher Columbus (1451–1506) named this vast diverse group of people "Indians" because he thought that he had arrived in Asia. This could indicate that being named by the dominant culture is not a new phenomenon. People eventually learned to deal with the naming and then reluctantly use that given name because it is also the case with the term "Hispanics." The term "Hispanic" or "Latino," although it makes sense from a political or marketing point of view, does not do justice to the diversity that characterizes the Latino people (Suárez-Orozco & Páez, 2002).

The encounter between European, Amerindian, Asian, and African cultures gave rise to a unique group of people of White, Black, and Amerindian backgrounds, but mostly of mestizo backgrounds, who continuously strive to live harmoniously with nature, others, and self. Thus, this multicolor policulture demands that researchers and clinicians be humble in their attempt to understand the complexity of what it means to be Latino or Latina.

In summary, Hispanic refers to a multicultural, multiethnic, mariachi, salsa, and tutti-frutti mosaic of people that sounds good, looks exotic, tastes great, moves quickly, and is found everywhere. The father-in-law of one of the editors (Esteban) often says that Hispanics are like the one-dollar bill: they are everywhere and everybody likes them. The first part of this statement has some elements of truth, but the second half is far from the truth because discrimination continues to be rampant at personal and institutional levels (Comas-Diaz, 2001; Montalvo, 1991; Rivers & Morrow, 1995).

CHARACTERISTICS OF THE POLICULTURAL FAMILY

At the heart of the Latino community is the family. Family, seen as a community of people connected by blood, adoption, marital agreement, and/or emotional links with a strong sense of togetherness, belonging, and interdependency, is the main source of support, care, guidance, and healing for the Latino people (Briones et al., 1990).

There are as many types of families as there are Latinos and Latinas in the world. This family diversity implies that there is not a single model or pattern of family relationship that Hispanic families must follow to be functional and healthy. The idea is to treat or approach each Hispanic family with its idiosyncrasies and distinctiveness. Furthermore, because clinicians are accustomed to use standards to measure people's behaviors and patterns of relationships by comparing them to a "prototype," it becomes a challenge for those working with Latino families to distance themselves from the process of applying Eurocentric family constructs such as differentiation, dependency, homeostasis, autonomy, and systemic thinking.

Traditional understanding of family therapy and counseling has been helpful in the sense that the impact of the internal psyche of an individual, as well as the social and contextual influence for individuals' cognitive, affective, behavioral, and relational functioning, is now considered. However, when clinicians try to apply traditional theories and family therapy approaches to multicultural families, the risk of harm is high because many of these assumptions ignore the contextual and ecological family implications to clinical practice (Luepnitz, 1988; Rogoff, 2003). Furthermore, the notion of the family coming once a week for therapy for a determined number of sessions does not have applicability with many Latino families. They might come for one session to complement the therapeutic work that is taking place through relatives, friends, comadres, compadres, and other social and health care professionals and return weeks or months later for more consultation.

This intermittent style of counseling and therapy has often been interpret-ed as a resistant or an uncooperative spirit on the part of the client. It is impor-tant to remember that most Latinos and Latinas see therapy or counseling as a collaborative effort among clinician, self, relatives, and friends (Rojano, 2004). The role of the clinicians is not that of the "only expert" and protagonist, but rather that of a collaborator and companion traveler. Moreover, because of the idea of community, the life journey is a communal experience in which several persons or a caravan of people are involved in the healing process.

Because of family diversity, there is not a single way of experiencing or being a family. No standard is acceptable for all families; therefore, it is difficult to compare one family with another. There is no one way of being married and no typical marriage. The most common denominator in Latinos is family diversity in terms of numbers of family members, socioeconomic status, living arrangements, composition, education level, structure, age, values, faith, style of functioning, and multigenerational households (Marin, 2003). Unfortunately, many well-intentioned clinicians with the illusion of a "typical" family have understood some Latino family diversity as pathologies—supposedly because some of these families do not reflect "the normal" Eurocentric view of family (Okun, 1996).

Family diversity, with its structure, continues to be the cornerstone and the building block of the Hispanic community, society, and culture. For most Hispanics, the family is the place from which they draw their strengths, celebrate their achievements, lament their losses, perpetuate their values, learn and maintain their motivations, and experience the fullness of what it means to be human. Indeed, it is in family where they triumph and fail, where they get sick, and where they heal. In addition, the family is charged with the process of enculturation as older members transmit the cultural knowledge, awareness, and skills into the next generations (Casas & Pytluck, 1995).

Iberian, African, and Amerindian views of family relations have shaped the Latino or Hispanic understanding of family (Lockhart & Schwartz, 1984). Highly influenced by the Roman Catholic Church and Islam, Iberians saw the father as the head of the house with the authority to make all decisions regard-ing the future of the family. The patriarch ran the family as a small estate where each member—wife, children, and servants—was expected to function, con-tribute, and work toward the well-being of the family unit or property.

Most Amerindian family members were interdependent, living and work-ing together toward sustaining the community or tribe. The family, consist-ing of the father, mother, sons, daughters, and close and distant relatives, along with other members of the household and tribe, was in charge of the education, care, discipline, and formation of the children. The flora, fauna, and cosmos were seen as part of the family that deserved respect and care. The elders of the tribe or community were in charge of passing the wisdom, culture, values, religion, art, music, and principles from one generation to the next. They used storytelling as the main avenue to pass that heritage. That kinship system defined the direction, ethos, responsibilities, administration, relationships, and future of the family.

Most Amerindian marriages served as an alliance between families who decided to join efforts and strengths to better protect, educate, preserve, nurture, and guarantee the well-being of the community. Parents and elders of the community were mainly the people in charge of studying the history, physical health, personality, talents, and preferences of the future couples with the intention of finding matching characteristics that would secure the success of the relationship. Cristina Torres (2001) from the World Health Organization estimates that 10.18% of the Latin American total population (520 million) is Amerindian.

The African family with the mother, father, grandparents, siblings, relatives, close friends, and neighbors forming the network and kinship necessary for the appropriate development of family members was very influential in shaping what is known today as the Latino family (Willie & Reddick, 2003). The African American family includes features such as solidarity, cooperation, sharing, caring, cross-generational support, charity, awareness of the impact of oppression, sense of humor, respect, religiousness, and faith, which are all common elements within the Latino families. A large number of Blacks are Hispanics—for instance, countries such as the Dominican Republic (84% of the entire population is Black), Cuba (62%), Brazil (46%), Colombia (~21%), Panama (14%), Venezuela (>10%), Nicaragua (>9%), Ecuador (>5%); the rest of Latino countries range between 1 and 4% (Torres, 2001). For centuries, Latinos and Latinas have mutually enlightened, supported, and developed each other.

Familismo—or the sense of loyalty, solidarity, cooperation, and interdependence—seems to be the cornerstone of most Latino families (Falicov, 1996; Gloria & Peregoy, 1996). It is common to hear from *tios* and *tias* (uncles and aunts) this dicho (saying): "*El que le pega a su familia se arruina,*" denoting that family must be the priority and that under no circumstance is betrayal to the family encouraged. The idea that problems and conflicts belong and stay within the family is very much part of the Latino families' belief system.

This issue of loyalty along with a healthy and necessary paranoia present in most Hispanic families needs to be taken into consideration when working with them. Culturally sensitive clinicians keep this in mind at the beginning as well as throughout the therapeutic relationship. Clinicians do their best to establish an environment of safety, trust, respect, reciprocity, or *personalismo*. This will allow the family to feel *en casa* (at home) and that, by consulting with a counselor, they are not betraying the unwritten family code about loyalty, but rather, seeking to strengthen the family relationship. Furthermore, multicultural competent clinicians will be ready to process Latinos' and Latinas' issues of guilt and shame resulting from their sharing their family issues with an "*estranger.*" Failure to address these issues may promote a premature termination of the therapeutic relationship.

ACCULTURATION OF LATINOS AND LATINAS

Acculturation is thought of as the process of enriching one's culture and roots by incorporating many of the lifestyles and worldviews found within the culture encountered in a life journey. This mutual and reciprocal process of interchanging values, beliefs, customs, attitudes, and relationships becomes the cornerstone of growth, learning, development, and advancement. Some Latinos seem reluctant to use the word acculturation because it generally implies discarding one's cultural roots in order to embrace the dominant culture. Perhaps, this way of seeing acculturation reminds Latinos and Latinas of what the Iberians did in forcing Amerindians to abandon and destroy their worldviews and ways of connecting with themselves, others, nature, and divine beings.

Acculturation (Berry, 1980, 1997) refers to "integration." Some Hispanic families going through this period of integration may experience an array of emotions and stressful events that include a sense of alienation, psychosomatic symptoms, parenting confusion, identity issues, and interpersonal marital conflicts (Flores, Tschann, VanOss Marin, & Pantoja, 2004; Leyendecker & Lamb, 1999). However, most Hispanic families, perhaps for their instinctual indigenous openness to embrace other cultures, show no signs of distress in incorporating values, customs, and religious practices from other cultures (Moyerman & Forman, 1992).

Acculturation as suggested by Berry (1997) consists of assimilation, separation, marginalization, and integration. Assimilation implies that the person must abandon, disengage, and mutilate his native cultures and values to adapt to those found in the dominant cultures (LaFromboise, Coleman, & Gerton, 1993). In other words, one takes all the cultural "*ropaje*" (clothing) and burns it or gives it away to make space for the new ones. Separation refers to people retaining their cultural heritages and backgrounds but rejecting those of the majority culture (Berry). The marginalization mode implies rejection of "mother" and dominant culture. Berry's last mode includes integration, which suggests that people retain their ethnic culture but embrace many of the dominant culture's features.

SPIRITUALITY AMONG HISPANIC FAMILIES

"*Hay de todo en la viña del Señor*" (in the Lord's vineyard there is a little of everything). Faith and religion are two elements present in most experiences of Latino people. The spiritual realm is consulted and used in issues related to life, educational, health, economic, political, familial, and personal challenges. The religious phenomenon is so prevalent and pervasive that it is not seen as something that one has but rather as who one is. In this way, people are spiritual beings trying to be humans. The abundance of symbols and rituals with religious meanings used by Hispanics to connect with the transcendent is a demonstration of the need of Latino peoples to live in harmony with nature, the universe, and self.

The policultural nature of the Latino people is also seen in their diverse expressions of faith and its way to connect with that, which is transcendent. Perhaps a most common path to experience their spirituality is from a syncretic religious practice that combines Amerindian, Christian, Islamic, Jewish, and African religion features. The Roman Catholic faith was cautiously and overtly imposed, but native Amerindians and African slaves were still able to preserve their religious rituals and beliefs by incorporating them into the dominant Roman Catholic tradition. For instance, in Bolivia, an Amerindian sculptor made two images of their ancient gods of nature and told the priest that these images were those of St. Peter and St. Paul. Curiously, the number of attendants at the Sunday religious service increased remarkably (González, 2003; Wiarda & Kline, 2001).

Today, although less than 20% of Latinos and Latinas attend church regularly, the majority of them profess to ascribe to the Roman Catholic faith. A second large group of Latinos and Latinas see themselves as spiritual people but maintain a level of suspicion of traditional faith groups such as the Roman Catholic and Evangelical movements. Some see the Roman Catholic Church at times as exploiting Latinos and Latinas and the Evangelical movement as an instrument of the North American empire. The Protestant and Evangelical faith tradition is increasingly becoming more popular with Hispanics, represented in some Latino countries by 12% (Chile) and in others by up to 25 to 35% (Guatemala) of the population (Wiarda & Kline, 2001). Other faith traditions include Islamic, Jewish, and Eastern religious practices. In summary, the Hispanic people value and treasure their spirituality, but this is as diverse as the culture is.

Spirituality, religion, and faith are central to Latino families' survival and resilience. In practice, it is difficult to separate these conceptual constructs because they are seen as concrete attitudes, affective expressions and actions that are read through the lenses of the community. The faith is lived within the context of the community. Respect and reverence for the transcendent, the universe, nature, and neighbors is expressed through many rituals and symbols that vary from family to family. Therefore, religion, faith, and spirituality are intimately connected and better understood when seen as an undivided whole.

Spirituality is about relationship and intimacy with the transcendent, self, and others. This web of relationships is what Latino families have historically used to face adversities, to celebrate achievements, and to make sense of their existence. The human being, seen as a social and holistic being with an indissolubly connected body, mind, and spirit that influence each other, achieves wholeness within these three types of relationships. Culturally sensitive clinicians and researchers working with Latino families will understand that spirituality or connectedness is an integrated part of their daily functioning and that tending to the whole person within the community context is essential for the healing process.

COMMUNITY AND COLLECTIVISM

As social beings, Hispanics are relationship oriented. They exist in order to be in community. Hispanics are born, reproduce, grow, unfold, mature, and die in community. Because of their gregarious nature, they need the community in order to receive the healing power of relationships. Human interactions do not take place in isolation; rather, they occur in connection with others, self, and the transcendent. Family counseling and therapy approaches with Hispanic families must take place within the context of the community.

Persons cannot survive by themselves and it is only in connection with others that it is possible to experience life to the fullest. In that direction, Jordan (2000) asserts that the main thrust of human development is the movement toward mutuality and relatedness. She goes further to suggest that the source of most human suffering is disconnection and isolation. The cognitive, emotional, social, and spiritual healing occur mainly in the presence of caring communities in which love, sharing, interdependency, and cooperation characterize the interaction and in which the clinicians and consultees join efforts to make meaning of the experiences and embrace each other in the journey to wholeness (Montilla, 2005).

Throughout history, particularly in European and North American cultures, a tension has existed between the individual and the community. Perhaps this friction is due in part to lack of balance in honoring and celebrating people's individual uniqueness, self-determination, and individual responsibility, while at the same time acknowledging the importance and well-being of the community. A healthy and balanced approach calls for valuing the person's uniqueness and freedom, while recognizing that the maximum human potential is experienced in relationships.

Most Latino families do not negate the value, respect, and dignity of each person but capitalize on the importance of coming together, caring for each other, and recognizing interdependency needs. They celebrate the reciprocal connection between the individual and community in which principles of equality, justice, and freedom are mutually respected. The idea is to value the uniqueness of each member of the community while keeping in mind the social responsibility of working together for the common good.

The meaning of community is illustrated in *Fuenteovejuna*, Felix Lope de Vega's play. The story is about the small town of Fuenteovejuna, which is under the tyrannical rule of Don Fernan Gomez, Knight Commander of the Order of Calatrava. After much suffering, the townspeople finally rebel and kill the commander, placing his head on a pike as the banner of their freedom. Their battle cry is "*Fuenteovejuna, todos a una*" (Fuenteovejuna, all are one). When the Grand Master of the Order hears of this, he appeals to Ferdinand and Isabella, who appoint a judge–inquisitor to find the guilty parties and punish them.

The judge, however, finds that he can make little progress in his inquiry because, whenever he asks, "*¿Quién mató al comandante?*" (Who killed the commander?), the answer is always the same: "*Fuenteovejuna, señor*" (Fuenteovejuna, my lord). Irritated, he puts 300 of the local inhabitants to torture. Still, from all of them—men, women, children, and people in their old age—the answer is the same: "*Fuenteovejuna, señor.*" Finally, the judge asks for instructions from Isabella and Ferdinand, who respond that, given such unanimity, there must have been just cause for the commander's death. Gonzalez (1990) asserts that the entire town realized that the community, and not any individual in it, killed the commander. Likewise, if one member of a community is facing some emotional, cognitive, social, or spiritual challenges, the entire community joins in the hurting.

EMOTIONS FROM THE LATINO PERSPECTIVE

Latinos and Latinas are emotional beings that experience life as a whole. Indeed, they are emotional beings trying to be humans. Emotions are natural physiological responses to internal and external stimulus (Greenberg, 2004), but they are read or interpreted through psychological and sociocultural lenses. The reading of these experiences through Hispanic eyes is very particular because "the Hispanic alphabet of emotions" has been composed with the help of Amerindians, Africans, and Iberians.

The emotions as a physiological phenomenon might be universal, but the ways of displaying them vary almost from family to family. Emotions are also symbols that could communicate love, care, disgust, or disapproval (Okun, Fried, & Okun, 1999), as well as values and concerns. Expressions of happiness, sadness, surprise, fear, disgust, anger, and contempt might have some universal elements (Ekman & Friesen, 1975), but the way in which they are uttered and used among Latinos and Latinas is very peculiar. For instance, a person who is crying at a funeral might not be feeling sad, but rather knows that, within the culture, weeping conveys the idea of caring, so the person joins in the crying.

Most Hispanics would not refrain from expressing negative or positive emotions in public because the idea of privacy seems to be of lesser importance than to be transparent. Again, stereotyping Hispanics as *alborotados* (wild, roaring) is not prudent because the person, cultural setting, and situation dictate greatly which and how emotions are conveyed. Socially related emotions such as shame (*verguenza*), guilt, indebtedness, *simpatia*, and respect are encouraged in community-oriented societies (Matsumoto, 1994).

CONSIDERATIONS WHEN WORKING WITH LATINO FAMILIES

The case of Maria and Pedro mentioned earlier in this chapter reflects the diversity within a Hispanic family. They represent at least five different cultures, each one with its set of values, customs, and beliefs. These different worldviews at times collide but, generally, at the end, family members realize that maintaining the community's well-being is the priority. Thus, individual divergent opinions, although valued as important, would yield space to the collective feeling and agreement.

The "person in-authority" of the family (usually maternal grandmother, oldest sister, or the woman that the family recognizes as an authority within the community) could be the most influential person in the decision-making process. She would encourage each family member—females and males, as well as children—to have a voice in the matter. It is very important for clinicians working with Hispanic families to be aware of the persons in positions of authority and leadership because the failure or success of the family intervention and therapeutic process will be highly shaped by the level of involvement of the "leader" of the family.

Their decision to include the family (43 members) in the process of defining ways of taking care of Maria's health situation mirrors the belief that, for healing to take place, the entire community needs to participate. The "expanded family" (Horowitz, 1997) composed of husband, wife, children, grandparents, siblings, aunts, uncles, cousins, and close friends (*compadres y comadres*), who might or might not live in the same household or neighborhood, plays an important part in the decision process.

Hispanics face family issues the same way they approach diseases of the body. As the disease appears the entire family is mobilized and comes together to join forces, struggle together, and find meaning. "*En la unión está la fuerza*" (there is power in togetherness). If the family resources seem limited or insufficient to combat the "intruder and disruptive situation," outside help is solicited. The "healer" or family counselor/therapist must approach the family respecting their values, traditions, and idiosyncrasies. By building on the family resources, the clinician becomes an active part of the family and, in togetherness, they tackle the issues. Multiculturally sensitive clinicians could help the Hispanic family use its resourcefulness, permeability, resiliency, and adaptive characteristics to face the psycho–socio–relational trials at hand.

The "healer" or family counselor would be most effective when he or she "becomes" a family member. This process of becoming part of the family starts with the establishment of the relationship that must be based on trust, truthfulness, respect, and reciprocity of thought, feelings, and relationship. This "joining" (Minuchin, 1974) stimulates family members to engage in sharing their personal stories, their "living human webs" or network of support, their hopes and dreams. Because the healer or clinician is not the single protagonist in the healing process, he or she would welcome the participation of the wider community to include, perhaps, educators, social workers, religious leaders, traditional healers, and medical personnel (Bronfenbrenner, 1979).

Most importantly, the multiculturally competent and sensitive clinician must strive to connect and be present with each family member. Equality, power sharing, compassion, "availability," and love characterize this connection and "being with" relational experience. Marcel (1950) suggests that being present is a gift of grace in which two or more human beings engage in self-sharing and mutual availability. The implication of this way of being present is that "healers" dispose themselves to be completely connected with the other, which in turn will facilitate "the discovery of depth through togetherness."

This chapter has included a case as well as a personal look at the Latino cultures and Latino history. In chapter 3, Celia Jaes Falicov continues with a close examination of how Latino families are organized and why the safety net of closeness is so important. Salvador Minuchin begins the journey of looking at the family in therapy in chapter 4.

REFERENCES

Berry, J. W. (1980). *Acculturation as a variety of adaptation.* In A. M. Padilla (Ed.), Acculturation: Theory, models and some new findings (pp. 9–25). Boulder, CO: Westview Press.

Berry, J. W. (1997). Immigration, acculturation and adaptation. *Applied Psychology, 46,* 5–68.

Brea, J. A. (2003). Population dynamics in Latin America. *Population Bulletin, 58*(1), 1–39. March 2003. Washington, D.C.: Population Reference Bureau.

Briones, D. F., Heller, P.L., Chalfant, H.P., Roberts, A. E., Aguirre-Hauchbaum, S.F., & Farr, W. F. (1990). Socioeconomic status, ethnicity, psychological distress and readiness to utilize a mental health facility. *American Journal of Psychiatry, 147,* 1333–1340.

Bronfenbrenner, U. (1979). *The ecology of human development.* Cambridge, MA: Harvard University Press.

Casas, J. M., & Pytluck, S. D. (1995). Hispanic identity development: Implications for research and practice. In J. G. Ponterotto, J. M. Casas, L. A. Suzuki, & C. M. Alexander (Eds.). *Handbook of multicultural counseling* (pp. 155–180). Thousand Oaks, CA: Sage.

Comas-Diaz, L. (2001). Hispanics, Latinos or Americanos: The evolution of identity. *Cultural Diversity and Ethnic Minority Psychology, 7*(2), 115–120.

Ekman, P., & Friesen, W. V. (1975). Unmasking the face: A guide to recognizing emotions from facial clues. Englewood Cliffs, NJ: Prentice Hall.

Falicov, C. J. (1996). Mexican families. In M. McGoldrick, J. Giordano, & J. Pearce (Eds.), *Ethnicity and family therapy* (pp. 169–182). New York: Guilford Press.

Fernandez-Armesto, F. (2003). *The Americas: A hemisphere history.* New York: The Random House Ballantine Publishing Group.

Flores, E., Tschann, J. M., VanOss Marin, B., & Pantoja, P. (2004). Marital conflict and acculturation among Mexican American husbands and wives. *Cultural Diversity and Ethnic Minority Psychology, 10*(1) February 2004, 39–52. Educational Publishing Foundation.

Gloria, A. M., & Peregoy, J. J. (1996). Counseling Latino alcohol and other drug abusers: Cultural issues for consideration. *Journal of Substance Abuse Treatment, 13,* 1–8.

González, J. L. (1990). *Mañana: Christian theology from a Hispanic perspective.* Nashville, TN: Abingdon Press.

González, J. L. (2003). *Historia del cristianismo: Tomo 2.* Miami, FL: Editorial Unilit.

Greenberg, L. S. (2004) Emotion-focused therapy. *Clinical Psychology & Psychotherapy, 11*(1), 3–14.

Horowitz, R. (1997). The expanded family and family honor. In M. Hutter (Ed.), *The family experience: A reader in cultural diversity.* Boston: Allyn & Bacon.

Jordan, J. V. (2000). A model of connection for a disconnected world. In J. Shay & J. Wheelis (Eds.), *Odysseys in psychotherapy.* New York: Ardent Media Publisher.

LaFromboise, T., Coleman, H. L. K., & Gerton, J. (1993, November). Psychological impact of biculturalism: Evidence and theory. *Psychological Bulletin, 114*(3), 395–412

Leyendecker, B. & Lamb, M. E. (1999). Latino families. In M. E. Lamb (Ed.), *Parenting and child development in "nontraditional" families* (pp. 247–262). Hillsdale, NJ: Erlbaum.

Lockhart, J. and Schwartz, S. B. (1984). Early Latin America. A history of colonial Spanish America and Brazil. New York: Cambridge University Press.

Luepnitz, D. A. (1988). *The family interpreted: Feminist theory in clinical practice.* New York: Basic Books.

Marcel, G. (1950). *The mystery of being.* Vol. I. London: The Harvill Press.

Marin, H. (2003). Hispanics and psychiatric medications: An overview. *Psychiatric Times, 20*(10), 80–83.

Matsumoto, D. (1994). *People: Psychology from a cultural perspective.* Pacific Grove, CA: Brooks/Cole.

Minuchin, S. (1974). *Families and family therapy.* London: Tavistock.

Montalvo, F. (1991). *Phenotyping, acculturation, and biracial assimilation of Mexican Americans. Empowering Hispanic families: A critical issue for the 90s.* Milwaukee, WI: Family Services America.

Montilla, R. E. (2005). Grieving and reconnecting in community. In Weaver, A. and Stone H. (Eds.), *Reflections on grief and spiritual growth.* Nashville, TN: Abingdon Press.

Montilla, R. E. (2004). *Viviendo la tercera edad. Un modelo integral de consejería para el buen envejecimiento.* Madrid: Editorial Clie.

Moyerman, D. R. & Forman, B. D. (1992). Acculturation and adjustment: A meta-analytic study. *Hispanic Journal of Behavioral Sciences, 14,* 163–200.

Okun, B. (1996). *Understanding diverse families. What practitioners need to know.* New York: Guilford.

Okun, B. F., Fried, J., and Okun, M. (1999). *Understanding diversity. A learning-as-practice primer.* Pacific Grove, CA: Brooks/Cole.

Rivers, R. Y., and Morrow, C. A. (1995). Understanding and treating ethnic minority youth. In J. F. Aponte, R. Y. Rivers, & J. Wohl (Eds.), *Psychological interventions and cultural diversity* (pp. 164–180). Boston: Allyn & Bacon.

Rogoff, B. (2003). *The cultural nature of human development.* New York: Oxford University Press.

Rojano, R. (2004). The practice of community family therapy. *Family Process, 43*(1), 59–77.

Suarez-Orozco, M. M. and Páez, M. M. (Eds.). (2002). *Latinos: Remaking America.* Los Angeles: University of California Press.

Torres, C. P. (2001). Equidad en salud: Una mirada desde la perspectiva de la etnicidad. Washington, D.C.: Programa de Políticas Públicas y Salud/División de Salud y Desarrollo Humano OPS/OMS.

U.S. Census Bureau (2004). Hispanic and Asian Americans increasing faster than overall population (Report No. CB04-98), Washington, DC: US Government Printing Office. Public Information Office. June 14, 2004.

Wiarda, H. J., & Kline, H. F. (2001). An introduction to Latin American politics and development. Boulder, CO: Westview Press.

Willie, C. V. & Reddick, R. J. (2003). *A new look at Black families.* Blue Ridge Summit, PA: Altamira Press.

CHAPTER 3

Family Organization

*The Safety Net of Close and Extended Kin**

CELIA JAES FALICOV

I do not belong to the culture of 911 (there is always a relative I can depend on to rescue me).

Latina client (1996)

CONCEPTS OF CONNECTEDNESS

As mentioned throughout this text, the basic social unit of Latino culture is the extended family. *La gran familia* comprises three or four generations of relatives and includes horizontal relationships between adult siblings, cousins, and myriad others who place considerable value on their day-to-day, or at least weekly, interactions. The sheer size of the household changes the texture of family life. There is a buzzy, noisy, chatty atmosphere in small spaces. Many people are part of a family's daily life, and a grandparent, an uncle, an aunt, or a godparent can always be counted on to change a diaper, keep an eye on a toddler, or monitor an adolescent's high jinks in the neighborhood. Overwhelmed parents get a much needed break and their children find some individual attention as this relative or that lends a hand.

---

*From Falicov, Celia Jaes, *Latino Family Therapy: A Guide to Multicultural Practice*. Copyright 1998 The Guilford Press. Reprinted with permission of The Guilford Press.

What accounts for this connectedness among such large kinship groups? Scholars and researchers use such concepts as *familismo* and the "familial self" to describe the cultural meaning systems that are the ingredients of a richly connected family.

FAMILISMO

Familismo encompasses meanings about inclusiveness and participation in large family networks. In many Latino extended families, visits are frequent and helpful exchanges commonplace. Rather than move away from extended family, as Anglo American adults often do, Latinos migrate toward them (Mindel, 1980). Also, unlike the dominant culture, boundaries around the Latino nuclear family are flexible, expanding to include grandparents, uncles, aunts, or cousins with natural ease (Alvirez, Bean, & Williams, 1981; Keefe, 1984; Ramirez & Arce, 1981; Vega, 1990). Children who are orphaned or whose parents are divorced may be included in the household of relatives, along with adults who have remained single, become widowed, or been divorced. Vertical and lateral kinship ties, up to third and fourth cousins, are often close.

Familismo also suggests collectivism or interdependence. Many family functions, such as care taking and control of children, financial responsibility, companionship, emotional support, and problem solving are shared. The emphasis is on collective rather than individual ownership or obligation, and on affiliation and cooperation rather than confrontation and competition.

The Role of Family Rituals

Nowhere is *familismo* better reflected and reinforced than in family rituals—a key component of Latino family life. Latino rituals are extended family celebrations that proclaim and reaffirm unity and connection. They may mark special events or occasions, but they also have a place in daily life.

Larissa Adler Lomnitz and Marisol Pérez-Lizaur (1987), a Chilean anthropologist and a Mexican anthropologist who live and work in Mexico City, comment that to be part of a Mexican family is to participate in a complex system of symbolic actions that amount to a way of life. Not one week goes by without one or both extended families requesting the presence of all nuclear family members for some type of gathering. The most common ritual for many families is *la comida semanal* (the weekly meal) at each of the two sets of grandparents' households, which usually takes place on weekends. This weekly custom includes all the unmarried or married offspring with spouses, children, and drop-in relatives of all ages. Visitors of any of the regular members may also be present.

Middle- and upper-class families from Mexico, Puerto Rico, and Cuba often continue some form of these gatherings in the United States, in part because they have the space and economic means. However, most immigrant families are poor and have shrunken extended networks. Still, informal rituals may persist or emerge—a weekly stroll through a city park, a family picnic in a public space, or a get-together for no other reason than to watch TV.

As a great believer in the weekly shared meal and its importance for family connection and identity, I often ask immigrant clients whether they might create a modified version of *la comida semanal*, perhaps eating together after church on Sunday or going for an ice cream after the children's soccer game. A weekly family meal may involve parents and adolescent children in cooking and cleaning, and this ritual in turn may renew the tradition of inviting significant others, if only to share a pizza and eat group style. Whatever their form, these gatherings symbolize *familismo*—solidarity, family pride, loyalty, and a sense of belonging and obligation to one's blood ties.

The Familial Self

An Anglo American therapist raised with values of autonomy and independence may wonder how the individual functions in such a collective world. A partial explanation lies in the concept of *personalismo* (Levine & Padilla, 1980), which denotes a high level of emotional resonance and personal involvement with family encounters. The term "familial self" may also explain how Latino individuals participate in life among many.

Observing Japanese and Indian people, psychoanalyst Alan Roland (1988) coined the term "familial self" to describe a sense of self that includes one's close relationships as part of who one is. This self-family construction is useful in understanding Latinos' dedication to children, parents, family unity, and family honor. Money, objects, home, and other possessions are shared easily, perhaps because a familial self is tied to a different concept about individual rights and property.

The familial self is balanced by an inner reserve of unshared feelings, which Roland calls a "private self," behind which all kinds of secret feelings and fantasies are kept. This inner separateness may explain in part how Latinos can individuate from their parents' nurturance and controls while maintaining considerable emotional closeness and mutual dependency for a lifetime. Over the years, the brilliant Mexican writer Octavio Paz has offered his interpretations about the Mexican national character, particularly in his book, *The Labyrinth of Solitude* (1961). Many of his ideas about Mexicans' ideations and communications coincide with the construction of a private self, shielded and evasive (Bartra, 1987; Ramirez, 1977).

Closeness Pathologized

Familismo and the familial self extend understanding of the Latino's preference for close connections with family. They also serve as important comparisons with mainstream Anglo American ideas about family life and, in turn, help therapists refrain from applying inappropriate diagnostic labels (such as "enmeshment"). Indeed, what constitutes "excessive" connectedness in one culture may have an entirely different meaning in another.

Tamara, my daughter, attended graduate school in San Diego and lived at home with me. The money that she earned covered only her university fees and minor expenses. She obtained free room and board at home. We got along very well, and each of us had total autonomy to travel, socialize, work, and shop at her own discretion. Even today, we share many meals, events of the day, news or gossip, and entertainment at home. Like many Latinas, we think a shared daily life is a rich life and have no resentment toward the small curtailments of freedom, the collective economics, or the emotional dependency. Her somewhat bewildered American classmates questioned Tamara frequently about our arrangement. They found it odd. They worried that she was not meeting all the challenges of growing up as defined by the Anglo American cultural narrative about "leaving home."

Although Anglo American therapists run the risk of pathologizing normative Latino closeness, they may also incorrectly label the behaviors that characterize such close family connections. For example, gender socialization motivates women to be supportive of their children and their husbands and to "sacrifice" themselves in silent ways that may be alien to Anglo American culture. In mainstream American psychotherapy, this could easily be perceived as codependence.

Jaime Inclán and Manuel Hernández (1993), two Puerto Rican psychologists who work at the Roberto Clemente Family Guidance Center in New York, wrote an interesting and useful cultural critique of codependence, a construct used widely as the basis for self-help and treatment approaches to chemical dependency. Inclán and Hernández argue that the concept of codependence is embedded in Anglo American values of separation/individuation and individualism. Clearly, the notion of codependence needs critical review before its application to Latinos because the changes expected of these "codependent" clients amount to a total rejection of *familismo*. *Familismo* stresses the duties of family members to help one another always, but especially in the face of serious problems such as alcohol or drug addiction.

Poverty and family honor also play a role in intensifying *familismo* because they promote even stronger family ties as a survival safety net. Furthermore, family honor dictates shielding family conflict, shame, or deviation from external scrutiny. Misunderstanding of these Latino values can result in labeling *familismo* as pathological codependency or enmeshment, particularly in families that have been in this country for more than one generation.

In multicultural work, therapists must therefore examine their personal and professional values and philosophies about family structure and connectedness, while exploring the specific meanings of closeness and attachment for each family.

THE CAST OF CHARACTERS, ROLES, AND HIERARCHIES

Understanding the unique brand of connectedness of many large Latino family networks helps one "read" and compare maps of family organization. Just as crucial to this familial drama, however, is knowledge of the players and their specific roles and relationships. This section explores cultural meanings related to "family members" who are not kin, godparents, the unquestioned authority of parents, the devotion between mother and son, and the lifelong bond among siblings.

Kith and Kin

A therapist working with Latinos may be fascinated by the gradual appearance of new characters in the family drama of clients. The nuclear family models that most therapists use are too narrow for application to many Latinos, so it is necessary to think beyond their confines. It is important to ask whether other people live with the family that the therapist is seeing in treatment. For new immigrants and poor and working-class Latinos, it is not uncommon to have seven or eight people sharing a room, with three or four people sleeping in one double bed. The family will likely reveal these important "others" as the barriers of institutional mistrust melt away.

I recently encountered a family consisting of mother, father, and three children who, after a few sessions, began talking about "the other family." In their rented apartment, they were housing another family of four who had recently arrived from a town near their own native home in Oaxaca, Mexico. The "new" family was paying to rent one of the two bedrooms. Both families shared one bathroom and kitchen. Although it helped pay the rent, the arrangement was creating serious tensions and jealousies rather than the anticipated help and child care and may have aggravated marital problems and fighting between the children.

Another family from Ensenada, Baja California, Mexico, consisted of a mother, three grown daughters, and a wealthy father who apparently lived with them on and off and paid for their therapy. However, this was the family that the father kept "on-the-side"—his *casa chica*. He had another legal family of wife and five grown children, his *casa grande*. He was very reluctant to participate in therapy because he was already going to therapy with his other, legal, family and his therapist forbade him from seeing his second family while he was solving problems with the first. The other therapist had quickly undertaken an acculturative stance and wanted the father to conform to monogamy with his "first" family, not considering the possible disservice to his "second" family.

Raised and trained in Anglo American culture, clinicians may back off in these situations and feel somewhat inhibited, to the detriment of the therapeutic process. It is best to ask questions politely and give each family member an opportunity to voice his or her feelings and opinions: "Is this type of family composition common in your culture? Is it common among your family and friends? How does it work? Does it cause any problems?"

Another family consisted of a single, professional Puerto Rican mother who had raised her two teenage daughters "alone" since they were babies. Then I learned that Lupita—maid, cook, babysitter, and "Jill"-of-all-trades— had lived with the three of them and slept with the girls for the past 10 years. Lupita had just brought her 12-year-old son back from Mexico to join this "family." When Lupita came, at my request, for an information session, not only did she know much more about the girls than the mother did, but she also turned out to be the best cotherapist I have ever had and the mother's most sensitive coach.

Maids have a silent presence in as well as a great impact on the lives of children and adults in Latino families, and they should be considered part of the extended family network (Chavez, 1994). They are present in middle- and upper-class families, as well as in many working-class families. Maids allow mothers to work outside the home for profit, perhaps experiencing less stress around child care issues than their Anglo American counterparts. The emotional attachment between these helpers and children, and occasionally between the adults, is often very significant.

Nelly was an illiterate, indigent 18-year-old Argentinian Indian who came from the north down to Buenos Aires to work for my family when I was a baby because my mother had become pregnant again. She quietly vanished from my life 19 years later, just prior to my wedding, when she was "no longer required" in my parents' household. Although she never told me, I always suspected that she had wanted to leave much earlier, but must have known that I so very much needed her warm and comforting presence in my life. That she could no longer be part of the family once she ceased to be *una empleada* (an employee) represents another excruciating social injustice toward "service" people. I later learned that she had a baby girl and had named her Celia Beatriz, my first name and my sister's first name.

The involvement of extended family, nonrelated helpers, and friends with the client family should always be explored. To what degree are these other players part of the problem or part of the solution? Would therapy with the nuclear family be enriched by participation from others? A simple question such as, "Does anybody else live with you?" or "Who helps you with the children when you are working?" begins this exploration.

For example, unmarried Latino men and women whose parents have died may be more likely to live with married siblings than on their own. The presence of a maternal or paternal aunt is so commonly seen among my client families that I have come to label it *la tia* (the aunt). The therapist usually discovers the importance of *la tia* serendipitously, similarly to "the other family" pattern mentioned previously. In some cases, the aunt serves useful affective and instrumental functions while subsystem boundaries are maintained. In other cases, depending on her age and role interactions within the family, the aunt may form a cross-generational coalition with a parent or child or may attempt to act as an intermediary between the two, sometimes benefiting growth but other times blocking it, as in the following example.

Charito Pérez, an unmarried, 33-year-old woman, moved in with her brother, his wife, and their children. She quickly formed a coalition with Maria, her 14-year-old niece, against Maria's father, Mr. Pérez. Maria claimed that her Aunt Charito understood young people much better than her father, especially in areas of fashion, curfew, and friends. There was some truth to this, in that the aunt had recently arrived from Cuba with "more advanced" ideas than Mr. Pérez, who had migrated 20 years before and held to traditional ways, especially with regard to his expectations of women. The aunt's role as mediator was a resource at times, but her protective stance sometimes prevented Mr. and Mrs. Pérez from reaching agreements directly with their daughter. In addition, this coalition also inflamed the covert conflict between Charito and Mr. Pérez, who exerted his control as older brother rather sternly.

In these situations, the therapist needs to be careful not to conceptualize automatically the presence of the unmarried "stranger" in the family as a problem. The therapist should also not believe that a triangle always reflects underlying marital conflict. Sometimes, sibling therapy among the adults is helpful in addressing old ledgers and loyalties from the family of origin.

Relationships with same-sex peers, whether relatives or friends, are so important for Latinos that it is not unusual for them to be implicated in the presenting problem of an individual or family. Occasionally, these relationships are a source of support, but often they are conflictual and comprise a stressor that affects the individual client and, in turn, his or her family. Whether working with individuals, couples, or other groupings, therapists are challenged to expand their unit of observation beyond the nuclear family, while keeping in mind that problems often reverberate as part of *familismo* rather than pathology.

The Value of Godparents

In Anglo American culture, godparents typically play an honorary role in family life. In Latino culture, godparents may be vital participants with significant status in families. The Latino custom of *compadrazgo* establishes two sets of extended family relationships: one between *padrinos y ahijados* (godparents and their godchildren) and the other between the parents and the godparents who become *compadres* and *comadres* (coparents). Many Mexicans and Mexican Americans live in the same towns as their *compadres* and use their help in a variety of ways (Keefe, Padilla, & Carlos, 1978).

Godparents are equivalent to an additional set of parents who have acquired formal kinship through a religious ceremony. They may act as guardians or sponsors of the godchild and care for him or her in emergencies, and they may be chosen from among members of the extended family or from outside. Godparents perform different roles and functions at various life cycle transitions and rituals, such as baptisms, communions, weddings, and funerals.

In many instances, migration separates the family from the godparents. However, near or far, godparents can have auxiliary functions as advocates for the child, adolescent, or even the parent. They can provide temporary relief for a sick or stressed parent or become an intermediary between parents and children. They can be especially valuable resources when therapy is addressing lifecycle impasses. In the case of an out-of-control adolescent, a godmother provided a "demilitarized zone" so that the parents and adolescent could begin to deal with their conflicts. Given their relative formality and emotional distance, godparents are often more effective with unruly adolescents than are the biological parents and even the grandparents, who sometimes are too partial to the child. Although godparents are seldom mentioned by Latino families in therapy, therapists might find a valuable resource if they take the initiative to ask about any *compadres* and *comadres*.

The Unquestioned Authority of Parents

Despite the presence of godparents, aunts, uncles, maids, and other players in the life of a Latino family, parents clearly have top billing. Although parents certainly care for and enjoy their children, affectional closeness and cohesion do not necessarily mean permeable boundaries, or even a great deal of self-disclosure, because too much closeness could threaten another strong organizing value: parental authority. Rules organized around age are the most important determinants of authority, with older men and women granted the greatest leadership and influence.

Latino parents command the *respeto* (respect) of children. Although the word *respeto* easily translates into English ("respect"), the meaning of the word is quite different in Spanish. For Anglo Americans, it reflects a fairly "detached, self-assured egalitarianism." For Mexicans, *respeto* means a relationship involving a "highly emotionalized dependence and dutifulness within a fairly authoritarian framework" (Díaz-Guerrero, 1975). For example, a 40-year-old Mexican woman recently said that she considered it a sin to be disrespectful of one's parents' needs for contact, involvement, and financial support in the way that her American boyfriend was with his parents.

In general, the status of parents is high and that of children low, although there are spoiled Latino children too, particularly in the upper classes. Complementary, vertical transactions between parents and children are stressed; symmetrical, horizontal transactions are discouraged or tolerated only in jest (Lomnitz, 1996). The unquestioned authority of parents persists throughout life, only slightly attenuated for adult children (Clark & Mendelson, 1975). Compare this situation with the Anglo American concept of "personal authority"

(Williamson, 1981), which underlines autonomy from parental approval as the hallmark of optional adult development.

The Status and Sacrifice of Mothers

Certain cultural prescriptions pertaining to gender also bolster parental status. The idealized role of the mother has been equated with self-denial and abnegation. When her patience is exhausted, a mother may become upset, nervous, or quietly suffer, but she is not expected to take time off or demand collective cooperation. A therapist may fail to convince a Latina mother that she needs time for herself and relief from her children. She may not share the Anglo American mother's resentment at being "other invested" rather than "self-invested," a value that underlies the individualistic nature of most dominant therapeutic goals.

The role of mother comprises a "mixed blessing." Latina mothers may experience considerable anxiety in relation to their children's safety and an excessive sense of responsibility. Mexican and Puerto Rican mothers may feel especially anxious about the dangers of the street and the vulnerability of their children to Los Angeles or New York gangs; they may believe that this danger may increase in proportion to the child's separation from his mother's lap.

On the positive side, the social position of "mother" carries considerable status and commands respect. A 52-year-old Mexican woman who is married to an Iranian man was totally devoted to mothering and homemaking. She considered these roles as the highest calling for an individual, because "it passes on the essence of family to the next generation." Furthermore, she felt that the household atmosphere she created played a very decisive role in enticing a great fellow to marry her daughter. "When he saw my clean house and the fresh, warm food I prepare," she said, "he was smitten with my daughter."

In payment for their sacrifice and dedication, mothers are the subject of much devotion, especially apparent in the lavish Mother's Day celebrations of Mexico. Indeed, mothers enjoy a lifelong reverence by their children—especially by their sons.

The Mother–Son Bond

Nowhere is parent–child closeness and devotion greater than in the relationship between mother and an oldest, an only, or a favorite son. This bond is mutually supportive. The mother may have a strong influence even over a grown adult son, and he in turn may always worship and side with his mother. A number of hypotheses about this powerful attachment go beyond mere emotional connectedness and enter the realm of family politics (Del Castillo, 1996). Some writers speak of the emotional isolation of the mother from her husband and the subsequent formation of a supportive subfamily unit of mother and children that excludes the husband. Still others regard a mother's instilling a fierce loyalty and devotion in her son as a way of undermining the authority of the patriarch and gaining ascendancy over him (Lamphere, 1974).

In the earlier discussion of connectedness, I addressed the danger of pathologizing *familismo* as enmeshment or codependency. At the other extreme lies the danger of romanticizing Latino family connectedness, including mother–son bonds that may be maladaptive. Clinicians who endeavor to be culturally respectful may be at risk of disregarding a number of fairly extreme, possibly universal, human problems that may appear as "closeness" but actually transcend cultural stylistic preferences. These problems are evident in repetitive, rigid behaviors and in imbalances of interpersonal influence that lead to developmental impasses and undifferentiation instead of growth. Such was the case of the family of Frank González Torres, Jr. This family of three illustrates parent–child connectedness gone awry, even though it has a culturally consonant flavor.

Frank Jr. was 9 years old when he was referred to therapy for night terrors and multiple fears. His mother, Mrs. Eudora González Torres, was a heavy-set and very properly attired 45-year-old woman who looked much older. She was born and raised in Mexico and lived with her parents before she got married in her mid-30s. She had wanted to go to nursing school but her mother did not let her for fear that she might become sexually active. Meanwhile, Frank's father had come from a very poor and chaotic family. He left his family in his early teens and fended for himself on the streets, ultimately becoming very suspicious and distant from almost everybody. When Eudora met Frank Sr., he was a single, very heavy, slow-mannered man a few years older than she. Frank Sr. was ready to get married then, but Eudora felt that she had to wait until her ill mother died before she could leave home. After her mother died, Frank Sr. and Eudora got married and migrated to the United States.

Their initial marital adjustment was smooth until Frank Jr. was born. In their words, "the apple of the discord" was planted. Instantly, mother and son became an inseparable unit. They slept in the same bed, displacing Mr. González Torres to the living room sofa. Disagreements about raising the boy mounted. Eudora protected her son and called his father a brutal and uncaring ugly monster. My impressions were to the contrary: the father's thoughts about his son's needs made more sense to me than did those of his wife.

The family first attempted to get help for Frank Jr. in kindergarten when he developed extreme separation anxiety. Prior to the boy entering first grade, mother and son suffered a conjoint psychotic break and were hospitalized and heavily sedated. The psychiatrists felt that the mother–son symbiosis was a hopeless situation and sent the boy to Mexico to live with relatives. Although Mrs. González Torres said that the separation was "like death to me," she complied with the plan.

After some time, Eudora recovered, Frank Sr. returned to the matrimonial bed, and the marital discord subsided. However, very soon after, the relatives in Mexico reported that Frank Jr. was having nightmares again. Immediately, the mother went to fetch the boy. Like a powerful magnet, mother and son embraced each other again and locked the father out in mind and body. Soon Frank Jr. developed terrors about everyone and everything. He could not go anywhere alone, not even to the bathroom.

I supported and engaged the father in therapy because he offered a hope for movement in a rigidly closed system. However, when Frank Sr. began to respond, Eudora wanted him out of the session. Creating an alliance and a boundary by seeing her alone prior to the conjoint sessions proved fruitless. She kept on repeating, "Poor me and poor little boy." I decided to challenge the rigidity indirectly by going with the flow and prescribing the symptom.

The paradoxical "ordeal-like" intervention required that Eudora go to school every day with Frank Jr., sit with him at all times, and monitor each and every one of his activities, including lunch and bathroom breaks. Eudora needed to ask written permission from the school principal for each of the activities every day. Contrary to my expectations, Eudora did not balk at the amount of work involved and cheerfully agreed to do everything. Gradually, however, Frank Jr. began to react. The other boys were teasing him and calling him a baby. He asked his mother to stop treating him so. One day, Frank Jr. abruptly said that he wanted to have his own apartment with no mother, father, or wife—just two pets: a cat and a dog. He would train the cat and the dog to live together from an early age because "if you get them old, they fight all the time, like they [his parents] do." Perhaps Frank Jr. would begin to separate and grow up a little after all. Like other breakthroughs with this family, this insight was short lived.

The González Torres family continued to have severe problems and failed to achieve any greater degree of individuation or separation. This type of extreme overinvolvement, fusion, or symbiosis is of a different magnitude and quality than the stylistic preference for connectedness and interdependence described here for Latinos. An article by Robert Jay Green and Paul Werner (1996) makes a very important contribution by rethinking the concept of enmeshment into two different concepts: functional "closeness–caregiving" and "dysfunctional intrusiveness." Green and Werner argue that some family relationships have a "superficial form of closeness" (high levels of contact, high degrees of disclosure) that derive from coercion, collusion, and anxious attachment rather than from mutuality.

The Meaning of Fatherhood

In the public's narrative of cultural ideals, Latino fathers are expected to protect the mother by demanding that the children obey and help her, while being only peripherally involved with daily caretaking, if at all. In reality, fathers may be playful and affectionate and do quite a bit of caretaking, particularly of young children (Gutmann, 1996).

The traditional pattern of father in the role of disciplinarian and mother as mediator between father and children may become more evident and rigid during the child's adolescence. Furthermore, the stresses of migration and culture change may contribute to a weakening of the father's authority. Sometimes, a father who appears controlling and intrusive with his adolescent children may simply be trying to be included in the family in the only way he knows how. I asked Elena's father, Mr. Morales, a Mexican immigrant, if this might be the case.

A congenial, feisty man, Mr. Morales rapidly answered me in the third person (with an *indirecta*): "He who appears to have military manners has in fact suffered a civilian 'coup d'état' years ago and has never been able to regain the presidency of the country." This metaphor for the ousted father became a central theme in the therapy. Mr. Morales explained that he felt guilty toward his wife because, in spite of great effort, he could not offer to the family the financial stability that he had originally envisioned. Mr. Morales recalled that, because of complications after Mrs. Morales had their fourth child, the lack of medical insurance led to medical bills that took many years to pay. To compensate for his failure, Mr. Morales tried to enlist the older children's cooperation in housework, hoping to make Mrs. Morales's life easier. The more that the father insisted, the more the adolescents resisted, rendering him frustrated arid ineffective. Now Mr. Morales could see that some of his attempted solutions become part of the problem.

Although some theories regard Latino men's dominance as based only on traditional cultural values (Mirandé, 1988), other theories (Baca-Zinn, 1982) see it as a response to structural factors in society. Male dominance may take on greater significance when social stratification systems exclude members of a minority from public roles, access to resources, or fair recognition for effort or other social rewards. This issue would seem to be particularly relevant to immigrant Latino men. The father who remains a disciplinarian in a culturally isolated situation is less acceptable to the children because he no longer represents a community of adults who uphold the same views.

The aloofness may be increased if he migrated first and his wife and children came later. The spouses may have never totally recovered from the separation, or the father's promise of a better future may never have materialized, decreasing permanently his prestige and influence. This situation may be exacerbated if the wife has joined the workforce to help out financially. The husband may forcefully assert his authority with his wife, who in turn signals to the children that their father is domineering and unfair. The children may see the mother as victimized and begin to protect her, or they may feel bound by gratitude to her. This type of family triangle may present special difficulties with adolescents who become scornful and distant from the father, perhaps irreversibly. (For an analysis of the positive and negative meanings of family triangles from a cross-cultural perspective, see Falicov, 1998.)

The widespread cultural stereotype of the Latino father as the dominant, authoritarian figure who makes all the decisions, is master of the household, and uses corporal punishment to discipline the children is contradicted by other images, views, and research data. Even as early as 1970, two studies supported a more egalitarian perspective on decision making for Mexican migrant farm families in California (Hawkes & Taylor, 1975) and a more equal division of household labor in Los Angeles and San Antonio (Glebler, Moore, & Guzman, 1970). In Mexico, Bronstein (1984, 1988) found no differences between mothers and fathers in scolding and criticizing or other exertions of authority. Although mothers were more physically nurturing in caretaking that comprised feeding and grooming, fathers were more emotionally nurturing in their playfulness with and verbal instruction of school-age children. Another recent study found that Latino fathers, when asked, believe that a family works better when husbands make the major decisions and wives support them, but agree that husbands should share in household responsibilities (Powell, 1995).

These findings coincide with my observations, although I have also encountered the more traditional authoritarian father and self-sacrificing mother, particularly in my clients' genograms of their families of origin. My interpretation is simply that, with any large group of people, considerable diversity will be found to support a variety of patterns. The fairest statement seems to be that Latino families are in transition, perhaps no different from families everywhere, and they display a mixture of traditional and egalitarian preferences.

The Sibling Bond

Fraternal Solidarity

Within the collectivistic Latino ideology, sibling ties are strong. Fraternal solidarity is an ideal that parents instill in their children from an early age. During childhood, siblings—along with cousins, or *primo hermanos*—may be constant companions. Parents prefer that their children have their brothers, sisters, and cousins as playmates, and children seem to be happy to do so. Competition and fighting among siblings is sometimes tolerated, although cooperation, sharing, and even sacrifice for a brother or sister are stressed. These values and the sibling bonds that they support endure throughout life. It is interesting that many adult, nondocumented immigrants live with a brother or a sister (Chávez, 1985).

The strength of this family tie provides a rich therapeutic resource, especially in multiproblem, underorganized families (Lewis, 1988). Sibling therapy eases generational, language, and value differences at any point during the life cycle and with members of any social class. It can be part of an effective method of cultural–generational mediation for immigrant families. The therapist can first interview the parents separately, then interview the siblings, and later bring the whole family together for a feedback session. In separate interviews, siblings can negotiate issues that they might not bring up with their parents present, or their cooperation may be enlisted to extricate an overprotected or a parental child from the parental subsystem.

As a separate modality, sibling therapy provides a good alternative when conventional family therapy is difficult or impossible, a frequent dilemma when family members are separated or disrupted because of migration, economics, or other struggles.

One of my first cases of sibling therapy was with the Robledo brothers: Gilberto (13), Rafael (11), and Chui (9). These three Puerto Rican boys were inhaling airplane glue together to get high. After numerous failed attempts to engage their mother, grandmother, or any other adults at home, the boys' probation officer was asked to bring whomever he could get. He came in with the three boys. My cotherapist, an American man in his mid-30s who had learned Spanish in the Peace Corps, and I spent the first two sessions building trust, discovering the individuality of each youngster, and understanding their relationships.

We spared them talking about their home situation. Their mother was functionally and emotionally unavailable—engaged in drug abuse and prostitution. Their daily home life seemed dismal and utterly hopeless. We talked about their neighborhood, their experiences with school, and what it meant for each of them to be Puerto Rican in Chicago. John and I talked about our ethnicities, gender, race, migrations, sibling groups and birth order, and the good and bad things in these categories and experiences. We were friendly and genuine, and even shared some of our questionable youthful experiences.

The five of us managed to feel a little closer to each other and were able to diffuse the hierarchies and the differences somewhat, but inevitably they were there. Thus, John and I decided to face the three youngsters as squarely as we could, by talking about our differences. We started with our differences in age, race, and gender. John and I stepped out of our roles as therapists briefly and talked about our roles as parents, in contrast to the boys' roles as children. I mentioned that I was a rather strict parent who did not like it when my children escaped their obligations to themselves, such as when they watched TV before doing their homework. Somewhat in jest, I confessed that I went around telling my children that if they watched too much TV their brains would turn into mashed potatoes. The roaring, cracking, writhing laughter that followed went on and on until Gilberto intervened forcefully saying, "Yeah! Hey, hey! Listen, listen, listen to this: can the stuff [airplane glue] turn your brains into mashed potatoes? Can it, can it? Hey, tell the truth, the truth!" We said that we thought that it did.

In the remarkable process that followed, Gilberto, the oldest sibling, became inspired to be almost primitively controlling of himself and his younger siblings. He instituted a system of surveillance and organized each brother to become a "cop" for the other, in a fashion reminiscent of William Golding's Ralph in *Lord of the Flies*. Anyone going near a hardware store or a parking lot was punished by the other two. Once, when Rafael and Chui teamed up and violated both rules, Gilberto abandoned them in the streets, did not talk to them for days, and came to a session by himself. Gilberto taught me about the power of sibling love and leadership when adults cannot nurture or control, but he also taught me about the human wish to care and be cared for, whatever it takes.

The Influence of Birth Order

Parents accord clear authority to older siblings and usually delegate some supervisory and caretaking functions to them. In large families, complex allocations of roles, division of labor, and individual compatibilities stimulate the formation of subgroups. Traditional gender role assignment encourages girls to do household chores for the boys, who in turn are supposed to chaperone and protect their sisters outside the home.

The oldest child tends to be "parentified," in part a consequence of migration (the child acts as cultural and language translator) and a common pattern in large families from collectivistic cultures. The parentified child's role as intermediary may persist throughout life, especially for daughters. This situation may work well but can also present difficulties during important life transitions, as happened in the following case.

Mariana Valdez brought her family of origin to therapy when she was 28 years old. She felt that her parents needed to develop a better relationship with her 16-year-old sister, who had become defiant and disrespectful. Although there were two older brothers, they had moved to the East Coast when they got married. Mariana lived with her second husband next door to her parents who, in spite of being in this country for 19 years, did not speak English or drive a car. Mariana took care of many of their public obligations and those of her two younger sisters, who were now 16 and 14 years old. Although this was not clearly stated as the reason for the consultation, Mariana had been recently diagnosed with advanced ovarian cancer. She feared for the well-being and social survival of her family as much as for her own life, and she knew that some drastic shifting of responsibilities had to take place.

Mariana was painfully ambivalent about her power in the family. On the one hand, she was proud of having been such a fundamental part of their adaptation. Yet, she was also deeply resentful about the constraints that this role entailed. Her first husband was a Mexican man who was abusive to her, but he had been approved by her parents because he was of the same culture and kept Mariana close to home. Another source of frustration for Mariana was that her sisters did not speak Spanish and used her as a translator and advocate to obtain freedoms, such as going out to movies and dances that the parents did not allow. The parents and the two younger sisters constantly turned to Mariana to mediate, causing her the stress of trying to be fair to both cultures and languages. Now she was very ill, very sad, and very tired, and she needed a replacement.

Mariana thought that if her role was indeed indispensable, somebody else should assume it, perhaps a therapist. This was a structural trap for me, given my own parentified role in my immigrant family of origin. Instead, I believed that a reshuffling of roles, more direct communication between the parents and younger children, and greater flexibility to make room for coexisting values seemed more appropriate therapeutic goals. (For an extensive description of this case, see Falicov, 1997.)

The influential position of an older sibling, particularly with immigrant parents, can be used to help a less favored or scapegoat sibling. Margarita Alonso had migrated to the United States from Mexico and was later joined by her mother and children. This case in more detail here shows how an older brother's intervention alleviated an interdependent, conflictual relationship between his mother and sister.

Soon after Margarita's mother and children joined her in San Diego, the young mother found herself struggling with the consequences of years of estrangement from all of them. Margarita was especially distressed by conflictual feelings toward her mother, Alma. She felt gratitude over the crucial role played by Alma in taking care of her children while Margarita sought a better life in the United States. However, Alma was critical of her daughter's lifestyle and her relationships with men. Margarita had been raised with values of *familismo y personalismo*. *Respeto* had stopped her from responding to Alma's criticisms until Margarita could not take it anymore and exploded in anger.

Gender issues played a definite role in that Alma relied on and respected the opinions of her sons—particularly the oldest, Agustin—but treated Margarita like a second-class citizen. When Agustin visited San Diego, I seized the opportunity for a sibling interview and presented it to Margarita as a way to obtain information about the family and enlist her brother's help.

Agustin's input was very enlightening. He was very supportive of Margarita, had a lot of empathy for her predicament, and offered his own perspective by telling Margarita a family secret. Agustin's theory was that Alma's pressure on Margarita over issues such as a woman's honor and reputation stemmed from her own shame regarding what Agustin called her "questionable past." There were many indications that, during her youth, Alma had worked as a barmaid and prostitute in a tiny Mexican town. Apparently, one of Margarita and Agustin's siblings, Ramona, had died of an acute infectious disease in her adolescence. Agustin had heard that their mother interpreted this death as punishment for her own "low life" and that was why she intensely returned to the Roman Catholicism of her childhood. Thus, Agustin attempted to dispel Margarita's anguish over her mother's accusations by shifting the blame and by promising Margarita that he would talk to Alma about relaxing the controls and criticisms and stressing, instead, all the good things about Margarita's hard work and accomplishments in the United States.

Continued emotional support, advice, and practical help among adult siblings are a tribute to the enduring connectedness of family ties among Latinos. Perhaps because of this closeness, quarrels and resentment among adult siblings are also common. These may occur because some siblings attempt to establish a more egalitarian relationship with each other during adulthood, but birth order and age hierarchies continue to be compelling. Sibling quarrels may also be caused by parental favoritism, disagreements about inheritance, unpaid debts, or the persistence of a controlling attitude on the part of an older sibling toward a younger one. Rifts among siblings, however, are seldom permanent. New family transitions often serve as points of reunion and pathways to rejuvenate brother and sister ties.

COMMUNICATION STYLES AND THERAPY

Ideologies about connectedness and hierarchies as reflected in the cultural meaning systems of *familismo* and *respeto* significantly shape the Latino family's style of communication. This final section explores some of the nuances of Latino communication and their implications for treatment.

Language and Politeness

The *amabilidad* (amiability), gentility, and civility of the Spanish language no doubt contribute to a politeness of demeanor, deportment, and address. From early in life, Latinos are raised with the notion that much can be achieved interpersonally if people talk nicely, explain a lot, and give compliments.

Maintaining Harmony: *Indirectas*, *Choteo*, and *Dichos*

In keeping with their desire to preserve family harmony and avoid interpersonal conflict, most collectivistic cultures favor indirect, implicit, and covert communications. People publicly agree—or at least do not disagree—with each other in order to "get along" and not make others uncomfortable. Conversely, assertiveness, open differences of opinion, and direct demands for clarification are seen as rude or insensitive to others' feelings.

The use of impersonal third-person rather than first-person pronouns is one aspect of this style. For example, by stating that "one could be proud of…" rather than "I am proud of…," the Latino individual is viewed as appropriately subtle and selfless. The use of allusions, proverbs, and parables to convey an opinion is commonplace, especially among Mexicans. Cubans seem more adept than Mexicans and Puerto Ricans at directness, softened by a mordant, piquant, and sometimes even outrageous sense of humor. The result of all this is an apparent harmony, sometimes at the expense of a clear understanding of the other's intent.

Indirectas are also used to maintain harmony when the emotion at hand is anger. A Mexican saying states that "the one who gets angry loses." Thus, criticisms often take the form of allusion (e.g., "Some people never change"), diminutives used in a sarcastic way, and belittlement. Similarly, Boswell and Curtis (1984) describe a Cuban's use of *choteo* (humor) as a way of ridiculing or making fun of people, situations, or things. *Choteo* may involve exaggerations, jokes, or satire to modify tense situations (Boswell & Curtis, 1984).

Harmony is also maintained by the formation of "light" triangles. Rapport-based alliances, especially when based along gender lines, provide an emotional outlet in the form of gossip and secrets. Rather than being detrimental, these light alliances may enhance the stability of a marriage (Komarovsky, 1967). As in other cultures, women's proclivity to "trouble talk" may be a basic ingredient of Latina intimacy (Tannen, 1990). In fact, Mexican working women consider it permissible to be disrespectful about their husbands' traits when talking to other women (Beneria & Roldan, 1987).

In addition to the use of *indirectas* and *choteo*, positive emotional expression is highly valued in the Latino culture. Words of endearment, compliments about a person's appearance, dress, or smile, or support for his or her positive qualities spice up conversations among intimates. Indeed, closeness is demonstrated not only by these verbal expressions but also through physical proximity and gestures. A couch in my office that accommodates only one American parent and one child comfortably seats one or two Latino parents with two or three children! Touching, kissing, and hugging are other manifestations of close family relationships, particularly between Latino parents and children. However, they extend to other friendly relationships too: in Mexico, Puerto Rico, and Cuba, teachers kiss pupils, hairdressers kiss their clients, and children kiss the parents of their friends.

In setting examples of *indirectas* and emotional closeness, Latino parents teach their children to have a "proper demeanor" and a considerate, helpful, and warm approach toward others. Later, they will be praised and liked for displaying *simpatía*—the ability to create smooth, friendly, and pleasant relationships that avoid conflict (Comas-Díaz, 1989; Levine & Padilla, 1980).

IMPLICATIONS FOR THERAPY

The Latino culture's emphasis on smooth relationships, social graces, and *personalismo* has significant implications for family functioning and family therapy. On occasion, communication styles that emphasize indirectness and civility in the name of avoiding conflict can become excessive and lead to concealment, lies, and intrigues. At other times, they may provide veiled messages sent on circuitous routes. Consider again the case of Margarita Alonso, her mother, Alma, and Margarita's brother Agustin.

Agustin had suggested that his mother might be having difficulty in her relationship with Margarita because of a "secret past" in which Alma, their mother, had worked as a barmaid and prostitute. However, the story did not end there. Margarita asked to see me alone 2 weeks after that sibling session. She started by telling me that she believed the story Agustin had told; she now vaguely recollected hearing rumors about their mother's past. However,

Margarita's main fear was that perhaps Agustin also meant the story as an indirect communication toward her. Margarita started weeping, pouring forth a confession about her own involvement with prostitution. In fact, she never could have paid for the three airplane tickets to the border, the "coyote" (smuggler) that brought them through, or the downsizing of their apartment had she not supplemented her meager salary with prostitution (Castillo, 1996). I will never know whether the brother really knew or just suspected these events in Margarita's life, but this type of indirect communication, by allusion, is fairly typical of a style that avoids direct confrontation.

Distinguishing the degree to which such patterns of indirect communication are maladaptive for a particular family is part of the therapist's task. Attention to style of communicating between client and therapist also has important implications at different points during treatment. An initial social phase that transmits the therapist's interest rather than focusing on procedures (such as referral sheets and appointment schedules) is critical when joining with a new client family. Manifesting real interest in the client, the problem, their theories about why the problem exists, and the attempted solutions is essential, given the Latino emphasis on *personalismo*, or building personal relationships.

A tone of acceptance that avoids direct confrontation or does not demand greater disclosure is essential throughout treatment. The therapist's use of humor, allusions, and diminutives softens the directness of treatment and is often a more effective delivery because these mirror preferred cultural transactional styles. Disclosure can be facilitated when the therapist becomes a philosopher of life through storytelling, anecdotes, and metaphors. Use of analogies, proverbs, popular songs, or a mysterious, unexpected communication that transmits an existential sense of the absurd or the reversals of life is consonant with Mexican cultural themes. A therapist's knowledge and timely use of *dichos* (proverbs) is an invaluable aesthetic communications resource (Dow, 1986; Fischer, 1988) for many groups, but Latinos are particularly adept with these metaphorical statements.

An intense emotive style and person-centered approach is more appealing than a businesslike, structured, or task-oriented approach. When feelings are subtly elicited by the therapist, Latinos respond much more openly than when they are directly asked to describe or explain their emotions and reactions. An experiential approach that emphasizes "telling it like it is" or "baring one's soul" and interpreting nonverbal language may well inhibit clients.

Similarly, although contracts and behavioral treatment goals might be too task oriented (most Latinos would not be comfortable scheduling certain times to be intimate or to resolve problems), the therapist can assign "conditional homework," perhaps asking the family to think about how it would feel to engage in a particular task if the occasion should arise. Such a technique is not only more collaborative and less presumptive, but also consonant with a culture that values serendipity, chance, and spontaneity in interpersonal relationships.

Whatever the theoretical orientation or type of intervention used, therapists should invite the family's feedback about the process of treatment. In a culture that emphasizes cooperation and respect for authority, clients may feel that it is impolite to disagree openly with the therapist. Encouraging the family to express their positive and negative reactions to the therapist's opinions helps to establish a tone of mutuality.

In conclusion, the client who said, "I do not belong to the culture of 911" was right: the Latino community seems to have little need for the assistance of 911. A plethora of others can be turned to for help, and many close and distant relationships occupy one's life. Therapists usually know little about the resources provided and the constraints imposed by large nuclear and extended family arrangements.

The challenge is to constantly be aware that a different model of individual development and family relationships from that of the conventional, middle-class Anglo American version may be operating. The extended family model may be in action even when families are fragmented across countries and undergo frequent expansions and contractions in family composition. The dimensions selected for discussion in this chapter—namely, connectedness, the cast of characters with their positions in the family hierarchy, communication, conflict resolution, and emotional expression—are particularly important domains, especially when one considers the degree of consonance or dissonance between the "maps" of the family and those of the therapist. These are also dimensions of family life in which cultural continuity, cultural change, temporary culture clash (with its ensuing clinical correlates), and eventual resolution through alternation or hybridization take place.

REFERENCES

Alvirez, D., Bean, F. D., & Williams, D. (1981). The Mexican American family. In C. H. Mindel & R. W. Habenstein (Eds.), *Ethnic families in America: Patterns and variations* (pp. 271–292). New York: Elsevier.

Baca-Zinn, M. (1982). Familism among Chicanos: A theoretical overview. *Humboldt Journal of Social Relations, 10*(1), 224–238.

Bartra, R. (1987). *La jaula de la melencolía: Identidad y metamorfosis del Mexicano.* Mexico, D.F.: Editorial Grifalso.

Beneria, L., & Roldan, M. (1987). *The crossroads of class and gender: Industrial homework, subcontracting and household dynamics in Mexico City.* Chicago: University of Chicago Press.

Boswell, T. D., & Curtis, J. R. (1984). *The Cuban-American experience: Culture, images, and perspectives.* Totowa, NJ: Rowman & Allanheld.

Bronstein, P. (1984). Differences in mothers' and fathers' behaviors toward children: A cross-cultural comparison. *Developmental Psychology, 20,* 995–1003.

Bronstein, P. (1988). Father–child interaction: Implications for gender role socialization. In P. Bronstein & C. P. Cowan (Eds.), *Fatherhood today: Men's changing role in the family* (pp. 107–124). New York: Wiley.

Castillo, A. (1996). *Goddess of the Americas/La diosa de las Américas: Writings on the Virgin of Guadalupe.* New York: Riverhead Books.

Chavez, D. (1994). *Face of an angel.* New York: Warner Books.

Chávez, L. (1985). Households, migration, and labor market participation: The adaptation of Mexicans to life in the United States. *Urban Anthropology, 14,* 301–346.

Clark, M., & Mendelson, M. (1975). Mexican-American aged in San Francisco. In W. C. Sze (Ed.), *Human life cycle,* New York: Jason Aronson.

Comas-Díaz, L. (1989). Culturally relevant issues and treatment implications for Hispanics. In D. R. Koslow & E. Salett (Eds.), *Crossing cultures in mental health.* Washington, D.C.: Society for International Education Training and Research.

Del Castillo, A. R. (1996). Gender and its discontinuities in male/female domestic relations: Mexicans in cross-cultural context. In D. Marciel & I. D. Ortiz (Eds.), *Chicanas/Chicanos at the crossroads: Social, economic and political change.* Tucson: University of Arizona Press.

Díaz-Guerrero, R. (1975). *Psychology of the Mexican: Culture and personality.* Austin: University of Texas Press.

Dow, J. (1986). Universal aspects of symbolic healing. *American Anthropologist, 18,* 58–59.

Falicov, C. J. (1997). So they don't need me anymore: Weaving migration, illness and coping. In S. Daniel, J. Hepworth, & W. Doherty (Eds.), *Stories about medical family therapy.* New York: Basic Books.

Falicov, C. J. (1998). The cultural meaning of family triangles. In M. McGoldrick (Ed.), *Re-visioning family therapy: Race, culture, and gender in clinical practice.* New York: Guilford Press.

Fischer, M. M. (1988). Aestheticized emotions and critical hermeneutics. *Culture, Medicine and Psychiatry, 12*(1), 31–42.

Glebler, L., Moore, J., & Guzman, R. (1970). *The Mexican American people.* New York: Free Press.

Green, R. J., & Werner, P. D. (1996). Intrusiveness and closeness caregiving: Rethinking the concept of family enmeshment. *Family Process, 35*(2), 115–134.

Gutmann, M. C. (1996). *The meanings of macho: Being a man in Mexico City.* Berkeley: University of California Press.

Hawkes, G. R., & Taylor, M. (1975). Power structure in Mexican and Mexican-American farm labor families. *Journal of Marriage and the Family, 37,* 807–811.

Inclán, J., & Hernández, M. (1993). Cross-cultural perspectives and codependence: The case of poor Hispanics. *American Journal of Orthopsychiatry, 62*(2), 245–255.

Keefe, S. (1984). Real and ideal extended familism among Mexican Americans and Anglo Americans: On the meaning of "close" family ties. *Human Organization, 43,* 65–70.

Keefe, S. E., Padilla, A. M., & Carlos, M. L. (1978). The Mexican American family as an emotional support system. In J. M. Casas & S. E. Keefe (Eds.), *Family and mental health in the Mexican-American community* (Monograph No. 7). Los Angeles: University of California, Spanish Speaking Mental Health Center.

Komarovsky, M. (1967). *Blue collar marriage.* New York: Random House.

Lamphere, L. (1974). Strategies, cooperation, and conflict among women in domestic groups. In M. Zimbalist Rosaldo & L. Lamphere (Eds.), *Women, culture, and society*. Palo Alto, CA: Stanford University Press.

Levine, E. S., & Padilla, A. M. (1980). *Crossing cultures in therapy: Pluralistic counseling for the Hispanic*. Belmont, CA: Wadsworth.

Lewis, K. G. (1988). Sibling therapy with muliproblem families. *Journal of Marital and Family Therapy, 12*(3), 291–300.

Lomnitz, L. A., & Perez-Lizaur, M. (1987). *A Mexican elite family: 1820–1980*. Princeton, NJ: Princeton University Press.

Lomnitz, L. A. (1996). *A comparative study of political cultures in Mexico and Chile: An anthropological approach*. Research Seminar on Mexico and U.S.–Mexican Relations, University of California, San Diego, CA.

Mindel, C. H. (1980). Extended families among urban Mexican American, Anglos, and Blacks. *Hispanic Journal of Behavioral Sciences, 2*(7), 21–34.

Mirandé, A. (1988). Chicano fathers: Traditional perceptions and current realities. In P. Bronstein & C. P. Cowan (Eds.), *Fatherhood today: Men's changing role in the family* (pp. 93–106). New York: Wiley.

Paz, O. (1961). *The labyrinth of solitude: Life and thought in Mexico*. New York: Evergreen Books.

Powell, D. R. (1995). Including Latino fathers in parent education and support programs: Development of a program model. In R. E. Zambrana (Ed.), *Understanding Latino families*. Thousand Oaks, CA: Sage.

Ramirez, O., & Arce, C. H. (1981). The contemporary Chicano family: An empirically based review. In A. Baron, Jr. (Ed.), *Explorations in Chicano psychology* (pp. 3–28). New York: Praeger.

Ramírez, S. (1977). *El Mejicano, psicología de sus motivaciones*. Mexico, D.F.: Editorial Grifalso.

Roland, A. (1988). *In search of self in India and Japan: Toward a cross-cultural psychology*. Princeton, NJ: Princeton University Press.

Tannen, D. (1990). *You just don't understand: Women and men in conversation*. New York: Ballantine Books.

Vega, W. A. (1990). Hispanic families in the 1980s: A decade of research. *Journal of Marriage and the Family, 52*, 1015–1024.

Williamson, D. (1981). Termination of the intergenerational hierarchical boundary between the first and second generations: A new stage in the family. *Journal of Marital and Family Therapy, 7*(4), 441–452.

CHAPTER 4

The Family in Therapy*

SALVADOR MINUCHIN

As emphasized in an earlier chapter, the concept of universality among families has some truth in it. Many of my suggestions of therapy in this chapter can and have been applied to families representing different backgrounds and cultures and they work with Latino families. However, it is important to acknowledge and understand also the differences within cultures including the cultures and subcultures of Latinos.

What often brings a family, including Latino families, into therapy is the symptoms of one member of the family. This is the identified patient, whom the family labels as having problems or being the problem. However, when a family labels one of its members as the "patient," the identified patient's symptoms can be assumed to be a system-maintaining or a system-maintained device. The symptom may be an expression of a family dysfunction or it may have arisen in the individual family member because of his particular life circumstances and then been supported by the family system. In either case, the family's consensus that one member is the problem indicates that, on some level, the symptom is reinforced by the system.

As open sociocultural systems, many Latino families are today continually faced by demands for change. These demands are sparked by biopsychosocial changes in one or more of the members and by various inputs from the social

---

*"The Family in Therapy" reprinted by permission of the publisher from *Families and the Family Therapy* by Salvador Minuchin, pp. 110–122, Cambridge, Mass.: Harvard University Press, Copyright 1974 by the President and Fellows of Harvard College.

system in which every family is embedded. A family having difficulty is a system that has responded to these internal or external demands for change by stereotyping its functioning. Demands for change have been countered by a reification of the family structure. The accustomed transactional patterns have been preserved to the point of rigidity, which blocks any possibility of alternatives. Selecting one person to be the problem is a simple method of maintaining a rigid, inadequate family structure.

The family therapist's function is to help the family by facilitating the transformation of the family system. This process includes three major steps. The therapist joins the family in a position of leadership. When joining, small talk is important with all families and particularly important with Latino families. This process unearths and evaluates the underlying family structure and creates circumstances that will allow the transformation of this structure. In actual therapy, these steps are inseparable.

As a result of therapy, the family is transformed. Changes are made in the set of expectations that governs the family members' behavior. As a result, the extra-cerebral mind of each family member is altered, and the individual's experience changes. This transformation is significant for all family members, but particularly so for any identified patient, who is freed from the deviant position.

In family therapy, the transformation of structure is defined as changes in the position of family members vis-à-vis each other, with a consequent modification of their complementary demands. Although change and transformation are similar terms, in this context they belong to different grammars. In family therapy, transformation, or the restructuring of the family system, leads to change or the individual's new experience. Transformation usually does not change the composition of the family. The change occurs in the synapses—the way in which the same people relate to each other.

When the therapist joins the family, he assumes the leadership of the therapeutic system. This leadership involves responsibility for what happens. The therapist must assess the family and develop therapeutic goals based on that assessment and must intervene in ways that facilitate the transformation of the family system in the direction of those goals. The target of these interventions is the family. Although individuals must not be ignored, the therapist's focus is on enhancing the operation of the family system. The family will be the matrix of the healing and growth of its members. The responsibility for reaching this state, or for failing to do so, belongs to the therapist in collaboration with the family.

DISEQUILIBRIUM IN TRANSFORMATION

In order to transform the family system à la structural family therapy, the therapist often must intervene so as to unbalance the system. This is generally true of all family systems, including Latino families. Jay Haley (1971) pointed out the pitfalls of forming a strong affiliation with one member of the family, indicating that if the therapist enters into a coalition with one spouse against the other in a particular session, he should soon repair and recreate the balance by coalescing or allying with the other. This kind of balancing technique is helpful in some cases because the therapist can increase the flexibility of the family and its ability to negotiate conflicts by helping it to attain balance.

However, in other cases, balancing techniques may crystallize the rigidity of the family. For example, if a therapist is working with a rigidly pathogenic family in which the only daughter, a 14-year-old girl with anorexia nervosa, is the identified patient, the therapist's family map reflects an overinvolvement of daughter and mother. The husband and maternal grandmother may be joined in a coalition that isolates the mother within the adult subsystem. The mother's only possibility for effectiveness and competence lies in her relationship with her daughter. The therapist's goal here is to create distance between the mother and daughter and to define a boundary around the spouse subsystem that will make it possible to free the girl and the mother from their deviant positions.

The therapist whispers to the girl, "Tell your mother that she does not love you enough and that is why you look like a scarecrow." The girl, seeking the therapist's support, obeys. Some therapists would question this intervention because the family therapist is encouraging the girl to be openly aggressive toward her mother, on whom she is pathologically dependent. The therapist might worry about the girl's inevitable guilt feelings. Perhaps she is not expressing her unconscious rage openly but is merely parroting the therapist's words. To blame the mother for the daughter's symptom would seem like minimizing the girl's responsibility for her actions and supporting the mutual dependence of mother and daughter. Finally, the tactic could be viewed as unfair to the mother, who is undercut by her husband and her daughter.

I believe, however, that the therapist is by this means taking a step toward the therapeutic goal. The only possibility for improvement in this family lies in the creation of distance between mother and daughter. The therapist's tactics are designed to separate mother and daughter. Accordingly, this tactic forms a coalition with the identified patient against the mother. The intervention skews the balance of all four family members. The mother, deprived of the outlet of her daughter and further stressed by the therapist's criticism, will have no choice but to increase her demands on her husband. The proximity between husband and wife will make it possible to separate the mother and daughter and to free them from their deviant positions.

The structurally oriented therapist (discussed in this chapter as an approach in working with Latino families) may appear to be unfair to individual family members. At any particular transitional moment in therapy, the process will look one sided. The therapist will seem to be ignoring the complexity of individual dynamics and may even appear to show insensitivity to the needs of individual family members. However, the total process of therapy will reveal that the therapist is maintaining a sense of contact with the family members in such a way that they follow even at times when they are experiencing this as unfair. The therapist must be sensitive to the dynamics of the family members, supporting them and confirming some aspects of their personality even when disqualifying them in other areas. Any therapist who does not have the capacity to imbue the family with a strong sense of his respect for each one of them as individuals and a firm commitment to healing will lose the family in the processes of transformation. This is particularly true when working with Latino families.

The family's reliance on the therapist is extremely important in the skewing process. When the therapist unbalances a family system by joining with one member, the other members experience stress. Their response may be to insist on system maintenance. The therapist must counter this by insisting that the family members move in the direction of the therapeutic goals while enduring the uncertainties of the transitional period. This movement is facilitated by the therapist's understanding, support, and confirmation of the family members' experiences and felt needs.

The therapist's use of self to support family members is particularly crucial in work with pathologically enmeshed families. However, as stated earlier in this text, one must be careful not to make a pathology of Latino family enmeshment. Some families' lack of differentiation makes any separation from the family an act of betrayal. The sense of belonging dominates the experience of being, at the expense of a sense of a separate self. Entering this situation, the therapist works to demarcate psychological and interactional turfs.

However, if one tries to yank a member of the family system away, the system will pull more strongly than the therapist can. It is impossible to disengage a member from the system unless he is engaged at a different level. For example, if as part of a rigid triad a child is deeply involved in the affairs of the spouse subsystem and closely allied with one of the parents, one therapeutic goal would be to block the rigid transactional patterns, preventing the use of this child and the reinforcement of his or her symptoms. One tactic, as well as a goal, would be to return the child to a rewarding position in the sibling subsystem. This role of the child is more in line with most Latino families.

Sometimes the interweaving of engagement and disengagement is feasible within the family. For example, while a child is being disengaged from a rigid triad and engaged with the sibling subsystem, the boundary around the spouse subsystem can be strengthened to increase the spouses' engagement. At other times, the therapist may have to use himself as a transitional channel for extrafamilial engagement in order to facilitate the disengagement from the family. Extrafamilial resources can be hooked into the system, such as by prodding a mother to find an activity that yields satisfactions outside her family or introducing as "cotherapist" an adolescent companion to facilitate the movement of a withdrawn adolescent toward the world of his peers. The therapist must monitor the impact of therapy and of life circumstances on the family and be ready to offer support. Change through therapy, like any other family change, is accompanied by stress, and the therapeutic system must be capable of dealing with it. Extended family members in Latino families can provide needed support.

The disequilibrium produced by the therapist's entrance into the family and its accommodation may be valuable in itself, but may not always be in the direction of the therapeutic goals. The suction of the system may pull the therapist into a contraindicated position. For example, a family comes into therapy because the husband has migraines. He is ashamed of his humble origins, having been the first of his family to go to college. He married a woman whose family he admired for their intellectual accomplishments, and he has great respect for his wife's opinions. She is the rule setter to whom he accommodates and defers, possibly not as in the traditional Latino family.

One therapeutic goal in this case might be to change the relative power positions of the spouses, transforming the family structure so that the man will gain status, securing more respect from his wife and achieving self-respect. To that end, the therapist affiliates with the man in initial sessions, supporting him and sometimes joining him in a coalition that is critical of the wife.

After four sessions, the wife calls to say that she wants an individual session. She is thinking of having an affair but does not want to hurt her husband by presenting this material in a joint session. When the therapist sees her in the individual session, she lets him know, without making it explicit, that he is the man with whom she wants an affair. He thinks that, as an analyst, he could have interpreted the woman's feeling as a transferential phenomenon or as resistance to therapy. As a structural family therapist, however, he cannot use this formula. He is faced with two questions. First, how can he help the woman to leave the session without a loss of self-esteem so as not to handicap therapy? Second, what has he done in previous sessions to downgrade her husband vis-à-vis the therapist and what can he do to repair that?

The therapist tells the woman to look at an abstract picture on the wall of his office and imagine that she is on a date with the man whom she wants as a lover. When she describes her fantasies, he tells her that they are very thin. Her descriptions of the man, he says, are so global and lacking in quality that it is obvious that she would only be exploited in a sexual relationship with him. Indirectly, this represents an attack on the woman in several ways. Because she is an actress, she resents having her fantasy description called thin. As an advocate of women's liberation, she reacts strongly to the suggestion that she is seeking a relationship in which she will be exploited. She leaves the office angry and disappointed at the therapist's insensitivity and obtuseness, but ready to continue therapy with her husband. She tells her husband about the session, without telling him that the therapist was her intended lover.

During the next session with the couple, the therapist treats the man with great respect, concentrating on his statements and paying close attention to the quality of what he says. He attacks the woman in such a way that the man comes to her defense and attacks the therapist. This helps to correct the skew caused in the previous sessions. Now both spouses have joined in a coalition against the therapist. Within this coalition, they occupy positions of parity. This makes it possible to create a therapeutic system based on the cooperation of peers.

ALTERNATIVE TRANSACTIONS IN TRANSFORMATION

A man separates from his wife, who has manic depressive episodes, when his daughter is 6 and his son is 5. Later he remarries and has another boy. After 5 years, he brings the two children of his first marriage to live with him and his new family. The family comes into therapy because of his daughter's undue sensitivity, crying spells, and feelings of being unloved.

The second wife, 2 years older than her husband, has a limited capacity to express feeling. Some therapists, after watching a session, might be very concerned about the stepmother's inhibited affective range. Perhaps the identified patient has a great joy of living, which could be made potential in therapy. The situation might dampen this.

The family therapist replies that if he had to search for a stepmother for the daughter of a manic-depressive woman, he would look for a woman with a narrow affective response. The family is suffering from transitional problems. A family of three is being forced to incorporate two new members and become a family of five. The ensuing problems of mutual accommodation and change in structure are what have brought them into therapy.

The father is trying to act as a buffer to protect his wife from his daughter. He enters into power struggles with the daughter, from which the stepmother is excluded. These conflicts escalate without resolution, leaving father and daughter furious and frustrated. The father, having experienced many similar conflicts with his first wife, tells his daughter that she is too much like her mother. He expresses concern that she too will grow up to be crazy.

The therapist's goal is to free this girl from her mother's "ghost" and to help the family through the processes of transition (Figure 4.1).

Accordingly, the strategy is concentrating on the stepmother, eliciting her comments, responding respectfully to her meager inputs, and stating that she is the key to change in the family. This reinforces and increases her activity in the sessions. The therapist forms a coalition with her, saying that her acceptance of the man's children is vital to the family and a meaningful thing for the marriage. However, the therapist questions her acceptance of the ghost of the first wife that her husband is bringing into their household. The second wife must help her husband exorcise this ghost. The father is attacked for failing to

$$\frac{FD_1}{MD_2} \quad \text{becomes} \quad \frac{FM}{D_1D_2}$$

Figure 4.1 The family transition.

recognize that his daughter is a teenager, not a peer with whom it is appropriate to enter into power struggles. He is also told to realize that she is a person in her own right, not an extension of her mother. The coalition of therapist, wife, and children transforms the family, transitionally making the husband the deviant and freeing the daughter.

This kind of treatment, which focuses on how people can affect and help each other, characterizes the therapist who regards the family as the matrix of healing. The goal is mutual accommodation and support. The stepmother, a wife who has always been afraid to challenge her husband, learns from her young stepdaughter. While the stepmother is learning from the girl how to challenge, the girl is learning from her stepmother how to retreat.

MOVEMENT IN THERAPY

Family members' experiences change as their positions relative to one another are transformed. The question arises as to why family members accept repositioning and why the transformations are maintained when the therapist is no longer part of the unit. The family comes into therapy asking the therapist only to alleviate the presenting problem. The wonder is that its members then allow and assimilate the therapist's probes, challenges, and insistence on change.

Like all therapists, the family therapist challenges people's perceptions of reality. It is conveyed to family members that his experiences are questionable because the therapist knows that reality is more complex. Family members' certainty of the validity of their experiences is eroded. This is not a confrontation technique. Rather, the therapist supports the family members, but suggests that there is something beyond what they have perceived. In effect, this is saying "yes, but…" or "yes, and…."

The therapist convinces the family members that the "yes, but" or "yes, and" suggestions are derived from their own natures. Statements that the family members find correct based on their previous experiences must support this position of doubt. Although challenges are made on grounds beyond what they can see, families are hooked into alternative possibilities of experience or alternative codes, already available. In such cases, it is helpful to understand the Latino family's worldview. Therapy must be a part of the family member's existing repertory.

For example, a wife makes an appointment for therapy because her husband has personal problems and also has great difficulty relating to their two sons. In the first session, the therapist sees the spouses alone. The husband says that he is the member of the family who has the problems. He describes himself as intellectual and logical. Because he is logical, he is sure that he is right; therefore, he tends to be authoritarian.

The therapist interrupts, after appropriate joining, to say that a man who is so concerned with logic and correctness must often be frustrated in life. He criticizes the man for never allowing his wife to perceive the depression he must feel and never allowing her to help him. By this means, the therapist is blocking a well-oiled but dysfunctional relationship in terms of an expanded reality. This observation feels right to the man, who acknowledges his depression, and fits the woman's never expressed wish for an opportunity to support her husband. Both spouses experience the therapist's challenging, change-requiring input as familiar and welcome because it recognizes the woman's felt needs and suggests some alternatives available to the man. The therapist then assigns a task based on his "yes, but." Under specified circumstances, when the wife feels her husband is wrong, she is nevertheless to side with him.

The parents bring the children to the next session. The adults have performed the assigned task and feel closer. The husband believes that his wife supports him, and she is gratified by the increased sensitivity and decreased authoritarianism that he has displayed in response to her support.

When the entire family is seen in therapy, it becomes clear that the children and mother are in a coalition that has isolated the father, making him peripheral and leaving too much of the socialization process to the mother. The children act as a rescue squad. When father sets rules, he does so in a pompous, *ex cathedra* manner, which makes the mother feel frustrated and helpless. The children begin to misbehave in ways that deflect their father's wrath to them. The younger child is particularly expert at this, and the relationship between him and his father is particularly tense.

The therapist's tactics are to break up the coalition of mother and children, clarifying the boundary around the spouse subsystem and increasing the proximity of husband and wife and of father and children. Accordingly, his strategems must support the father, even though the therapist disagrees with him. Tasks are assigned that will bring the father and younger son together, excluding the mother. This task also confirms the father in his evident skills of logical thinking and detached observation of behavior, but now directs these skills positively toward a son whom he has always regarded as irritating. The father is to meet with the son at least three times during the week for a period of no longer than 1 hour. During this period, he is to use his capacity for clear observation and analysis by studying his son so that, during the next session, he can describe the son's particular characteristics to the therapist. In this way, the therapist is brought into the contact between father and son as a distant observer. The father, who has always related to this child with impulsive, derogatory, controlling movements, will feel the therapist encouraging him to use his logical skills in relating to his son, inhibiting his impulsiveness. The mother, who has been stressed by her exclusion from this interaction, will nevertheless feel supported in an important area: her wish that her husband become a good father.

The father, mother, and son are all repositioned by the therapist's interventions. Originally, they accepted these position changes because the therapist offered them alternatives within their range and held out a promise of more satisfactory arrangements. The family transformation is maintained when the therapist is not there because new dynamics among the family members have been activated by the transformation, and the new transactional patterns are supported by them. The new transactional patterns thus tend toward self-maintenance.

Patients move for three reasons. First, they are challenged in their perception of their reality. Second, they are given alternative possibilities that make sense to them. Third, once they have tried out the alternative transactional patterns, new relationships appear that are self-reinforcing.

THE ROAD IS HOW YOU WALK IT

The concept of transformation deals with large movements in therapy that take place over time. The therapist must know how to map goals and how to facilitate the small movements that carry the family toward those goals. Help is presented in such a way that families are not threatened by major dislocations. A person's ability to move from one circumstance to another depends on the support received because he or she will not move toward the unknown in a situation of danger. Therefore, it is vital to provide systems of support within the family to facilitate the movement from one position to another. This is particularly true when working with Latino families.

Therapeutic contact occurs on a level of interpersonal immediacy within a specific context. As the poet Jimenez wrote, "The road is not the road, the road is how you walk it." The content of a session depends on many idiosyncratic factors, such as the family's worldview, transactional style, and the therapist's personality. It is not surprising, therefore, that therapeutic descriptions seeking to generalize discuss techniques of treatment in isolation. However, therapeutic content relates closely to the current life experience of a family. The family dynamics and structure are conveyed by the content of the communications among its members as well as by the order of those communications.

The content of a session is also influenced by the therapist's input. Two therapists might arrive at basically the same goals and tactics for a family, but the means to those goals would differ markedly because the therapists' styles, as the product of their life experiences, are different. For example, my style is partly a product of a childhood spent in an Anglo-described "enmeshed" family with 40 aunts and uncles and roughly 200 cousins, all of whom formed, to one degree or another, a close family network. My hometown in rural Argentina, with only one main street that was called "Main Street Number Eleven," had a population of 4,000. My grandparents, two uncles, a cousin, and their families lived on our block. Like an inhabitant of Chinatown, when I walked the street, I felt that a hundred cousins were watching me. Thus, I had to learn as a child to feel comfortable in situations of proximity, yet to disengage sufficiently to protect my individuality.

As a young professional, I tended to empathize with children and to blame their parents. After I was married, had children of my own, and was making the mistakes that parents inevitably make, I began to understand parents and to sympathize with them. My life in Israel, where I worked with Jewish children from many cultural backgrounds, and in the United States, where I worked with Black and Puerto Rican families, sensitized me to the universality of human phenomena, as well as to the different ways in which specific cultures prescribe a person's response to these phenomena. I became particularly aware of the manner in which societies coerce their underdogs (Minuchin, 1967).

Through the years, I have had a number of successes and made innumerable blunders; these have given me a sense of competence and authority. In my worst moments, this sense of achievement is expressed in an authoritarian stance, and at other times it allows me to operate as an expert. In the measure to which I have learned to accept myself and to recognize areas in which I will never change, I have developed a sense of respect for the diversity of people's approaches to human problems.

My therapeutic style is organized along two parameters: how to preserve individuation and how to support mutuality. I am always concerned with preserving the boundaries that define individual identity. I do not let one family member talk about others who are present in a session. This rule can be brought alive by telling a family member, "He is taking your voice." I often separate people who are sitting together, and may gesture like a traffic officer at interruptions or inappropriate requests for confirmation. I tend to discourage the use of one family member as the repository for others' memories. I approve descriptions of competence and encourage family members to reward any competence that is displayed in a session. I am generous with positive statements about individual characteristics, clothing, a well-turned phrase, or a creative perception. I encourage and join family underdogs, supporting them so that they can win acceptance and change their position. In particular, I support the struggle of growing children for age-appropriate independence. It is often possible to state a problem in this area in terms of comparative ages: "Sometimes you act like a 6-year-old, and sometimes you act like a real 17-year-old." This formulation becomes a tool for encouraging the development of behavior of a 17-year-old.

In encouraging mutuality, my best technique is to display a sense of humor and a general acceptance of the foibles of humans. I tend to challenge the existence of an "I" without a "you." Instead of telling a family member to change, I tell another member, who has a significant complementary relationship with the first, to help the first to change because the first cannot do it alone. This tactic utilizes the power of the family's own system of mutual constraints, which make it difficult for one individual to move without support and complementarity from the others. In effect, I turn other family members into my cotherapists, making the larger unit the matrix for healing. I avoid making individual interpretations. When a husband is overcontrolling, for example, I may challenge the wife for encouraging her husband's dominance. This collaborative approach seems to work well with Latino families.

I approach family conflicts through sequential interpretations so that the same pattern is highlighted from different points of view. For instance, in a situation in which a 14-year-old child is having difficulties in school and his parents are in conflict about how to deal with this, I might make three interventions. Joining the husband, I would say, "A coalition between your wife and your son is making you helpless." Joining the wife, I would say, "The inability of your husband and son to resolve conflicts is overburdening you, making you responsible for taking care of both of them." Joining the son, I would say, "Your father and mother are arguing about your difficulties in school without giving you any chance to participate. They are keeping you younger than you are." I then ask them to enact a change in the session.

In general, instead of letting people talk about past events, I tend to give situations immediacy by bringing them right into the session. For instance, if I am working with an anorectic patient, I eat with the family. If spouses talk about a conflict, I ask them to enact it. I use space to express proximity and distance, asking people to move about as a way of facilitating or blocking communication and affect.

I have learned to disengage and to direct family members to play out their drama while I am observing. I am spontaneous with interventions because I have learned to trust my responses to families. However, I continuously observe the order and rhythm of family communications, making conscious decisions about when to talk to whom.

As a therapist, I tend to act like a distant relative. I like to tell anecdotes about my experiences and thinking and to include things relevant to the particular family that I have read or heard. I try to assimilate the family's language and to build metaphors using the family's language and myths. These methods telescope time, investing an encounter between strangers with the affect of an encounter between old acquaintances. They are accommodation techniques, which are vital to the process of joining.

My approach and activities during the course of therapy are always sensitive to the background, values, beliefs, and worldview of the family. For all therapists, including me, it is important to understand, respect, and be sensitive to the diverse cultures of Latinos when working with Latino families.

REFERENCES

Haley, J., (Ed.) (1971). *Changing families: A family therapy reader.* New York, Grune & Stratton.

Minuchin, S., Montalvo, B., Guerney, B. G., Roman, B. L., and Schumer, F. (1967). *Families of the slums: An exploration of their structure and treatment.* New York, Basic Books.

PART II

Strategies That Work With Latino Populations

CHAPTER 5

Multicultural Competencies and Family Therapy Strategies With Latino Families

PATRICIA ARREDONDO

De padres sanos, hijos honrados (from wholesome parents, honorable children)

(Rovira, 1984, p. 68)

The purpose of this chapter is to discuss approaches to therapy with the Mirandas, a contemporary, middle-class Latino (Mexican American) family from the southwest. Although only one family is presented, the Miranda case introduces interacting issues and dynamics that are best understood from Latino orientations. To focus only on the issues and possible therapeutic interventions is insufficient, however. Therefore, the next few sections will provide a foundation for a more informed discussion of the role of therapists who may work with families such as the Mirandas and others who present with different issues but perhaps hold similar value orientations.

Therapy typically is centered on the individual, but for Latinos socialized with an overriding sense of *familismo*, this is often countercultural. A recent study by the American Counseling Association's (ACA) Practice Research Network found that counselors report a great need to involve family members

in counseling, not just the individual with the presenting issue. We anticipate that the Miranda family may look like other non-Latino families and that,
in those cases as well, a family counseling approach is indicated.

OVERVIEW

The legitimacy of ethnic-specific counseling knowledge and practices is fairly
recent. Therefore, a brief historical discussion will be provided for the multicultural counseling competencies paradigm (Arredondo et al., 1996; Sue,
Arredondo, & McDavis, 1992) because these inform Latino-specific counseling competencies (Santiago-Rivera, Arredondo, & Gallardo-Cooper, 2002).
Culture-specific information about Latinos will be introduced, touching on
value orientations, help-seeking behavior, health and mental health beliefs,
and the role of religion and spirituality. Environmental and structural barriers
to the access of mental health services will also be reviewed. The Miranda
family will be introduced as a case study, followed by considerations for assessment, treatment, and limitations to treatment. Suggestions for future directions
for family counseling with Latinos will also be offered.

Ultimately, parents want to have children who are *bien educados* (well
mannered). This chapter will not respond entirely to how this can be achieved
with the Miranda family, but the case will heighten awareness of cultural values
and nuances that will lead to more culturally responsive family counseling.

THE CONTEXT FOR CULTURALLY COMPETENT COUNSELING

The past 25 years have witnessed a mandate for multicultural and culture-specific competence in the fields of counseling and psychology. Important statements about competence in education and training, research, and practice
(American Psychological Association, 2003; Arredondo-Dowd & Gonsalves,
1981; Arredondo et al., 1996; Sue et al., 1992, 1998) have propelled and
reinforced multiculturalism as the "fourth force in counseling" (Pedersen,
1990). These documents are of a more macro or etic nature addressing
domains of awareness, knowledge, skills, and systems change, charging the
mental health professional with the responsibility to become culturally competent. Heretofore, deficit perspective about the "other" (typically, an ethnic
minority group) had been employed. The expectation expressed was that this
other would adapt to the status quo (Sue et al., 1992), absolving the mental
health professional of any responsibility.

The multicultural counseling competencies paradigm was shaped during
the past 25 years by professional development committees of the Association
of Multicultural Counseling and Development (AMCD), a division of the ACA
and Division 17 Society of Counseling Psychology, American Psychological
Association (APA). The Governing Council of ACA approved the multicultural

counseling competencies in 2002, the same year in which the APA Council of Representatives approved the *Guidelines on Multicultural Education and Training, Research, Practice and Organizational (Policy) Development* (APA, 2003).

The similarity in these documents begins with the definition of the scope of the competencies and guidelines. Both are inclusive of historically marginalized ethnic/racial minority groups in the United States—specifically, Asian American Pacific Islander, sub-Saharan Black Africans, Latinos and Hispanics, and American Indians/Native Americans. The discussion also specifies that, in most situations, the mental health professionals are individuals of European American heritage. However, the writers of the competencies and guidelines also indicate that *all* psychologists and counselors are responsible for their multicultural competency development, irrespective of ethnic or racial group membership or heritage. A brief discussion of the multicultural competencies paradigm follows.

Domains of Multicultural Competence

Knowing oneself as a cultural being has been posited as fundamental to cultural competency development (Arredondo et al., 1996; Fouad & Brown, 2000; Pedersen, 2000; Sue et al., 1982, 1992). The premise is that individuals' worldview is shaped by familial and societal influences that reinforce values, norms, and behaviors that promote or limit openness to others of different cultural backgrounds. Of course, this holds true for counseling professionals. Although some may not have knowledge or care to have knowledge about their cultural heritage, how one is socialized by family, education, and society at large will inevitably influence how one considers culture and cultural diversity in counseling.

For the discussion about family counseling with Latinos, cultural self-awareness is essential. Negative stereotypes about persons of Latino heritage have persisted for decades in the United States, primarily fueled by media portrayals. Contemporary discourse about Latino families is one of depreciation with a focus on illegal immigration, associations with drugs and gangs, and a disregard for education. These are messages to which all mental health professionals have been exposed regardless of contact with Latino families. In the context of multicultural competence, culturally competent mental health professionals are comfortable with their cultural heritage and respect the cultural differences of Latinos (Santiago-Rivera et al., 2002).

The second domain of multicultural competence refers to developing knowledge about the worldview of others. In so doing, attention must be given to the ease with which categorization of others into in-groups and out-groups occurs (Fiske, 1998; Tajfel & Turner, 1986). This unconscious process leads to assumptions about privilege that because one is White male, he holds higher professional status (Fouad & Brown, 2000), and is part of an in-group (Swim & Mallett, 2002). Thus, in the midst of becoming knowledgeable about the "other's" worldview, professionals may easily fall into the trap of automatically distancing or minimizing interpersonal differences because of the color-blind approach, fears based on limited previous contact, and beliefs of their ethical commitment to respect for the dignity of all persons.

Knowledge about the worldviews of Latinos is complex. Heterogeneity is based on country of origin and experience with entry into the United States, as well as colonization by the U.S. government, generational status, and any number of differences based on dimensions of personal identity (e.g., age, gender, religion). Santiago-Rivera and her colleagues (2002) have proposed a Latino dimensions of personal and family identity to describe the complexity among Latinos. When conducting family therapy, it is incumbent on the clinician to consider all of the dimensions in order to personalize the treatment and to avoid stereotype-based practices (Falicov, 1998; Flores & Carey, 2000; Santiago-Rivera et al.).

The cultural competency domains are interdependent. Awareness and knowledge building are ongoing educational processes that can continuously inform clinical practice. The third domain of multicultural competence encompasses culturally synergistic and relevant interventions. As clinicians approach their work with Latino families, consideration must be given to language differences and preferences, expectations about counseling and the role of the counselor, issues of confidentiality within the family, location of services, and other factors that may support or limit access. These contextual factors are essential to supporting the actual counseling intervention. For effectiveness, multimodal approaches must be applied. No one theory applies to counseling with Latinos, and no one type of intervention will work with all families. Although this seems overly simplistic, at times clinicians have proposed reality therapy versus insight therapy with Latinos. It is best to begin with the Latino dimensions of personal and family identity as a way to determine whether *cuento* therapy, behavioral therapy, or a feminist model is indicated.

Space does not permit a lengthier discussion about Latino-specific competencies. However, in the next few sections, factors of importance related to multicultural competence are discussed.

Familismo

Familismo is the emphasis on family interaction and structure and represents many confounding factors (Ho, Rasheed, & Rasheed, 2004). Expectations about family loyalty and *hermandad* (friendship) with friends and family members trump individuality.

Personalismo

This refers to the respect for relationships as well as some unspoken expectation of reciprocity. In the context of counseling and based on generational differences, some individuals will have a greater need for a sense of *personalismo* with the therapist. A perceived absence of this feeling may engender mistrust and disengagement from therapy. The culturally competent counselor will likely anticipate the relational values that many Latinos hold and spend time building rapport rather than getting down to business immediately, if this is indicated.

Respeto

The emphasis on *respeto* also signals the expectation of hierarchy and clear lines of authority within the family structure. Immigrant parents or parents who are second and third generations will likely have strong messages about parenting and gender role expectations. Socialization is influenced by the values of *machismo* and *marianismo*. Boys are taught to be men (*ser hombres*), indicating several objectives: being responsible for one's family; being in control; and, at the negative end of a continuum, being the dominator in the family.

Messages for women are similar to those given to women across cultures (Arredondo, Psalti, & Cella, 1993). Among these are the expectation to be mothers, dutiful, long-suffering, and the glue that holds the family together. The concept of *marianismo*, or the expectation to live according to the example of the Virgin Mary, is communicated explicitly and implicitly to young Latinas (Gil & Vazquez, 1996).Understandably, *marianismo* may introduce personal conflict for a woman and interpersonal conflict with her partner and in a family situation.

Espiritismo

Espiritismo refers to spiritism; among some Latinos, sickness is sometimes thought to be caused by spiritual forces that cause physical and emotional suffering. *Santeria* and *curanderismo* are ways to cure such sickness by restoring balance through diverse rituals that range from using herbs to spiritual possession (Aponte, Rivers, & Wohl, 1995). Mental health services are sought out after all else has proven ineffective (Ancis, 2004). Often, the medical office or the emergency room is the initial point of contact. It is more acceptable to refer to a migraine or back pain, rather than to report that one is depressed.

Though many issues, such as immigration, acculturation, and assimilation processes; language barriers; and socioeconomic concerns, create stress and associated mental health issues, studies have shown that Latinos do not consider mental health services a solution to their familial or emotional problems (Ho et al., 2004). Latino psychology authors have spoken about the interrelationship of religion and spirituality and the Latino spiritual soul (Flores & Carey, 2000) and the influence of the indigenous spiritual system (Ramirez, 1998) from a Mestizo worldview. Expressions such as *si Dios quiere* (if it is God's will) suggest a deference to or acceptance of a higher power to determine the outcome of life situations. Thus, when counseling with Latino families, the culturally competent therapist will need to inquire about spiritual and religious belief systems and preferences for different health care practices, indigenous and Western alike.

THE MIRANDA FAMILY

Background

Marisol and Julio are parents to Cecilia, 16, Julio Jr., 15, and Rosa, 10. Julio has a B.S. in computer science and Marisol is a registered nurse. He works for a local computer chip manufacturing firm and she works at the children's hospital. Marisol only returned to full-time work within the last 5 years when her youngest child, Rosa, started kindergarten.

Marisol was born in Sonora, Mexico. Her father and mother have a strong identification with their native Yaqui culture and know many of their Yaqui traditions, as well as the indigenous Yoemi language. Since moving to the United States, the family is typically thought to be Mexican because of their appearance and because they primarily speak Spanish. At the time of immigration, Marisol was 10 years old. She grew up strongly identifying with being *Mexicana*, reinforced by the local Mexican neighborhood. Marisol grew up in a migrant farm worker family, in which her mother and father worked in the fields. She also worked in the fields alongside them during the summer.

Julio was born in El Paso, Texas, as were his parents. His grandparents were from Juarez, Mexico, just 10 minutes away from the El Paso border crossing. He identifies strongly with *Tejano* culture and being Mexican American. Julio's father was a foreman in a factory and his mother stayed home to raise the family's four children. Education was strongly encouraged; Julio's father attended a trade school through his union.

Marisol and Julio met through his twin sister, Estella, who was a classmate when both were attending the University of Texas, El Paso (UTEP), with Marisol. He graduated college at the University of Texas, Austin. The couple was married immediately after Marisol graduated from UTEP with her nursing degree; they have been married for 17 years. Their three children—Cecilia, Julio Jr., and Rosa—were born in the United States. They have a strong Catholic belief system. They currently live in Tucson, Arizona, where they moved for employment opportunities and to be near Julio's twin sister.

Cecilia (Ceci) is Julio and Marisol's eldest daughter. She is 16 and a very outgoing young woman. She enjoys the arts, with a particular interest in painting. Ceci is a good student but must work very hard in her academics to maintain an A average. She has her sights set on going to college to study fine arts. This is a point of contention with her parents, who do not view art as a career.

Julio Jr., or Junior, is 15 and just starting high school. He excels in playing baseball, which is his main focus. He is a mediocre student, getting mainly a grade of C in his classes. Junior struggles with paying attention in class and is often disruptive, using his sense of humor to distract other students. He is often labeled the class clown. He has had behavioral issues over the years, leading to many parent–teacher conferences and disciplinary measures by the school.

Rosa, age 10, is a quiet child. Phenotypically, she is darker and more heavy-set than her siblings. She has struggled with her weight ever since she entered first grade and has dealt with teasing from peers and family. The affectionate nickname is "*la gordita*" (fatty or little fat one). She is a high achieving student and is performing well above grade level. She loves animals and spends much of her time at home with the family's many pets, most of which are animals that she has adopted or strays that she shelters. Her mother is tolerant of her affinity for animals, but her father thinks that "it's disgusting" and that animals are not to be in the house.

Extended Family

Julio's parents still live in El Paso, as do three of his five siblings. Julio and his twin sister are the eldest children. He has three younger sisters and one brother. His twin sister lives in Tucson, Arizona, and works as teacher. She is divorced with two children. His youngest brother is a senior in college at the University of New Mexico. Julio's grandmother, Juana, lives with his parents, Inez and Julio Sr. Juana and her late husband, Pedro, were born in Hermasillo, Senora, Mexico.

Marisol's parents, Carlos and Dolores are from Sonora and live in El Centro, California, near San Diego. Marisol was born in Sonora, as were four of her siblings. Her parents started their migration north when she was 10 years old. They lived in Mexicali for 2 years without her father before moving to El Centro, California. He migrated first with her eldest brother during the *bracero* program. Because her parents were farm workers, they often moved to different parts of the state. However, they always wanted to return to El Centro and eventually did. Of Marisol's seven siblings, only one remains in El Centro: her youngest sister, Carla. Marisol's siblings, who include five sisters and two brothers, live in different places throughout California and her eldest sister lives in New York. Marisol's grandparents still live in Sonora.

Presenting Issues

The Miranda family was referred to counseling by Ceci's school counselor and the family doctor. The school counselor referred them because she believed that Ceci was underperforming. The counselor had been told by some of Ceci's teachers that she seemed withdrawn and preoccupied with constant daydreaming. The counselor, who had supported Ceci's interest in painting and her pursuit of an art school, also noticed that her grades had slipped and her personality was changing. The family doctor became involved because of Ceci's weight loss and self-reports of sleeplessness and fatigue. To both professionals she had confided that her parents did not love her and that they did not support her desire to become an artist.

Initially, the Mirandas were reluctant to meet with a private counselor. They told the new counselor, Ms. Gallagher, that Ceci had changed; she was not studying for all of her courses because she was spending too much time with "those drawings." Marisol and Julio consider Ceci to be defiant and "out of control." They describe her as having *coraje*, anger in her heart. Julio strongly objects to Ceci's desire to be an artist. ("Painting a picture is a hobby, not a career. You can get a job painting a house but how are you going live painting pictures?") He does not support her desire to go to art school or seek a B.A. in fine arts. "Stay at home and save us money if you want to paint; the community college is down the street," he states impatiently in front of Ms. Gallagher.

Marisol is also concerned about her daughter's ability to have a successful career in art; her worry is that Ceci will be poor and disappointed. Marisol is not as affected by her daughter's interest in art because her grandmother and eldest sister are artists, although not college educated. However, Marisol notes that her grandmother was talented and painted around the house, but it was not her life's passion. She also explains that her older sister, Alejandra, is a graphic designer and often does her work on a computer. Marisol is most offended by the images that Ceci paints, which often involve images of the Virgen de Guadalupe and depict other religious issues (i.e., Ceci hanging on a cross), her family members, and abstract images of women. Marisol has told Ceci that it is a sin to "desecrate" sacred images or openly explore sexuality. ("In your own head, maybe, but in a painting—for everyone to see? How can you feel proud of that?") Marisol and Julio tell the counselor that Ceci is bringing shame to the family and this is reflecting on their roles as parents. It seems to Ceci that suddenly her parents are behaving in old-fashioned ways.

Peripheral Issues

Ceci feels that her parents do not give her brother, Junior, as much negative attention and scolding as she receives. She is aware that her brother has behavior problems in school and has relatively low ambition outside of his athletic interests. Ceci feels that Junior is favored by their father: His poor grades are often overlooked because of his athletic talent. Although he is often scolded "in the moment" for having troubles in school, there are few consequences other than an occasional grounding. She notes that her brother often steals money from her and other family members, disregards house rules, and pushes her and her younger sister around. Ceci is especially irritated with how Junior teases Rosa about her weight and dark color. He has also teased Ceci about being a "*gringa*" because she is fair. Junior may be resentful because Ceci can "pass" as being Anglo; she often drifts between worlds and has Latino and White friends, but feels somewhat like an outsider in both groups.

An important family dynamic is that Rosa, the youngest child, is relatively forgotten. Even though she is a high achiever, many of her accomplishments, such as having one of her paintings displayed in the school's art gallery, often go unnoticed. Her parents are concerned that, with her interest in art, she will become irreverent like Ceci. Although Rosa is praised by her parents for her academic achievements, she does not get the accolades that her brother receives for his athletic accomplishments. She is quiet and often does not express what she wants, leaving her needs unmet. Ceci is close to her sister but Ceci's personal problems often disrupt their relationship and she spends increasingly less time with Rosa. Marisol works full-time and has much less time with Rosa than she did with Ceci and Junior and knows her differently than she does her other two children. This is a point of guilt for Marisol because she feels neglectful and that she is not living up to her role as *una madre*.

Assessment of Family Strengths

It would be fairly easy to begin an assessment of the family with a traditional problem-oriented lens. On the surface, it appears that the tensions introduced by Ceci's change in personality and *coraje* are the lightning rod. Rather than focusing on the apparent family disorder, the culturally competent counselor would be aware that, for many Latinos, attending counseling may be a sign of weakness, a possible indictment of poor parenting. The Mirandas have come in voluntarily with Ceci and, though they may be resistant to talk to a stranger, this reluctance may be serving as an important indicator, ironically, of family strength. The Miranda family has many levels of emotional integrity and does not want to be dissected and changed. Thus, the counselor's role is to set the stage by indicating that some change is necessary to achieve balance within the family system and that she is there to facilitate constructive dialogue.

The astute counselor will also reframe Ceci's oppositional behavior as strengths: She is an outspoken young woman who can articulate her concerns well. Although her parents are not pleased with what she is saying and how she is acting, her ability to express herself is a strength. By discussing Ceci's affect and actions as a skill, instead of in the context of content, the counselor can help the parents to view Ceci in a different way. By focusing on the content of her words and artistic expressions, of which they disapprove, Marisol and Julio have overlooked Ceci's tenacity and creativity—important skills in the workplace and in life. In fact, Julio will note that Ceci is a lot like his twin sister, goal oriented and strong.

Marisol and Julio are concerned parents. It is important for a therapist to recognize and honor their desire for a more positive family dynamic. Though they may be expressing their feelings in a way that feels hostile and constraining to Ceci, the counselor can point out their intention and concern for her well-being. By highlighting the common goals of daughter and parents, which are essentially to have family harmony and have reduced familial tension, the counselor can facilitate more role-taking and active listening among the three.

Potential Barriers

Initially, barriers should not be the focus because they can be used as excuses why therapy does not work or why it is not worth the family's time. Though barriers are important for the therapist to recognize, they can alternatively be framed as "family concerns." For the Mirandas, these concerns could include leaving work early to attend counseling, the need to involve the other children eventually, and shame about speaking to an outsider. The therapist must anticipate these unspoken concerns and be prepared to address them at the appropriate time. These can then be viewed as part and parcel of the therapy setting as the counselor works to help the family deal with or eliminate them. Sometimes, family or environmental issues are so longstanding that they feel unchangeable or a family has minimized them and does not perceive them to be important concerns. For the Mirandas, this may relate to Junior's long-standing underachievement, behavioral problems, and their favoritism toward his athletics.

Julio has time constraints with the demands from work that he can use as a way to distance himself from the counseling sessions. Though he has valid reasons for being so busy, this may also be a reflection of his effort and energy level with familial issues and his comfort level with confrontation. For Latino men, being in control and *controlado* are highly prized behaviors.

Case Conceptualization

Of course, there are so many different issues but they may not need to be defined as "problems," as noted in the discussion of family strengths. Creating a porous structure in the session in which families can continue to redefine their needs within the context of the presenting issues creates a less restrictive therapeutic ambiance and allows family members to self-define and self-initiate within the counseling sessions. A Latino-centered needs assessment (Santiago-Rivera et al., 2002) would assist in helping the family to discuss their presenting needs within an appropriate values-based framework. Understanding how Latinos present their needs, referring to the family-centered, collectivistic manner, may also shed light on how Ceci is trying to differentiate herself from the rest of her family.

Because gender socialization is often integrated into the core concepts of the family, Ceci may be making a firm statement in contradiction to the *marianismo* concept of womanhood, which emphasizes that young women be pious, pure, and long-suffering (Santiago-Rivera et al., 2002). If Ceci perceives her personal passions to be in contradiction with her family values, she has two choices: She can abandon her personal goals and not utilize her talents or she can attempt to redefine herself within the family and try to change family structure. Changing the family is much more difficult to do and may not be beneficial to Ceci or the Miranda family. As previously discussed, the family has many strengths and is motivated to make changes that enhance the family dynamic. A counselor can assist family members in making change within their ordered framework. Because the Latino family entails certain values that can offer comfortable structure as well as feelings of constriction, a therapist should highlight the positive and flexible aspects of the family's core concepts.

Most families are not coming into counseling to be completely disman-tled. Focusing on what is working and using a strength-based approach and culturally appropriate frames of references can encourage family members to work within their family structure, work together, and be mindful of and sensi-tive to differences in individual interests and perceptions. Bringing to light that Ceci is not so different in many ways from other family members in her artistic ambitions and referencing the extended family network, like Marisol's older sister, can normalize Ceci's main point of contention with her parents. Emphasizing that Ceci does not need to attack the family in order to have her concerns heeded can help her to direct her angry energy towards constructive dialogue with her parents.

If Ceci feels confident that the family structure will accept her personal choices, she can learn different strategies to communicate her needs to her family and cope with their responses in a healthy way. It is already evident that Ceci has a level of comfort and security within her family structure because she is able to verbalize her concerns. In a highly restrictive family environment, a young woman may not express her feelings of angst or unhappiness because this could be interpreted as dissension and dishonorable. The consequence would be rejection. However, Ceci is open about her concerns, alluding to her comfort level with her family and her assurance that she will not be rejected.

Marisol and Julio may not understand Ceci's strategies for getting her needs met. Their family-of-origin structures entailed much more rigidity, especially Marisol's. Because Marisol's parents were migrant farm workers who had to emigrate with many small children across the Mexican–U.S. border, the focus was primarily to keep the family together or to make plans to re-unite the family. Because the environmental factors were so restrictive, familial patterns mirrored this. The emphasis on basic survival took the focus off indi-vidual needs. Marisol often worked with her parents in the field, regardless of whether she wanted to. Julio is the eldest male in his family. Traditionally, this is a role of responsibility and reverence—a privileged yet pressured position. Julio may feel the impetus to tell Ceci what to do and how to do it to protect her from possible consequences. He may feel responsible for Ceci's successes and potential failures, as well as obligated to structure her life so that she can achieve happiness and stability.

Using the Latino dimensions of personal identity can assist a family in looking at themselves as individuals and then as a family. It is also an impor-tant tool for a counselor to gain a more thorough, highly personalized cultural assessment. This can assist the therapist in helping the family to define impor-tant issues and enhance the case conceptualization. By having each member of the Miranda family explore their different dimensions, fill them out, and then share them, they can learn about and discuss their personal experiences.

This can serve as a facilitator for an important dialogue on personal and familial differences. It can also highlight intergenerational similarities. Ceci may be able to gain some understanding about her mother's fears for her and may also be able to see how her father conceptualizes the family and his role as a father. This can also be an important way to share personal information that is often overlooked or unspoken, such as Marisol's Yaqui heritage. Marisol and Julio can also develop an understanding of how Ceci conceptualizes herself. The counselor can then assist the family in contextualizing Ceci's personal and cultural growth within normal adolescent development. This can also bring to light unhealthy self-conceptualization or irrational beliefs.

Diagnosing the client should be a careful balance between a person meeting diagnostic criteria and a client having a situational response to certain life stressors. In different cultures, social stresses that promote anxiety may be associated with somatic symptoms. Feelings of anxiety could prompt a dissociative response to stressful life events such as family conflict (Castillo, 1997). Keeping this in mind, it is important to discern whether Ceci's symptoms are a response to her familial tensions and can be alleviated by changes in the family dynamic or are more individualized and need more specialized intervention. The least serious diagnosis and least invasive treatment is always a good first intervention if questions are posed in the case conceptualization. Because many confounding factors may be present, sorting through the information at the family system level is important because the Miranda family came into the counseling setting as a family.

A possible diagnosis for Ceci would be dysthymic disorder, characterized by a chronically depressed mood that occurs for most of the day more days than not for at least 2 years. Ceci presented with enough symptoms to meet criteria such as having feelings of hopelessness, poor eating, low self-esteem, and difficulty making decisions. Though teachers, doctors, and parents may have noticed the changes recently, she may self-report that she has been feeling depressed for a much longer time, which caused the buildup of emotion and the subsequent current behaviors.

Marisol and Julio may describe Ceci as often losing her temper, arguing with adults, refusing to comply with adults' requests or rules, angry and resentful, and touchy or easily annoyed by others. This would meet diagnostic criteria for oppositional defiant disorder, a pattern of negative, hostile, and defiant behavior lasting at least 6 months. A counselor must be careful in interpreting the parents' view of their child before labeling the behavior as an Axis I condition. Though Ceci may meet this description, oppositional defiant disorder is often associated with more severe behavior as well as a consistent pattern in different areas of a person's life. As the school counselor and family doctor reported, her current pattern of behavior was of concern because it was relatively new. The concerns were also oriented toward Ceci's passive versus aggressive reaction to stress.

The antagonistic behavior appears to be isolated to the family setting. This may be difficult for Marisol and Julio to hear or accept. The counselor can frame it as an important discovery, stating that an issue that can be isolated or particularly identified in a certain setting narrows the scope of the problem. Marisol and Julio want their daughter to conduct herself in different ways, but they also have obvious concerns for her physical and emotional health.

It is important to explore whether Ceci has an eating disorder such as bulimia nervosa, nonpurging type. After all, the doctor noted that she had lost weight and was reporting sleeplessness and a loss of appetite. This is a cross-cultural issue but is typically discussed more openly within European American culture (Castillo, 1997). Addressing health issues immediately is of primary importance. Asking Ceci and her parents about the duration and pattern of Ceci's sleeping and eating habits, as well as asking her to keep a log of these daily activities, would be helpful in assessing whether more diligent intervention is needed. As previously stated, her sleeplessness and weight loss could be a response to her familial conflict and her feelings of isolation and of not feeling valued and accepted by her parents.

Intervention

Because the Latino family structure is hierarchical and has strong role definitions, it is important for a practitioner to choose therapies that suit the familial style. It is of primary importance for a therapist to be aware of his or her worldview (Arredondo et al., 1996; Sue et al., 1992) regarding highly structured family systems in which gender and age are key defining features. Understanding that the structure in Latino families encourages integrity and enculturation is pertinent to appropriate intervention strategies. Assisting family members with more positive communication and coping skills so that they can navigate through their life stressors with the support of the family, rather than rebelling against or rejecting the family, can be a strong foundational asset for all family members.

Using strategies from cognitive behavioral therapy (CBT) and reality therapy can emphasize strategic skill building and the power of positive decision-making. CBT places heavy emphasis on family interaction patterns and how these experiences influence family members and the family dynamic. The concept of restructuring the schema, or core beliefs, can be an important process for the family. This is not to say that the family needs to be restructured. Rather, distorted beliefs, which are serving as a parasite on the family's integrity, are confronted and reoriented to appropriate reasoning (Corey, 2001).

For example, Julio views himself as a leader and caretaker and he states that he values his family more than anything in this world. Shedding light on his isolating and driving his daughter away by belittling and disregarding her personal passions can be an important, though difficult, revelation for Julio. Connecting personal values and goals with actual actions and expressions of these values can be a powerful reorientation technique. Asking Julio to define his goals and to look at how his actions are contributing to or detracting from those goals can be a call to action for him.

The A–B–C theory of personality can help family members explore their core beliefs. This entails pointing out that B (belief system/value orientation) affects A (activating event) and C (emotional and behavioral consequences) (Corey, 2001). If someone thinks that A causes C, he is placing the responsibility outside of himself and the family schemata, the jointly held beliefs about the family. In actuality, it is the person's belief about the event that causes a reaction. If Ceci feels as if her parents do not love her because her father has stated that he will not pay for college if she majors in fine arts, she is connecting an action with a consequence (father not paying for school = not being loved).

Ceci needs to see that it is *her* belief—not her parents'—that her parents do not love her if they are not unconditionally supportive of her personal desires. Discussing that her parents may disagree with her thoughts and ambitions, but that it does not lessen their love for her could assist her in coping with her parents' reactions. Ceci can gain a deeper understanding of her family when she is helped to understand that her parents are concerned about her well-being, influenced by their family-of-origin experiences, and feel that it is their responsibility to protect her. She can then convert feelings of loss and loneliness into an understanding of her family's devotion to her and of intergenerational differences, thus helping her to resolve her own feelings of inadequacy and isolation.

A key part of helping family members create positive change within the family structure is assisting them with communication skills. Because of the role definition and the busy life of a teenager and two working parents, Ceci, Marisol, and Julio may not be used to expressing their needs in a constructive way. Ceci may have been feeling isolated for some time, but she did not have the platform or skills to address her needs. Having the family practice positive and affirming communication by role playing or using reframing techniques (Santiago-Rivera et al., 2002) can facilitate dialogue while a counselor assists them with fine-tuning their skills.

Encouraging the Mirandas to set a time aside each week outside the counseling session to have a family meeting, or *reunión*, in which thoughts and experiences can be shared, discussed, and dealt with, will give each member a voice within a shared and consistent space. This can be a way to deal with difficult situations and/or a time to share accomplishments, big or small. Emphasizing the family's ability to empathize and rejoice with one another and that learning how to express these shared feelings is a positive communication and problem-solving skill (Ho et al., 2004) can encourage the family to make time for this *reunion*.

Integrating reality therapy into the counseling sessions can also be useful with Latino families because of Glasser's (2000) belief that to love and to belong are people's primary needs (Corey, 2001). Latino families can sometimes be wrongly thought of as overly enmeshed or codependent because of their closeness and feelings of obligation for one another (Santiago-Rivera et al., 2002). Keeping this in mind, an important technique for a counselor is to build on the strength of the value of family, love for family members, and the strong sense of and need for belonging in a family system. By looking at how Ceci feels unsatisfied by her relationships in her family and dealing with improving them, many of her somatic and depressive symptoms may be resolved when this root cause is addressed. Ceci feels as if her main source of support and identity, her family, does not accept who she is. This is an attack on her sense of self, which can cause acute responses. Because her identity as a Latina is so integrated into the family system, her response to this family conflict has been extreme and unhealthy by her not eating, isolating herself from hurtful stressors (undesirable parent responses), and withdrawing.

By not focusing on symptoms, reality therapy techniques enable a client to self-empower. A counselor and a family client already know that symptoms exist, that they are troubling, and that they want to cope better with their presenting issues. Focusing on the symptoms can negatively reinforce the existing problems. Encouraging accountability, showing that there is choice in almost all matters, and focusing on the present allows clients to move forward, instead of staying entrenched in their negative past experiences. Asking Ceci, Marisol, and Julio, "What do you want?" coupled with "What are you doing now to accomplish that?" gives a broader goal with a time-specific, smaller milestone to focus on as well. It also helps people focus on what they, as individuals, can do versus what they would like others not to do.

Proposing to Marisol that she focus on what she can do to improve her relationship with Ceci instead of focusing on all the negative things that Ceci does can serve many purposes. It takes a lot of pressure off Ceci and relieves Marisol of the belief that she can change and control Ceci's personal ambitions. Having Marisol look at how Ceci is responding to her fears and apprehensions about her daughter becoming an artist is a good reflective tool, but not the point of focus.

If this interaction is not producing the desired response, the counselor should ask Marisol the key question: "What do you want?" while helping her to focus on things within her scope of control. Instead of Marisol replying, "I'd like Ceci to be a more respectful daughter," a therapist can encourage her to reframe that. Marisol could refocus her attention on herself by stating, "I'd like to have a more respectful dialogue about things with my daughter." By following this question with, "What are you doing to accomplish that now?" and "What can you do this week to have a more respectful dialogue?" the counselor can place the problem into an action-oriented strategy. He or she can then follow up by looking at how Marisol accomplished her goal, part of her goal, or none of it. The continued dialogue can be around what stopped this accomplishment and how the family can work together as a system to improve the successful completion of their individual goals.

Within the Latino family system and with reality therapy, the state of the relationships is always at the forefront of the issues. Though each individual has choice and the personal power to make change, the delicate balance between getting individual needs met and maintaining a collectivistic structure must be carefully orchestrated within the counselor–family partnership. When a family starts to deal with persistent negative patterns of interaction, this can feel like a hopeless situation. Latino families are especially vulnerable to extreme responses to family conflict because *familismo* is a central tenet in Latino culture.

The counselor will also want to discuss the importance of bringing the other children into the counseling sessions at some time. Because familial integrity is so important in Latino families, problems are often difficult to address in isolation. Ceci has expressed concerns regarding her other siblings; therefore, it is important to address the family as a whole at some time. It is also pertinent for the counselor to keep in mind that, when the parents are having serious issues with one child, the other children are also affected by the change in their sibling as well as the attention diverted to the presenting issues. The family structure is fluid and a rock dropped in the family "pond" has obvious ripple effects. Bringing this to the parents' attention and making them mindful of the importance of acknowledging and addressing the other children's feelings and concerns is integral in creating balance within the entire family unit.

Rosa may feel tremendous anxiety about constant conflict between her older sister, with whom she is close, and her parents, whom she loves and upon whom she depends. She may also feel neglected because she does not have the problems that her sister has or the athletic talent of her brother, which her father openly glorifies. Julio Jr. may feel in competition with and resentful of the attention that Ceci is receiving because of her personal issues, even though the attention is mostly negative. Ceci may need to resolve relational conflicts with her brother, which may be another source of tension outside the presenting issues with her parents.

Discussion

Family conflicts may be exacerbated by experiences of discrimination and feelings of powerlessness. Latinos who feel marginalized by the dominant society may assume a position within the family that exerts destructive patterns of behavior to compensate for these feelings of societal oppression (Ancis, 2004). Using therapy techniques that can value the traditions and traditional values of the parents but assist them in differentiating their past experiences from those of their children can be important in mending the intergenerational divide.

The communication breakdown that the Miranda family is experiencing is often caused by the lack of intergenerational communication and understanding. By creating a comfortable forum for dialogue that emphasizes respect and family strength, counseling can assist a family in an important empowerment process—that of knowing and appreciating itself. The Mirandas have many positive attributes in their family. The parents have had tremendous personal successes and the family is intact, verbalizing their concerns, and seeking help. The children have defined ambitions and are full of different talents, interests, and creativity. Seeing the larger picture is extremely useful in creating a constructive dialogue. This assists the family in understanding that the work done in counseling is not to destroy or distort the family structure but to build upon its strong foundation.

Of course, in the scope of this chapter, not every presenting issue can be addressed. Important points to consider outside those discussed are intra-family issues regarding color, weight, and size. As mentioned in the family's introduction, some tensions and insecurities regarding phenotypic issues are deeply rooted in cultural feelings of otherness, inferiority, and powerlessness. Another issue is gender socialization and favoritism within the family system. Addressing religion and how that contributes to the family's worldview would also be very important.

THE ROLE OF PREVENTION

In the past, prevention models have sought to bring awareness to issues of oppression in the ethnic communities and raise consciousness regarding problems and community resources. By combining preventative curriculum with clinical practice, a multifaceted approach to community counseling can be conceptualized (Miller, O'Neal, & Scott, 1982). Minority members are often met with discrimination and institutional practices of racial prejudice that block their ability to transition into the host society. Prevention strategies that deal with these institutional barriers and subsequent acculturative stress while combining personal empowerment strategies may provide an appropriate, accessible, and useful program that addresses life skills along with mental health issues. Gaining insight from such programs may assist a counselor in helping Latino families within a context that feels comfortable.

A therapist must be aware of and familiar with historical and contemporary barriers and have an understanding of how to advocate and address issues outside the family structure. A Latino family may have issues outside the counseling session that need to be dealt with in tandem with personal issues, such as housing, immigration status, or transportation.

SUMMARY

As is evident with the Mirandas, Latino families are very diverse in cultural background, social economic status, belief systems, and coping mechanisms. However, within the counseling setting, some important similarities, such as the importance of family, can be found. When helping a Latino family, it is important to understand their value orientation and self-perceptions, and to gage their feelings on the therapeutic process. Focusing on strengths and encouraging families with proactive strategies to address problem areas are key.

Asking a family about their family traditions, philosophies, or *dichos* can create rapport and give a counselor a sense of who this family is. The family has a personality and a belief system. Focusing on the ways in which the family operates and the types of relationships that exist in the family, a counselor can help a family to mend from the inside out. Family members will sometimes place themselves on the outside because of internal chaos or a lack of understanding. Reintegrating people into this network can be extremely empowering. It is very likely that once Ceci mends her relationships with her family members, gains support from her parents, and develops an understanding of her strong and unique family system, she will have very different responses to family conflict. Instead of stress and isolation, she will know that she has a platform for dialogue. Instead of Marisol and Julio feeling afraid and acting brazen, they can learn to communicate their concerns in a way that works.

Having strategies and reinforcing techniques that work can create a new family dynamic within a traditional family structure. Understanding that parenting and relationship building among siblings entails time and demands that family members work on their relationships, instead of just letting them develop unattended, can be an important discovery for a family. A counselor should facilitate this process with an open mind, patience, and perseverance. The family will often respond to the personality and hope of a counselor. Creating this ambiance and relationship of trust can help a family actualize its potential.

REFERENCES

American Psychological Association (2003). Guidelines for multicultural education and training, research, practice, and organizational change for psychologists. *American Psychologist, 58,* 377–402.

Ancis, J. (2004). *Culturally responsive interventions.* New York: Brunner–Routledge.

Aponte, J. F., Rivers, R. Y., & Wohl, J. (1995). *Psychological interventions and cultural diversity.* Boston: Allyn & Bacon.

Arredondo-Dowd, P., & Gonsalves, J. (1981). Preparing culturally effective counselors. *American Personnel and Guidance Journal, 58,* 657–660.

Arredondo, P. Psalti, A., Cella, K. (1993). The woman factor in multicultural counseling. *Counseling and Human Development, 8,* 1–7.

Arredondo, P., Toporek, R., Brown, S. P., Jones, J., Locke, D. C., Sanchez, J., et al. (1996). Operationalization of the multicultural counseling competencies. *Journal of Multicultural Counseling and Development, 24,* 42–78.

Castillo, R. J. (1997). *Culture and mental illness: A client-centered approach.* Pacific Grove, CA: Brookes/Cole Publishing Company.

Corey, G. (2001). *Theory and practice of counseling and psychotherapy* (6th ed.). Belmont, CA: Wadsworth.

Falicov, C. J. (1998). *Latino families in therapy: A guide to multicultural practice.* New York: Guilford.

Fiske, S. (1998). Stereotyping, prejudice, and discrimination. In D. Gilbert, S. Fiske, & G. Lindzey (Eds.), *Handbook of social psychology* (Vol. 2, 4th ed., pp.357–411). Boston: McGraw–Hill.

Flores, M. T., & Carey, G. (2000). *Family therapy with Hispanics: Towards appreciating diversity.* Boston: Allyn & Bacon.

Fouad, N. A., & Brown, M. (2000). Race, ethnicity, culture, class and human development. In S. D. Brown & R. W. Lent (Eds.), *Handbook of counseling psychology* (3rd ed., pp. 379–410). New York: Wiley.

Gil, R. M., & Vazquez, C. I. (1996). *The Maria paradox.* New York: Perigee.

Glasser, W. (2000). *Reality therapy in action.* New York: HarperCollins.

Ho, M. K., Rasheed, J. M., & Rasheed, M. N. (2004). *Family therapy with ethnic minorities* (2nd ed.). Thousand Oaks, CA: Sage.

Miller, S. O., O'Neal G. S., and Scott, C. A. (1982). *Primary prevention approaches to the development of mental health services for ethnic minorities: A challenge to social work education and practice.* New York: Council on Social Work Education.

Pedersen, P. (1990). *Counseling across cultures* (3rd ed.). University of Hawaii.

Pedersen, P. (2000). *Hidden messages in culture-centered counseling: A triad training model.* Thousand Oaks, CA: Sage.

Ramirez III, M. (1998). *Multicultural/multiracial psychology: Mestizo perspectives in personality and mental health.* Northvale, NJ: Jason Aronson Inc.

Rovira, L. I. (1984). Spanish proverbs: A survey of Spanish culture and civilization. Lanham, MD: University Press of America.

Santiago-Rivera, A., Arredondo, P., & Gallardo-Cooper, M. (2002). *Counseling Latinos and la familia: A practical guide.* Thousand Oaks, CA: Sage Publications.

Sue, D. W., Arredondo, P., & McDavis, R. J. (1992). Multicultural competencies and standards: A call to the profession. *Journal of Counseling and Development, 70,* 477–486.

Sue, D. W., Bernier, J. Durran, M., Feinberg, L., Pedersen, P., Smith, E., et al. (1982). Position paper: Cross cultural counseling competencies. *Counseling Psychologist, 10,* 45–52.

Sue, D. W., Carter, R. T., Casas, J. M., Fouad, N. A., Ivey, A. E., Jense, M., et al. (1998). *Multicultural counseling competencies: Individual and organizational development.* Thousand Oaks, CA: Sage.

Swim, J. & Mallett, R. (2002). Pride and prejudice: a multi-group model of identity and its association with intergroup and intragroup attitudes. Manuscript submitted for publication.

Tajfel, H., & Turner, J. (1986). The social identity theory of intergroup behavior. In S. Worchel & W. Austin (Eds.), *Psychology of intergroup relations* (pp.7–24). Chicago, IL: Nelson–Hall.

CHAPTER 6

Counseling Latino Children

CATHERINE CUEVA

INTRODUCTION TO THE GONZALES FAMILY: SESSION 1

Jose and Maria Gonzales have made an appointment with you to discuss concerns about their 7-year-old son, Pedro. Specifically, the parents are concerned about Pedro's increasing aggression at home and his falling grades in school. In an effort to become more knowledgeable of the family's background and worldviews, you ask the parents to tell you about where they are from and learn that they were born in Mexico. As the conversation continues, you learn that Jose (34) and Maria (33) decided to move to the United States 4 years ago to provide a better life for their four children: Jose Jr. (14), Anna (12), Pedro (7), and Theresa (5). Both parents state that they value education and want their children to have a good education.

Jose and Maria indicate that the move has not been easy and describe some of the positive and negative experiences that they have had as immigrants. Jose mentions that his brother and his wife and children moved to the area at the same time and acknowledges that they have relied on each other for support. Jose and Maria contribute to the family income. Jose works full-time as a mechanic and occasionally does side jobs for extra money. Maria works part-time at a local restaurant, which allows her to be home when the children get home from school. Between Jose and Maria, the couple earns enough money to provide for the family's necessities.

Throughout the interview, the couple emphasizes that they want their children to understand the importance of family, respect others, and have faith in God. The family, including Jose's older brother and his family, goes to church every Sunday at the local Catholic church and the children attend religion classes once a week as well. It is important to Jose and Maria that their children are familiar with their native culture and they do their best to pass certain traditions and practices to their children.

The majority of the children's time outside school is spent with family. Jose's older brother, Juan, and his wife, Petra, have three children: Juan Antonio (13), Thomas (9), and Gabriella (6). The two families are very close and see each other several times a week. Jose and Maria believe that having family around who are also recent immigrants has helped everyone adjust and has brought them closer as a family. Although everyone in Jose's family seems to have adjusted fairly well, Pedro, their 7-year-old son, has been exhibiting negative behavior at home and school. Pedro's increasingly negative behavior has caused concern and embarrassment among the entire family. The family members have tried to talk to Pedro about his behavior, but it has not seemed to help.

Maria mentions that Pedro's teacher, Mrs. Garcia, recently expressed concerns about his behavior in school. Maria explains,

> Mrs. Garcia said that Pedro has not been paying attention in class. She said he has been distracted lately and has not been turning in his work on time, and as a result he's falling behind in reading. A couple of days ago Mrs. Garcia sent a note home telling us that Pedro has been teasing one of his classmates. He has never been a troublemaker. I just don't understand why he's acting like this.

As you listen to Maria, you notice that Jose seems to be thinking about something. After a while you ask Jose, "Is there anything you would like to add?" Jose sits quietly for a moment and then says, "We were wondering if Pedro is having trouble in reading because we speak Spanish." Aware that this is a common misconception among many individuals, you make sure to emphasize that Pedro's ability to speak two languages is a great asset and most likely is not interfering with his ability to learn (Woolfolk, 2004). In fact, as you listen to Jose's concern, you recall reading that "higher degrees of bilingualism are correlated with increased cognitive abilities in such areas as concept formation, creativity, and cognitive flexibility" (Woolfolk, p. 54).

Confident that you have enough background information from the parents, you tell Mr. and Mrs. Gonzales that you would like to meet Pedro and talk to him about his recent behavior. The parents agree to make an appointment for the next week so that you can begin working with Pedro. In the meantime, you suggest that Pedro get a physical from his pediatrician to rule out any physiological causes.

Aware that this is the first time that the parents and Pedro have seen a counselor, you begin by explaining that the goal of counseling is to help individuals and families overcome obstacles to their growth and development (Thompson, Rudolph, & Henderson, 2004). Because Pedro, the identified client, is a minor, you go over the consent forms with his parents. After reviewing the form, Maria asks, "Will you tell us what is happening in your sessions with Pedro?" You let Jose and Maria know that because Pedro is the client in this situation, it is your responsibility to act in Pedro's best interest. You assure Jose and Maria that, if Pedro indicates that he is being hurt or plans to hurt himself or someone else, you will disclose that information to them and the proper authorities. You explain that it is important for Pedro to feel safe sharing what is going on inside him so that you can help him deal with those thoughts and feelings.

Jose's body language conveys that he is a little troubled by this last comment. After a brief silence he asks, "Why doesn't Pedro feel safe talking to us? We care about him and want to help him with his problem. We've never done anything to hurt him or make him feel threatened." Maria adds, "In our culture, we turn to our family and God in times of need. We go to them for support and guidance because we know we can trust them to help guide us in making the right decision." Acknowledging their concern, you respond

> Sometimes children don't want to share what's troubling them with the people they care about because they think it might make them sad or trouble them. Other times children have trouble putting into words how they are feeling. Part of what I will do with Pedro is to help him find a way to express what is going on inside him and help him find constructive ways to deal with those feelings. Hopefully, through the counseling process, Pedro will feel more capable and comfortable expressing himself to others, including his family.

As the session comes to an end, Jose and Maria express confidence that you will help Pedro and their family work through this difficult time. Eager to get started, Maria asks, "Is there anything we can do between now and next week?" You tell the parents that if they are interested, they could keep track of what is happening before and after Pedro's disruptive behaviors. You show them a chart for doing an ABC analysis and explain that it may help identify things in the environment that may be maintaining Pedro's behaviors. The couple seems interested in using this method, so you give them several copies in English and Spanish. Because they have never done an ABC analysis, you fill one out as an example. Pleased with the information that you have given them, the couple thanks you and makes Pedro's first appointment with you for the next week.

Reflection

As you reflect on your session with Jose and Maria Gonzales, you are aware that there are many similarities and differences between your life experiences and the Gonzales's life experiences. You think about how your experiences have shaped your life and worldview and realize the importance of taking the Gonzales's cultural background and immigration experiences into consideration when working with Pedro. In an effort to remain aware of the role that culture plays in this relationship, you decide to keep a journal reflecting on your thoughts, feelings, and observations and the impact that they have on the counseling process.

In addition to your goal of increasing your awareness of the cultural variables that exist and play a role in this relationship, you have three other goals for your first session with Pedro. First, you want to build rapport with him to facilitate the development of a trusting relationship between the two of you, and you want to get to know Pedro. This will help you understand who "Pedro" is as well as help you identify possible avenues that you can use when working with Pedro. Establishing rapport and building a positive therapeutic relationship with Pedro will also facilitate Pedro's progress (Lambert & Cattani-Thompson, 1996). Second, you want to rule out the possibility of abuse, using nondirective approaches. Finally, you want to identify where Pedro is developmentally.

As you work with Pedro, you will continually assess how his physical, social, emotional, cognitive, and moral development affects his functioning. Understanding that culture affects human development, you are aware of the importance of taking the family's culture into consideration when assessing where Pedro is developmentally (Shonkoff & Phillips, 2000). Specifically, Pedro's development in all of these areas is learned by observations and experiences in his environment. In addition, you also understand the importance of looking at Pedro's development from a holistic perspective because each developmental variable is interrelated (Magnusson, 1995).

Finally, you are aware that the family's spiritual beliefs are very much a part of their values, decisions, and daily practices. As you read about this subject, you learn that, "for many Latinos, the interrelationship between spirituality and/or religion and cultural practices is extraordinarily close. In discussions about Latino world views, it is a challenge to separate the origin of beliefs and values" (Santiago-Rivera, Arredondo, & Gallardo-Cooper, 2002, p. 46). Although this information seems to be consistent with your observations of the Gonzales family, you are aware that each individual and family system is unique. You understand the negative impact that making generalizations can have on the counseling relationship.

SESSION 2

The following week Pedro and his parents arrive promptly for the scheduled appointment. Aware that Pedro may not feel comfortable being alone with you immediately, you greet the family and invite them into your office for a brief visit. Maria mentions that Pedro knows why he is here today and "is a little nervous" about the visit. Upon walking into your office, you notice that Pedro's eyes light up when he spots the art supplies. Maria asks Pedro to sit down in one of the chairs and he complies with her request. You talk with the family briefly about how the week has gone; towards the end of the conversation, Maria hands you the ABC analysis from the past week. You get feedback from Jose and Maria regarding the analysis and briefly review the chart.

Noticing that Pedro continues to gaze at the art supplies, you ask, "Do you see something you would like to do, Pedro?" Pedro looks at his mom, smiles, and nods his head, eagerly responding "I like to do art." You invite Pedro and his family to the art table and allow him to choose what he would like to use. Pedro turns to his mother and asks whether she will draw with him. Maria agrees to draw a picture and the two of them work quietly. Sensing that Pedro seems to be at ease in your office, you ask, "Do you think it's okay if Mom and Dad go back to the waiting room while we do some art?" Pedro nods his head and begins looking through the different art supplies. As Jose and Maria leave the office, Maria kisses Pedro on the forehead and reminds him that they will see him shortly.

As you sit back down at the art table, Pedro asks if he can draw another picture. You nod and Pedro immediately begins drawing a picture with the oil pastels. As you watch him work, you notice that he is drawing a family portrait. He holds the pastel with a firm grip and the lines on his drawing are smooth and well controlled, indicating that his fine-motor skills are well developed for a 7-year-old child. As the two of you begin talking, you learn that Pedro likes to play video games, draw, play with his siblings, and watch television.

As he completes his family portrait, you ask Pedro to tell you about his picture, and he willingly begins telling you about the portrait. You take advantage of this opportunity to learn about the family system from Pedro's perspective. During the course of the conversation, Pedro makes the comment, "I colored my dad with this color," and points to the peach-colored pastel. Curious about why Pedro chose the color peach, given that you intentionally have several shades of brown available, and why he thought it was important to point this out, you encourage Pedro to tell you more about the why he chose peach for his father's skin. Shrugging his shoulders, Pedro gets up from his seat and begins looking around the room at the artwork displayed on the walls. After examining the artwork, Pedro asks, "Can we put my picture up on the wall?" Nodding your head, you ask Pedro where he would like to place his picture. Aware of the time, you decide to wait until the following session to explore the issue of his father's skin tone. As Pedro is putting up his picture, you ask, "Would you like to invite your mom and dad back into the office to show them your picture?" Pedro agrees enthusiastically and the two of you invite Jose and Maria back into the office.

Pedro proudly shows his parents the picture and explains that he put the picture up all by himself. After some polite conversation, Maria mentions that they made an appointment for the same day and time next week. She also mentions that Mrs. Garcia, Pedro's teacher, is willing to talk with you about Pedro's behavior at school. You let Maria know that you will contact Pedro's teacher before your next session with him. Jose and Maria thank you and then remind Pedro to say thank-you and good-bye. Pedro obediently follows his parents' request and the family leaves.

Reflection

After your session with Pedro, you reflect on some of the observations that you have made regarding how culture may be influencing your interactions with the family. First, you are aware that, when you communicate with Pedro's parents, the conversation generally begins with some "small talk" and gradually moves toward your work with the family. You recall that the concept of *personalismo*, which refers to "valuing and building interpersonal relationships" was discussed at a multicultural conference you recently attended (Santiago-Rivera et al., 2002, p. 44). You see the personable conversations as a reflection of the Gonzales's "*personalismo* value orientation" (Santiago-Rivera et al., p. 116).

Second, because the couple has stated that they view Pedro's problem as a family problem, not just Pedro's problem, one way in which you have attempted to involve the family is by inviting Jose and Maria into your office for a brief visit before and after each session. Based on your observations, the family has responded well to this and, with each visit, the couple appears to feel more comfortable and relaxed.

Finally, Pedro's interactions with you sometimes give you the impression that he does not feel very relaxed during the sessions. Attributing this feeling to Pedro's noticeably good manners, which makes the interactions feel very formal, you wonder whether his behavior is a reflection of what his mother referred to as *respeto* (respect) rather than a sign of Pedro's uneasiness. Thinking back to your previous reading, you wonder whether this is an example of how spirituality and values are interrelated (Santiago-Rivera et al., 2002). As you read more about *respeto*, you learn that it "represents sensitivity to the individual's position and creates a boundary within which conversations should be contained to avoid conflict" (Santiago-Rivera et al., p. 113). You are aware that this behavior is often viewed by individuals from other cultures as submissive, rather than respectful.

As you reflect on each of your goals for the session, you are satisfied with your progress with regard to building rapport and assessing Pedro's developmental levels. Based on this session, you have some ideas for how you will continue to work with Pedro. At this time, you are not concerned that Pedro is abused or neglected but, as always, you will continue to watch for any warning signs. During the next session, you plan to continue building your relationship with Pedro and assess how he is functioning developmentally. Aware that 7 hours of Pedro's day is spent in school—a much different environment from his home or your office—you hope that talking with Mrs. Garcia will help you get a more accurate and complete view of Pedro's world.

This week, you would like to focus on Pedro's ability to verbalize and discuss his emotions because he will need these skills in future sessions. Encouraging and providing opportunities for Pedro to discuss and explore his emotions should allow him to begin to become more cognizant and more adept in processing his feelings (Denham, 1998). In addition, you plan to give the family their first homework assignment, a game that focuses on talking about and exploring emotions. This assignment should serve to help Pedro generalize what he learns in counseling to other environments, involve the family in the counseling process, provide an opportunity for the family to discuss emotions in a way that is comfortable to them, and hopefully increase Jose and Maria's awareness of how discussing emotions can help the family function.

Finally, you are very curious about Pedro's comment regarding his father's skin color. You are aware that Jose's skin color is significantly darker than Maria's and Pedro's and are unsure why Pedro wanted his father's skin to be lighter. Not wanting to make any assumptions, you decide to see whether this subject comes up in the next counseling session. Based on Pedro's response when you asked him to elaborate on the comment, you decide that an indirect approach may be a more effective way to explore the subject. In the meantime, you begin to review the literature regarding the development of ethnic identity.

Specifically, you are interested in how young children's ethnic identity develops. As you familiarize yourself with different ethnic identity models, you come across a social cognitive approach to understanding the development of children's ethnic identity (Knight, Bernal, Garza, & Cota, 1993). This model describes ethnic identity as part of what the child uses when trying to figure out who he or she is. The information regarding children's ethnic identity comes primarily from the child's family and members of the cultural group with which the child has contact (Knight et al., 1993). In Pedro's case, he has a great deal of knowledge about his culture. He speaks Spanish fluently, identifies himself as Mexican, and has knowledge regarding specific cultural traditions.

In addition to gathering information from members of his cultural group, Pedro gathers information about himself from members of the dominant cultural group. In this case, the group comprises children at Pedro's school, who come primarily from a European American background. Based on your reading, you are aware that interactions with the dominant culture can influence how children feel about their ethnic identity (Knight et al., 1993). In Pedro's case, conversations with his parents and teacher indicate that he has a healthy sense of self and is well liked among his peers. Pedro's parents and teacher have not noticed any problems or issues related to ethnicity. Based on the literature and what you know about Pedro, you decide to see whether Pedro brings up any more issues regarding skin color or ethnicity.

SESSION 3

The next session with Pedro begins like the previous one. Jose, Maria, and Pedro come into the office for a brief visit. After a short conversation, Maria expresses her concern about Pedro's reading grades. Recalling a prior conversation with Mrs. Garcia, in which she indicated that Pedro would probably need tutoring to bring his grades up, you ask Maria about the possibility of Pedro receiving tutoring. During one of your conversations with the family, you remember the couple saying that Pedro's older cousin, Miguel, was good in reading and ask whether it would be possible for him to help Pedro. Jose and Maria seem to think that this is a good idea and are willing to try it. Jose and Maria say good-bye to Pedro and remind him that they will see him shortly.

You begin the session by saying, "Pedro, I thought we could watch part of your favorite movie today." A big grin spreads over Pedro's face, "We're going to watch *Finding Nemo*?" As you put the movie into the DVD player, you tell Pedro, "We're going to watch a part of *Finding Nemo* for two reasons. First, we don't have time to watch the whole movie during our session. Second, I decided to watch *Finding Nemo* after you told me how much you like the movie, but I'm a little confused by a certain part and was wondering if you could help me understand it better." Pedro confidently assures you that he will help you understand the movie.

The purpose of this exercise is to assess to what extent Pedro is able to verbalize and discuss emotions. You chose to use an indirect approach because you want Pedro to feel comfortable engaging in discussion about emotions. Once you assess his ability to verbalize emotions and sense that he is comfortable doing so, you will gradually move to a more direct discussion of some of Pedro's emotions.

As the two of you watch the movie clip, you occasionally ask Pedro to label some of the different emotions displayed by the characters or explain why the character behaved in a particular way. Sometimes you ask Pedro what he thinks he would have done in a similar situation. At times, you carefully take a thought that Pedro had trouble expressing and restate it in a slightly more sophisticated way as a means of teaching or modeling the goal behavior of verbalizing emotions effectively (Bandura, 1986).

After the two of you finish discussing the movie, you set up a game that will help facilitate more discussion about feelings. You choose an "emotions bingo" game because it involves labeling different emotions based on facial expression and body language. The game has colored photographs of children from several different cultures and covers basic emotions that a 7-year-old child should be able to identify and discuss. As you play the game, you use the emotions expressed in the photographs to explore Pedro's feelings. At times, you ask Pedro, "Why do you think the boy is sad?" Other times, you ask more direct questions, "What's something that makes you feel sad?" You encourage Pedro to ask you questions for three main reasons: to help him understand that *everyone* has these emotions, to allow him to observe different ways of expressing emotions, and to practice asking others about their emotions.

Through this game, you are able to gain some insight into some of Pedro's behaviors. You find out that the classmate Pedro has been "teasing" at school is a little girl whom he bashfully admits is "very pretty." Upon discussing the issue in a little more depth, you assess that Pedro's attraction to this girl is healthy and appropriate for his age. You also learn that Pedro is upset that his mother has been giving more attention to Jose Jr. lately. Finally, you notice that Pedro consistently has difficulty talking about fear.

Aware of the time, you ask Pedro whether he would like to take this game home so that he can teach his family how to play. Pedro is excited about the prospect and the two of you invite Maria and Jose into the office for the last 10 minutes of the session. You ask Pedro whether he would like to tell his parents what the two of you did in session. After Pedro shares the information with his parents, you explain that the game is a type of "homework assignment" that will help facilitate discussion about emotions within the family.

Aware that emotions are often expressed differently across cultures, you show the family a description of the game written in English and in Spanish. The description emphasizes that everyone has his own way of talking about and communicating feelings and that no single way is the right way to express how they are feeling. Emphasizing that every culture has certain words to identify and discuss different emotional states, you encourage the family to use what feels comfortable to them. You encourage the family to try playing the game in English and Spanish to strengthen the communication of emotions in both languages. The family thanks you and says good-bye. As they are leaving, Pedro gives you *un abrazo* (a hug).

Reflection

As you reflect on your session with Pedro and his family, you consider how culture shapes emotion. You understand that every culture has specific rules and beliefs that have an impact on how and when emotion is described, expressed, and understood. During the game that you played with Pedro, you asked him to identify the emotion that he thought was being expressed in the photograph. This allowed you to learn what different facial expressions meant to Pedro, and it also allowed you to hear the language he uses to describe and discuss emotions. Aware that Pedro is exposed to different cultures at home and at school, you encouraged Pedro, and later his family, to use English as well as Spanish to describe and discuss emotions. Pedro needs practice using both languages to express his emotions in order to interact effectively with his family and peers.

You are aware that children learn rules and ways of expressing emotions primarily by observing their environment. Pedro has spent the majority of his first 5 years with his family and, consequently, most of what he has learned about emotion has been shaped by what he has seen at home. These observations have shaped what Pedro might consider to be of emotional importance, how Pedro responds when feeling a specific emotion, and how he copes with his emotions (Barrett & Campos, 1991). During the past 2 years, Pedro has been exposed to a very different environment that has new rules, situations, and ways of handling emotion. Based on your observations during the game, his interactions with his parents during sessions, and your conversation with Mrs. Garcia, Pedro seems to be effective in picking up and using cues regarding emotion in both settings.

You are a little curious about Pedro's difficulty in discussing fear. Aware that many of the symptoms that Pedro has been exhibiting, prior to and over the course of counseling, are frequently associated with anxiety, you consider how you will approach the next session. As the week comes to an end, you get a phone call from Maria explaining that Pedro has been having nightmares and is scared to go to sleep. You ask Maria how they have been handling the situation and she tells you, "I say a special prayer with Pedro before he goes to bed. We've also been letting him sleep in our room." You ask Maria how that has worked and she tells you that it has helped a little. You encourage Maria to continue to find ways to talk to Pedro and ease his fears and let her know that you will bring this up in the next session.

As you reflect on what you know about anxiety in children, you recall that it is not uncommon for children to exhibit anxiety or fear. Childhood fear may be conditioned as a result of an actual or vicarious experience (Kagan, 1984). For example, a child who falls into a swimming pool and nearly drowns may consequently develop a fear of water. Children's fear may also stem from the "anticipated loss of the love relation to a parent" (Kagan, p. 156). Thus, a parent who is unconsciously giving more attention to one of the children may produce anxiety in the other children. Finally, childhood fear may be "triggered by the unfamiliar," such as a child's first trip to the dentist (Kagan, p. 156).

In Pedro's case, you consider the source of his anxiety as well as the degree to which Pedro's behaviors are affecting his functioning at home and at school. Your goal for the next session is to provide a nonthreatening means for Pedro to discuss his fears. You plan to begin with an indirect approach to discussing fear and then gradually guide the conversation to Pedro's situation.

SESSION 4

As Jose, Maria, and Pedro enter your office, Pedro hands you the game and says thank you. The family shares some of their experiences, and Jose comments, "I don't think we've every really just talked about our feelings. I think we all learned something about each other." Pleased with the feedback, you ask Pedro whether he wants to give his mom and dad un abrazo before they leave. Pedro hugs his parents and, before walking out, Maria says, "I talked to Mrs. Garcia yesterday and she said that Pedro's grades have been improving." Glad to hear that Pedro is doing better in school, you say, "It sounds like you have *all* been working very hard!" Pedro smiles and waves good-bye to his parents.

You begin the session with Pedro by reading a story about a little boy who is having nightmares. You use the story to help open a discussion about fear. As the two of you discuss the story, Pedro is able to talk about the boy's fears and how he thinks they are making him feel. The two of you discuss some of the physical symptoms related to fear and how the body starts to feel different when someone is scared. You let Pedro know that everyone feels scared sometimes and the two of you discuss things that you find scary.

At one point Pedro mentions, "I don't like it when I have nightmares." As you begin talking to Pedro about his nightmares, you notice that he is having some trouble expressing himself. Taking out some paper and art supplies, you ask Pedro whether he would like to draw a picture about the nightmares that he has been having. Pedro nods his head and begins drawing. He draws a picture of his family inside their house. You notice that everyone is sitting together and no one is smiling in the picture. You also notice that Pedro colored his father's skin dark brown.

When he finishes drawing, you ask Pedro whether he will tell you about his picture. Pedro looks at the picture quietly for a couple of minutes and says, "I don't want to talk about this." After a while, you ask Pedro how he is feeling and he responds, "My stomach feels funny, like when I wake up from a nightmare." You respond,

> I can tell by looking at your face that you are very worried about something. I know it is very hard for you to talk about what is scaring you. I want to help you, but I'm not sure how I can help. Do you have any ideas?

Pedro thinks about the question for a while and then says, "I think my dad needs help." Curious, you ask, "What kind of help do you think your dad needs?" Pedro responds, "I don't know." Aware of the time, you ask Pedro whether the two of you can talk about this with his parents. Pedro hesitates for a while and then says okay. Unsure of where this is going, you invite Jose and Maria into the office, hoping that they can help clarify Pedro's concern.

As Jose and Maria sit down, you encourage Pedro to show his parents the picture about his nightmare. They look at the picture and Maria asks Pedro to explain his drawing. Pedro responds, "That's our family." Maria asks, "Why do we all look so sad?" Pedro is quiet for a while and then responds, "I don't know." Jose and Maria look at you and you respond, "Pedro seems to think that his dad needs some help, but he's not sure what kind of help." Jose and Maria sit quietly for a while trying to figure out why Pedro thinks his dad needs help. After several minutes, Jose asks Pedro, "Did something happen that makes you think I need help?" Pedro responds, "I heard you and mommy talking about some people that might take you away." Jose and Maria immediately appear to understand the conversation to which Pedro is referring. Jose turns to you and says, "My working permit is about to expire, and I'm in the process of renewing it." Uncertain of how the process works, you ask the couple to explain it to you. Jose explains,

> The working permit needs to be renewed every year. If the visa is still good, the Department of Homeland Security will renew the permit. However, this process is a source of concern for most immigrants, even more so after the September 11th terrorist attacks. We heard about the pressure that the government is putting on foreigners because some of our friends were required to go back to Mexico. But this is not the case with us, because my visa is good for 10 years and the company that I'm working for is in good shape financially. So, although we are concerned, I don't think I will have any problems getting my working permit. My immigration lawyer has told me that there is no need to worry.

When he finishes, Jose assures everyone in the room that the chances of his having to leave the country are slim. He explains that he has a lawyer and that Jose Jr. has been helping him with some of the paperwork. Maria adds, "Jose Jr. has helped us with some of this paperwork. It's very confusing sometimes." Jose turns to Pedro, "Is this what you've been worrying about?" Pedro nods his head and Jose continues, "I don't want you to worry about me leaving, okay? No one is going to take me away. No matter what happens, our family will stay together." Pedro smiles and gives his dad *un abrazo*. You let the family know that you would like to see Pedro two more times by himself and then see the whole family the following session. Jose and Maria agree and thank you for the session.

Reflection

Aware that your understanding of immigration issues is limited, you decide to do some research to learn more about the process and its impact on those involved. As you read, you learn that several factors influence the immigration process, including the reason for immigrating, who immigrates and when, the individuals' personalities, and the context in which immigration occurs (Santiago-Rivera et al., 2002). In Pedro's case, the family decided to immigrate to provide a better life for their children. Jose and Maria stated in the initial interview that they moved because they wanted their children to receive a good education. In addition, you know that the entire family, including some extended family, moved together. Based on your conversations with Jose and Maria, you are aware that this decision has made the transition somewhat easier for both families. As you continue to work with Pedro, you have been able to observe how the families work together and support each other. Your experiences with the different family members have been very positive, and it appears that the family members' values of dedication, hard work, and faith in God have contributed to their success during this challenging time.

Today's session with Pedro has helped everyone understand the source of Pedro's anxiety. You have asked Jose and Maria to keep you up to date on the matter and they have agreed to do so. During your next session, you want to make sure that Pedro is not holding on to other erroneous beliefs related to the immigration process or ethnicity. You would like to clarify with Pedro the issue related to his father's skin color. Although you suspect that it may be related, you do not want to assume that is the case. In addition to identifying faulty beliefs, you want to help Pedro find ways to express and cope with his anxiety.

Familiar with the literature regarding children and anxiety-related issues, you plan to utilize cognitive–behavioral techniques to achieve these goals (Albano & Kendall, 2002; Kendall & Choudhury, 2003). Specifically, you would like to help Pedro recognize the physical signs of anxiety, identify thoughts that lead to feeling anxious, and cope with the anxiety (Albano & Kendall). You plan to involve the family in the last two sessions of this process in an effort to facilitate lasting change. By involving the whole family, you hope to set up a support system for Pedro as well as provide everyone with tools that they can use in the event that a similar situation occurs in the future. Your belief that family involvement will facilitate this process is supported by the literature and your experience with the Gonzales family (Albano & Kendall; Barrett, Dadds, & Rapee, 1996).

SESSION 5

The session begins with a brief conversation and then the couple gives you an update regarding Jose's immigration status. Everything seems to be going well and the situation should be resolved soon. Maria also tells you that Pedro has not had any more nightmares, and his behavior at home has gotten much better. Jose adds, "It seems like once Pedro found out that I wasn't leaving, things have gotten a lot better." Maria nods her head in agreement and couple gets up, "We're going to let you two get to work." Pedro hugs his parents and the two of you begin the session.

You begin by asking Pedro how he is feeling, and he responds, "Better." Nodding your head, you ask, "Can you tell me more about how things are better?" Pedro responds, "I'm not having bad dreams anymore, and my grades in reading are good. I think I got a 100 on my test." Pleased with the news, you say, "I wonder what's making things better for you?" Pedro thinks about the statement for a moment and then responds thoughtfully, "My head isn't having trouble thinking anymore." Curious about his comment, you ask Pedro to tell you more and Pedro continues, "Before it was not really letting me think, like when I was in school, I wasn't really listening to my teacher because my head was thinking about my dad." Nodding your head, you say, "It sounds like when you were worried about your dad leaving it was hard for you to concentrate on your work." Pedro nods his head, "Yeah." After a brief silence you ask, "Is there anything else you are worried or unsure about?" Pedro shakes his head, but does not say anything. Taking out the family portrait and nightmare pictures, you say, "Well, I have one thing that I'm not sure about and I was wondering if you could help me with the answer." Pedro, who seems to enjoy helping others, eagerly responds, "Sure."

You show Pedro the family portrait and ask him to tell you about his picture. Pedro begins identifying the people in the picture; when he gets to his dad, he stops for a moment and then says, "And that's my dad." After some silence, you take out the picture of the nightmare and ask Pedro to tell you about this picture. Pedro looks at the picture for a while and then says, "In my nightmare, I was scared that my dad was going to leave. My whole family was sad in the dream." Nodding your head, you say, "That sounds like a very scary dream to have." Pedro responds, "It was very scary." After a moment, you place the two pictures next to each other and ask, "I was wondering why you colored your dad a differ-ent color in the second picture?" Pedro looks at the pictures for a long time and then says, "I want his skin to be lighter so that the police won't take him back to Mexico." Attempting to clarify his last comment, you ask, "Do you think that the reason your dad was going to have to leave was because his skin is dark?" Pedro nods his head but does not say anything. You spend some time trying to help Pedro understand why his dad thought he would have to leave. After the two of you discuss the issue at some length, you see that this is a lot of information for Pedro to take in and decide to shift gears a little bit.

You ask Pedro whether he remembers the story that you read last week. Pedro nods his head and says, "It was about a little boy who was having bad dreams." Nodding your head, you ask, "Do you remember talking about some of the things our bodies feel when we are scared?" Pedro responds, "Your stom-ach feels funny and your heart beats fast." Pedro begins beating his hand on his chest real fast, "Like this!" Impressed with his recall, you say, "Well, today I thought that we could practice doing some activities that can help us when we start to feel scared or anxious." You take out a game that helps teach children how to talk about their emotions. The game focuses on using "I messages" and on finding constructive things to do when something is bothersome, such as talking about it, drawing a picture, exercising, and spending quiet time alone. Before starting the game, you tell Pedro that "one thing we can do when some-thing is bothering us is to talk about how we are feeling."

You spend the last 10 minutes of the session teaching Pedro a relaxation exercise. After explaining the purpose of the exercise, you show Pedro how to take deep breaths. Once he has the hang of taking deep breaths, you tell him that you are going to play a CD and the two of you are going to lie down on the floor, close your eyes, and listen to the CD. The two of you go through the visualization exercise. When the exercise is over, you help Pedro process the experience. Excited about the experience, Pedro asks if he can show his mom and dad. The two of you invite Maria and Jose into the office and Pedro begins to tell them about the relaxation exercise. When he is finished, you explain the focus of today's session and tell them that they can take the game and the relaxation CD with them and do it as homework. You remind the family that next week will be the last session with Pedro and that, for the session following that one, you would like to invite the entire family.

Reflection

As you reflect on your session with Pedro, you consider how his cognitive abilities have an impact on his ideas of ethnicity. Pedro's limited cognitive abilities have led him to connect his father's skin color with the reason he was having to leave. Pedro's belief is consistent with most children his age who focus on concrete (skin color) rather than abstract (immigration status) constructs (Casas & Pytluk, 1995; Piaget & Inhelder, 1969). In addition, Pedro does not yet understand that certain characteristics, such as skin color, are constant. This is consistent with literature suggesting that the concept that one's race or ethnicity is constant generally develops around the age of 10 or 11 years of age (Semaj, 1980).

Part of helping Pedro deal with his anxiety involves teaching him to recognize his feelings, symptoms, and thoughts (Rapee, Wignall, Hudson, & Schniering, 2000). You have been working with Pedro for the past several weeks on recognizing his feelings and symptoms. The next few sessions will focus on Pedro's thought processes. Because Pedro is relatively young, you decide to use self-instructional training (Meichenbaum, 1977). This approach "has been shown to be particularly useful for very young children" (Rapee et al., 2000, p. 81). It involves teaching children to make statements that help reduce their anxiety (Meichenbaum, 1977).

You will begin by introducing self-instructional training in your last session with Pedro and will continue to utilize it in the following session with Pedro and his family. You want the family to be familiar with this type of training so that they can provide assistance and support for Pedro when necessary. Also, because treatment is coming to an end, you want to equip Pedro and his family with skills that they can use in the future if problems arise.

As you reflect on your final sessions with Pedro and his family, you review his progress over the past 5 weeks. Pedro is more open when discussing his feelings and has a better understanding of them; his symptoms related to anxiety continue to decrease. You have been preparing Pedro for your final session for several weeks, and he seems to be handling it well. Your goals for your final individual session with Pedro are to provide him with tools that he can use to deal effectively with his anxiety and to discuss feelings related to the end of the counseling relationship.

SESSION 6

Jose, Maria, and Pedro arrive on time for the session. As they walk into your office, Pedro smiles and hands you some flowers. Getting down to Pedro's level, you thank him and ask whether you can give him *un abrazo*. Maria smiles, "He picked them from our garden." You talk with the family briefly about their garden. As the conversation comes to an end, Jose hands you the relaxation CD and thanks you, "We did the relaxation exercise every night this week. It was nice, the whole family did it together." Pedro turns to his parents and gives them a hug, and Jose and Maria go to the waiting room.

You begin by reviewing the concepts that you discussed with Pedro in the previous session. After you have assessed the degree to which Pedro remembers and understands those concepts, you tell him that you want to teach him one more thing that he can do to help him feel better when he starts to worry. You show Pedro a recording sheet and explain that the two of you are going to watch different movie clips and write down three pieces of information. The first two pieces of information focus on what the character was thinking about and how the character was feeling. The final piece of information focuses on things that the character could have said to feel less worried.

You play several movie clips from *Finding Nemo* and *Shark Tale* to practice using this technique. You work with Pedro on the first several examples and after he seems to have the hang of it, you allow him to do several on his own. After Pedro has completed several of the forms successfully, the two of you discuss times during the past week or two when he could have used this technique to help him feel less worried. After Pedro identifies several examples of when he could have used the technique during the past week, you bring up how he feels about ending counseling. Pedro identifies several thoughts that he could use to calm himself if he begins to miss attending counseling sessions. You reassure Pedro that ending counseling does not mean that you will stop caring or thinking about him.

The two of you discuss any anxiety related to ending the counseling relationship and identify constructive ways of dealing with it. Pedro suggests that he could send you a picture if he misses you or wants to tell you something. You let Pedro know that it is okay for him to send you pictures and that you will give him some envelopes and stamps so that he can mail them. Sensing that Pedro is happy with the suggestion, you add, "I was thinking about taping our relaxation exercise and that way you can take it home and listen to it whenever you need." Pedro smiles, "I like that idea!"

You take the tape recorder out and insert a new tape. You begin the tape by saying, "Hello Pedro, how are you feeling today? I hope everything is going well. I want you to get ready for the relaxation exercise." You then play some quiet background music and begin the visualization exercise. When you finish the exercise, you conclude by saying, "I hope you are feeling better and more relaxed. Remember that you can use this whenever you need to relax. Say hello to your family for me." As you stop the tape, Pedro gets up and asks, "Can we show my mom and dad?"

The two of you invite Jose and Maria into your office and Pedro excitedly shows them the tape and explains what it is. His parents seem pleased and tell Pedro that they will listen to it tonight. Pedro tells them about the pictures and the movies that you watched. When Pedro is finished, you give Jose and Maria some of the recording sheets in English and Spanish and encourage Pedro to explain how they are used. You encourage the family to practice using them during the next week and let them know that the sheets can be modified if necessary. You remind them that, next week, the family is invited to the session. You let the family know that next week will probably be the last session. The family thanks you and as they leave Pedro gives you *un abrazo*.

Reflection

As you think about your final session with the Gonzales family, you review your reflections, exploring how cultural variables contributed to the counseling process. You consider how your increased awareness and understanding of the differences and similarities in backgrounds and worldviews helped you develop your relationship with the family. In particular, you recall how reading about spirituality in the Latino culture provided you with a more open and alternative view of some of the actions and beliefs expressed by the family.

You consider how the family's cultural values shaped the manner in which you communicated with them during sessions. Specifically, you extended each session so that you could spend some time with the family before and after your time with Pedro. This extra time provided the opportunity to engage in short, but personal conversations with the family. You believe that your time spent interacting with the family helped you develop a positive and trusting relationship with them that ultimately affected Pedro's progress. You also learned that, although your interactions with Pedro were more formal than those with other children with whom you have worked, it was a reflection of *respeto* rather than uneasiness.

Your experience with the Gonzales family also created a greater awareness and appreciation of the difficulties and stresses experienced by immigrants. You became more aware of the historical and political factors that affect individuals from different cultures (Arredondo & Arciniega, 2001). As your relationship and insight with the Gonzales family developed, you became increasingly aware of their resilience and strength. Your decision to involve the family in the counseling process was based on your awareness of this strength. Ultimately, you believe that the commitment and willingness of this family is what contributed to Pedro's progress. As you reflect on this point, you recall a statement that Maria made during the first session, "*La familia es el corazón y espíritu de la cultura Latina.*" (The family is the heart and soul of Latino culture.) (Santiago-Rivera et al., 2002, p. 19).

Aware that the strategies and techniques that you used throughout this process needed to fit with the family's culture and values, you utilized primarily Rogerian and cognitive–behavioral strategies and techniques. Your decision to use Rogerian techniques was based on literature citing the importance of establishing a positive and trusting therapeutic relationship with clients (Lambert & Cattani-Thompson, 1996). Your decision to use cognitive–behavioral strategies and techniques was based partly on literature indicating that it is well suited for children and those who prefer a more direct approach to counseling (Thompson et al., 2004). A statement that Maria had made early in the relationship also contributed to your decision to employ cognitive–behavioral strategies. As you were visiting with the family one day, Maria told you, *"De padres sanos, hijos honrados."* (From wholesome parents, honest children.) (Santiago-Rivera et al., 2002, p. 34). As the two of you discussed this saying, you became aware that the family believed firmly that children learn by watching others.

As you come to the end of your notes, you are aware of how you have grown as a therapist as a result of your experience with the Gonzales family. You have learned a great deal about their family and yourself, and you will miss working with Pedro and his family. Your goals for the final session are to discuss how the family will handle minor setbacks and future problems. You also want to attain a sense of closure with the family.

SESSION 7

Jose, Maria, Pedro, and his siblings arrive on time for the session. After introducing yourself and shaking hands with the family, you invite them to have a seat. In an effort to create a comfortable atmosphere, you ask Pedro whether he would like to show his siblings around the office. Pedro eagerly agrees and shows his brothers and sisters some of his favorite activities. When he finishes, Pedro asks, "Is it okay if my little sister can color?" You nod your head and invite the rest of the family to the art table.

As everyone gets situated, Jose and Maria give you feedback on the recording sheets from the previous week. You are pleased that the family found the cards helpful and that they would like to continue using them. You let them know that you will give them enough copies to last for a while and reassure them that they can always stop by the office and get more if necessary. You continue to talk with Jose and Maria as the children color. As the children finish their pictures, Pedro suggests that they take turns talking about their pictures. After listening to each of the children describe his or her picture, you invite everyone in the family to draw a picture about something that has changed since the family began attending counseling. You decide to draw a picture as well.

When everyone finishes their picture, you ask if anyone would like to share his work with the group. You gain a great deal of insight from this activity and learn that everyone in the family experienced change as a result of the counseling process. When the family finishes sharing their pictures, Pedro asks, "Are going to share your picture?" Nodding your head, you show Pedro and his family your picture and share how you have grown as a result of your relationship with them.

You spend the remainder of the session discussing any concerns the family has in regards to the termination of the counseling relationship. You let the family know that it is not uncommon to experience minor setbacks occasionally and discuss how they might handle them. You also discuss how they might apply what they have learned to future problems. Jose and Maria express their confidence that everything will be okay.

Finally, you let the family know that you usually send two letters to your clients to check on their progress—1 month and then 6 months after their last counseling session (Thompson et al., 2004). You ask the family whether it is okay for you to send a letter to see how they are doing. Jose and Maria are pleased with the idea and give you their permission to send the letters. As the session comes to an end, you thank the family for their hard work and wish them well. Jose and Maria give you a hug and thank you for helping their family. You say good-bye to Jose Jr., Anna, and Theresa and thank them for coming to visit. Finally, you give Pedro *un abrazo* and hand him some envelopes and stamps so that he can send you some pictures. You walk with the family out into the waiting room and wave good-bye.

Reflection

As you go back to your office, you write your final reflection on your experience with the Gonzales family. You are pleased with today's session and feel confident that the family has the tools, strength, and commitment to face whatever challenges may lie ahead. You are grateful for the opportunity to have worked with this family because your experience with them has contributed to your professional and personal growth. Through your experience with the Gonzales family, you are even more aware of the impact and enrichment that culture has on everyone's lives.

REFERENCES

Albano, A., & Kendall, P. (2002). Cognitive behavioral therapy for children and adolescents with anxiety disorders: Clinical research advances. *International Review of Psychiatry, 14*, 129–134.

Arredondo, P., & Arciniega, M. (2001). Strategies and techniques for counseling training based on the multicultural counseling competencies. *Journal of Multicultural Counseling and Development, 29*(4), 1–10. Retrieved on March 6, 2005 from EBSCO Host Research Databases.

Bandura, A. (1986). *Social foundations of thought and action.* Englewood Cliffs, NJ: Prentice Hall.

Barrett, K., & Campos, J. (1991). A diacritical function approach to emotions and coping. In E. M. Cummings, A. L. Greene, & K. H. Karraker (Eds.), *Lifespan developmental psychology: Perspectives on stress and coping* (pp. 21–41). Hillsdale, NJ: Erlbaum.

Barrett, P., Dadds, M., & Rapee, R. (1996). Family treatment of childhood anxiety: A controlled trial. *Journal of Consulting and Clinical Psychology, 64*, 333–342.

Casas, J., & Pytluk, S. (1995). Hispanic identity development: Implications for research and practice. In J. Ponterotto, J. Casas, L. Suzuki, & C. Alexander (Eds.), *Handbook of multicultural counseling* (pp. 155–180). Thousand Oaks, CA: Sage Publications.

Denham, S. (1998). *Emotional development in young children.* New York: The Guilford Press.

Kagan, J. (1984). *The nature of the child* (10th ed.). New York: Basic Books.

Kendall, P., & Choudhury, M. (2003). Children and adolescents in cognitive–behavioral therapy: Some past efforts and current advances, and the challenges in our future. *Cognitive Therapy and Research, 27*(1), 89–104.

Knight, G., Bernal, M., Garza, C., & Cota, M. (1993). A social cognitive model of the development of ethnic identity and ethnically-based behaviors. In M. Bernal & G. Knight (Eds.), *Ethnic identity: Formation and transmission among Hispanics and other minorities* (pp. 213–234). Albany, NY: State University of New York Press.

Lambert, M., & Cattani-Thompson, K. (1996). Current findings regarding the effectiveness of counseling: Implications for practice. *Journal of Counseling and Development, 74*(6), 1–15. Retrieved on March 5, 2005 from EBSCO Host Research Databases.

Magnusson, D. (1995). Individual development: A holistic, integrated model. In P. Moen, G. Elder, & K. Luscher (Eds.), *Examining lives in context: Perspectives on the ecology of human development* (pp. 19–60). Washington, D.C.: American Psychological Association.

Meichenbaum, D. (1977). *Cognitive behavior modification: An integrative approach.* New York: Plenum.

Piaget, J., & Inhelder, B. (1969). *The psychology of the child.* New York: Basic Books, Inc.

Rapee, R., Wignall, A., Hudson, J., & Schniering, C. (2000). *Treating anxious children and adolescents: An evidence-based approach.* Oakland, CA: New Harbinger Publications, Inc.

Santiago-Rivera, A., Arredondo, P., & Gallardo-Cooper, M. (2002). *Counseling Latinos and la familia: A practical guide.* Thousand Oaks, CA: Sage Publications.

Semaj, L. (1980). The development of racial evaluation and preference: A cognitive approach. *Journal of Black Psychology, 6*, 59–79.

Shonkoff, J., & Phillips, D. (Eds.). (2000). *From neurons to neighborhoods: The science of early childhood development.* Washington, D.C.: National Academy Press.

Thompson, C., Rudolph, L., & Henderson, D. (2004). *Counseling children* (6th ed.). Belmont, CA: Brooks/Cole–Thomson Learning.

Woolfolk, A. (2004). *Educational psychology* (9th ed.). New York: Pearson Education, Inc.

CHAPTER 7

Counseling and Family Therapy With Latino Adolescents

STEPHEN SOUTHERN

Adolescence is a period of tremendous growth and upheaval with multiple demands for coping and adjustment of adolescents and their families. Although some may consider *adolescence* a North American construction, Latino or Hispanic adolescents, especially those living within the United States, have predictable counseling and developmental needs. Working with adolescents can be a challenge because interventions for children and adults may not apply. In addition, evidence-based research to determine "what works" when counseling adolescents is scarce (Rubenstein, 2003). Nevertheless, counselors have implemented programs for adolescents and their families in community and school settings. Counseling with Latino adolescents requires cultural awareness and sensitivity in order to increase access to services, ensure participation in counseling programs, and establish maintenance of treatment gains.

Latino adolescents should be considered a population at risk for developing several, probably related, problems. Problem domains include poor school and vocational adjustment, delinquency and substance abuse, and community violence. These social problems reflect influences of larger social systems, including poverty, recent immigration status, prejudice and discrimination, and lack of community resources. The family mediates the influence of other social systems and presents opportunities for intervention or risk reduction.

117

The purpose of this chapter is to provide an overview of counseling programs and practices for work with Latino adolescents. The remainder of the chapter will be organized around three domains or problem areas: academic and vocational adjustment, delinquency and substance abuse, and violence. Selected counseling interventions are described in each of the areas.

ACADEMIC AND VOCATIONAL ADJUSTMENT

Although immigration to North America has been a dream for many Central and Latin American families, the life careers of immigrants and assimilated Latinos reflect harsh economic realities. Print and broadcast media report regularly on hardship, exploitation, and even death among illegal aliens smuggled into the United States to perform backbreaking labor for modest wages. Similarly, Latinos who have been in the country for generations have been relegated traditionally to poorly paying service and labor occupations (Arbona, 1989; De Leon, 1996). Many Latino adolescents grow up in poverty, with limited access to medical, educational, and social service resources. Education represents a promising means by which Latino youth can escape poverty and realize the American dream of freedom and independence. However, high dropout rates and underachievement confound the potential benefits of ongoing education.

Many factors contribute to barriers to academic and vocational adjustment. High school graduation rates are much lower for Latino than Anglo American students (Stanard, 2003). Educational attainment of Latinos is affected by ease of access to schooling, including problems of overcrowding, cultural insensitivity, and language barriers (Acosta, Weist, Lopez, Shafer, & Pizarro, 2004; Tashakkori, Ochoa, & Kemper, 1999). Schools in urban (Crean & Arvey, 1992) and rural (Talbot & Kuehn, 2002) settings have responded to the educational needs of Latino youth by integrating educational and social services, providing bicultural and bilingual professionals, and encouraging postsecondary education and college entrance.

Integrating educational, medical, and social services is an innovation that has helped many students from economically disadvantaged backgrounds. School-based programs enable Latino adolescents to access resources they need to become resilient. For example, a trauma-focused cognitive behavioral treatment program for Latino immigrant students and their families was implemented in a school setting (Kataoka et al., 2003). The school-based program produced declines in trauma-related symptoms, enabling the students to participate better in the educational program. Another school-based program offered services to adolescent Latinas who had been sexually abused (McGurk, Cardenas, & Adelman, 1993). This program used confidential interviews and follow-up therapy groups to provide counseling to the underserved population.

An innovative school-based intervention was devoted to enhancing life skills and problem solving in urban Latino students (O'Hearn & Gatz, 2002). The program enlisted specially trained high school leaders as role models and counselors to younger peers. It focused on setting positive goals, anticipating barriers to goal attainment, using social supports, and building on personal strengths in problem solving and negotiation. Because underachievement in Latino youth may be associated with poor self-concept (Baruth & Manning, 1992) and fatalism (Guzman, Santiago-Rivera, & Hasse, 2005), it is important that counseling programs include positive role models and active disputation of self-defeating behaviors.

Students who participated in an enrichment program designed to promote college success among Latino adolescents reported that the affective quality of attachments to parents facilitated educational attainment and career aspirations (Kenny, Gallagher, Alvarez-Salvat, & Silsby, 2002). Parental attachment or bonding improved grades and facilitated positive mental health. Families contribute to the academic adjustment of their children by valuing education and providing emotional support.

Once Latino students have entered college, they tend to underutilize support services and may experience academic difficulties. Ethnic-identified Latinos were less likely than bicultural or acculturated peers to use various counseling resources (Atkinson, Jennings, & Liongson, 1990). Having access to Spanish-speaking counselors and culturally empathic professionals would improve service delivery and retention of Latino college students. In addition, Latino college students tend to use informal support networks (Chiang, Hunter, & Yeh, 2004). Therefore, their development could be supported by providing relevant psychoeducational materials to student groups and using peer advisors and counselors when possible.

The academic and vocational adjustment of Latino adolescents can be enhanced through careful design and delivery of counseling services. Ideally, these services will be well integrated in school-based or college settings. Successful counseling programs can use role models and peer counselors to strengthen life-coping, decision-making, and problem-solving skills. Young Latino adolescents should receive accurate information about the world of work by means of interesting media that include Latino actors or examples. Vocational exploration programs should include opportunities to interview or *shadow* (i.e., follow through a working day) Latino adults who are realizing success in scientific, technical, administrative, and artistic occupations. Opportunities for high school graduation and college enrollment should be emphasized. Psychoeducational and therapy groups can be incorporated into the school day to offer access to help and promote resilience. Finally, counseling Latino adolescents should include careful consideration of the family system. Parents can help in the resolution of academic and other difficulties.

DELINQUENCY AND SUBSTANCE ABUSE

Parents and helping professionals in schools and communities across the United States are concerned about adolescent problems with delinquency and substance abuse, which may be considered separate problems. However, in most cases, they are intertwined (see Dembo, Pacheco, Schmeidler, Fisher, & Cooper, 1997). For the purposes of the present review, the problem areas will be treated as interrelated. Delinquency and substance abuse emerge as problems from known childhood factors.

In their classic text, Wilson and Herrnstein (1986) articulated the causes of crime. Factors contributing to the emergence of delinquent conduct, usually by age 9, included

- being born to a young mother
- being low in birth weight (typically less than 5 lbs.)
- having verbal or communication problems
- exhibiting symptoms of attention deficit disorder or impulsivity
- being raised without a father
- receiving harsh or inconsistent discipline
- associating with rule-breaking peers
- lacking a commitment or bond to school
- receiving reinforcement for offender behavior

Factors associated with reduced risk for criminality included (Wilson & Herrnstein, 1986)

- experiencing pair-bonding with a good-enough mother
- modeling positive or proactive behavior from one's father and mother
- learning adequate coping and problem-solving skills
- avoiding risky situations
- associating with achievement-oriented peers
- becoming involved in academic and extracurricular activities at school
- receiving fair and consistent discipline

Growing up in impoverished families with limited access to educational and support services places some Latino adolescents at risk for delinquency and substance abuse.

Early adolescence is a period of significant developmental reorganization (Liddle, Rowe, Dakof, Ungaro, & Henderson, 2004). During this period, vulnerable youth are at considerable risk for developing serious substance abuse and conduct problems. Regular drug use at an early age tends to set the stage for later drug abuse and antisocial behavior (Liddle et al., 2004). Interventions at the earliest stages of problem identification reduce risk by promoting protective factors in as many functional domains as possible. Protective factors include family, educational, social, and individual strengths or resources that would promote positive development in various aspects of life. Protective factors have been defined as influences that prevent, limit, or reduce drug use and may counter, buffer, or neutralize other risk factors over time (Newcomb & Félix-Ortiz, 1992).

Research and theory on the etiology of problem behavior in adolescence often focus on the role of the family in the development of problem behavior (Griffin, Botvin, Scheier, Diaz, & Miller, 2000). Poor parental monitoring has been associated with high rates of adolescent substance abuse, delinquency, and aggression. Poor parent–child communication and lack of parental support have been linked to increased adolescent substance use (Griffin et al., 2000). The literature indicated that problems with family structure contribute to the etiology of substance abuse disorders and behavior problems in vulnerable adolescents.

Family cohesion or connection has been associated with reduced risk for substance abuse and adolescent adjustment difficulties. Several studies have demonstrated the influence of family cohesion in preventing or reducing risk for substance abuse. O'Farrell and Feehan (1999) found that family treatment for alcoholism produced improvement in cohesion, resulting in improvements in psychosocial functioning. A family-based substance abuse prevention program in a rural community increased resilience and enhanced protective factors, including family cohesion (Pilgrim, Abbey, Hendrickson, & Lorenz, 1998). The prevention program increased appropriate attitudes about alcohol and tobacco use by adolescents.

A recent family-based prevention-oriented counseling program for high-risk adolescents (Hogue, Liddle, Becker, & Johnson-Leckrone, 2002) described counseling efforts that targeted family cohesion and school bonding, as well as other protective factors in reducing risk for substance abuse and conduct disorder. A major protective factor identified through research (Marsiglia, Miles, Dustman, & Sills, 2002) is that of enjoying a high degree of attachment and ongoing strong ties to their parents.

Another structural factor that provides some protection against family and community disorganization is maintenance of cultural identity or ethnic pride. A study of Mexican American adolescents established that ethnic pride and identity protected the young adults from becoming involved with alcohol use (Marsiglia, Kulius, Hecht, & Sills, 2004). Ethnic identity involves identifying with one's ethnic or cultural group; its variables enhance the effect of other protective factors (Brook, Whiteman, Balka, Win, & Gursen, 1998). A study of risk factors for drug use in a multiethnic sample of adolescents indicated deterioration of family environments was a stronger predictor of initiation in Hispanic immigrants than non-Hispanic immigrants (Gil, Vega, & Biafora, 1998). This conclusion illustrates the importance of family structural cohesion and the problems associated with the breakdown of the Latino family as it encounters the potentially disorganizing effects of exposure to majority or Anglo American culture. Family cohesion and ethnic identity interact or combine to strengthen protective factors against substance abuse and other rule-breaking behavior.

Acculturation, or the process by which minorities adjust to a majority culture, is related to a number of adjustment difficulties experienced by Latinos. Members of ethnic minorities have the challenge of acculturating into mainstream society while maintaining healthy pride and identity. Exposure to disorganizing environmental experiences or distressing community violence is the strongest predictor of delinquency (Taylor & Carey, 1998).

Family and cultural disorganization contribute to increased risk for delinquency and substance abuse. Latino adolescents may be considered especially at risk for adolescent adjustment difficulties due to the demands and stresses of poverty and acculturation. Enhancing ethnic identity and family cohesion can contribute to reduction of risk for substance abuse disorders and adjustment difficulties. Having strong religious beliefs, commitment to church attendance, and involvement in spiritual disciplines or religious rituals may also insulate some Latino adolescents from the myriad of disorganizing influences in contemporary American culture (Wills, Yaeger, & Sandy, 2003).

Counseling for delinquency and substance abuse among Latino adolescents involves a combination of treatment modalities, although family counseling may be the most important ingredient. Kazdin (2002) summarized the effective psychosocial treatments for conduct disorder in children and adolescents. Cognitive problem-solving training helped individuals resist provocation, impulsivity, and risky situations. Functional family therapy and parenting training were used to strengthen the structure of the family. Culturally relevant issues were integrated into this treatment program for Latino youth (Kazdin, 2002).

Counseling Latino male delinquents involved examination of attitudes toward masculinity and substance use (Arcaya, 1999; Black, Paz, & DeBlassie, 1991). Counseling may be most effective when adolescent males are encouraged to maintain ties with their traditional cultures while building coping skills that are effective in the cultural mainstream (Black et al., 1991). Misunderstanding of *machismo*, or the expected gender-role behavior of men, may lead some Latino adolescents toward aggressive and rule-breaking behavior (Bacigalupe, 2000).

Baptiste (1987) indicated that significant issues are related to loss in immigrant families. Immigrants lose contacts with their home countries and extended family members. They experience problems with language and expectations about their new home in the United States. Many immigrants fear losing their children to the new dominant culture (Baptiste). Parents may be concerned about their children's *culture shedding* behavior, while young people may become frustrated by their parents' holding onto the old ways, including perceived misuse of parental authority (Merali, 2002). Counseling Latino adolescents may involve exploration of grief issues and misperceptions about the motivations for parenting practices. Acculturation and assimilation are the systemic factors underlying experiences of loss, transition, and exaggerated role expectations.

Two family therapy research groups have examined systematically the effects of individual and family interventions upon delinquency and substance abuse. Howard Liddle and colleagues developed a multidimensional family therapy program for adolescent alcohol and drug abuse (2001). This approach was developed in response to advances in understanding adolescent development and accumulating research data regarding efficacy (Liddle, 1996). The overall multidimensional family prevention program combined standard curriculum-based prevention with assessment-based psychosocial treatment (Liddle & Hogue, 2000). The multidimensional model takes into account risk and protection theory, developmental psychopathology, ecological theory, and cultural issues. The program addresses family and peer relationships, prosocial behavior and school involvement, and health issues. The therapy is conducted in the family home, fostering close bonds, family resilience, and connections to prosocial institutions. Recently, the program was integrated in the national multisite trial of the cannabis youth treatment program (Dennis et al., 2002).

Another evidence-based treatment for delinquency and substance abuse was based on research by Richard Dembo and colleagues (Dembo et al., 1997; 1998). The research closely examined drug use and delinquent behavior in high-risk youth, including many Latino youth in Florida. Subsequently, the group developed the family empowerment intervention, a systems-oriented family counseling program offering structural interventions delivered in the family home by well-trained paraprofessionals (Dembo, Dudell, Livingstone, & Schmeidler, 2001). This intensive treatment program involves multiple contacts per week with at-risk families, empowering parents to communicate, monitor, discipline, and guide their adolescents (Dembo et al., 2001). The family empowerment intervention presents excellent follow-up data (up to 36 months) and evidence of efficacy in fostering adolescent psychosocial functioning and reducing recidivism (Dembo, Schmeidler, & Wothke, 2003; Dembo et al., 2001). The program has been integrated with good results with comprehensive initial assessment of youth and intensive probation services (Dembo et al., 2001).

The evidence-based approaches of Dembo and Liddle highlight the need for home-based, intensive family counseling services for Latino delinquents and substance abusers. Both programs are practical and culturally sensitive. They help parents address the rule-breaking and conduct-disordered behavior of adolescents who are moving away from the protective influences of the Latino family toward disorganization and peer influence over offender behavior. Although academic and vocational issues can be addressed in school-based programs, delinquency and substance abuse concerns must include some family counseling and parenting training in home-based programs. Adolescent problems with violence require school, family, and community responses.

VIOLENCE

Although violence occurs over the life span (see Peters, McMahon, & Quinsey, 1992; Wilson & Herrnstein, 1986), violent offenses against persons tend to peak in adolescence and young adulthood, especially among males. Violence is so pervasive in American society that it is now treated as a public health problem (Dulmus, 2003; Hammond, 2003). School counselors and mental health professionals need to conceptualize counseling services as public health interventions.

Latino adolescents may be victims or perpetrators of violence. They may be both because the cycle of violence predisposes some victims to become victimizers. Latino youth, especially those who are impoverished, are disproportionately the victims of crime (Rennison, 2002). According to the National Center for Victims of Crime (2002), 28% of Latino high school students reported being the victims of crime, compared to 25% of African American, 16% of Anglo American, and 11% of Asian American students. Effects of victimization include problems with mental health (MacMillan, 2001), substance abuse (Funk, McDermeit, Godley, & Adams, 2003), delinquency (Taylor & Carey, 1998), risky sexual behavior (Newcomb, Locke, & Goodyear, 2003), and partner violence (Ehrensaft et al., 2003).

Latino male youth who were violent in dating relationships and street fighting presented similar characteristics: regular exposure to community violence, reinforcement of exaggerated gender stereotypes, disorganization in the family system, and lack of consistent parenting (Gorman-Smith, Tolan, Sheidow, & Henry, 2001; Sheidow, Gorman-Smith, Tolan, & Henry, 2001; Ulloa, Jaycox, Marshall, & Collins, 2004). However, when Latino adolescents received skillful parenting in cohesive families, they were less likely to perpetrate violence, regardless of the extent of exposure to community violence (Gorman-Smith, Henry, & Tolan, 2004). As found in other problem areas, Latino adolescents are protected from community disorganization and violence exposure by emotional closeness in the family and good parenting practices. Latino adolescent violence emerges from family and community disorganization, especially when young men engage in externalizing or acting out behaviors perceived as normal within a gender stereotype of exaggerated masculinity.

Some Latino adolescents who have lost their way find their identities in gang membership and violence. Lost youth discover structure, hierarchy, and bonding in the gang system. Gangs offer social connection and meaning, especially when the adolescents have dropped out of school and family systems (Arfaniarromo, 2001; Becker, Felkenes, Magana, & Huntley, 1997). In gangs, youth find money, drugs, and excitement. In the process, they perceive that they are recovering aspects of Latino cultural heritage (Lopez & Brummett, 2003). Gangs reflect a stake in conformity to group norms (Wilson & Herrnstein, 1986). Chicano music and Latin rap contribute to the maintenance of gang culture and violence (Morales, 2003).

Gangs are, in effect, surrogate families and replacement for lost sense of community. The clothes, symbols, and rituals represent attempts to belong. Violent, delinquent, and substance-abusing Latino adolescents have lost their way. They do not experience the benefits of close family or school bonds so they turn to gang membership to feel supported and make meaning in daily life. Gang members are influenced especially by the peer network. They find heroes or idols whom they can admire, recovering lost parenting in the process. The experiences of gangs, as threatening as they seem, actually point to some potential solutions for Latino adolescent violence.

Faced with losses and disorganization, Latino adolescents are drawn toward deviant peers and mood-altering experiences. Lacking a stable sense of identity, a Latino youth may try to find himself in a gang or the lyrics of a violent song. Some counselors are capitalizing upon the adolescents' search for identity and meaning by telling stories and engaging creative imagination. Storytelling of prosocial and coping cultural norms can contribute to resilience (Constantino, Malgady, & Cardalda, 2005). Folktales and biographies provided models and heroes, advancing the developmental processes of internalization, introjections, and idealization (Constantino et al., 2005). Sharing family photos and constructing magazine photo collages represent creative adjuncts to the fundamental narrative experience of rebuilding one's family and community (see Landgarten, 1993).

The examples of Latino adolescent violence and gang activity contribute to an understanding of what has been missing in the lives of poverty-stricken and disenfranchised youth. They are seeking structure, sense of belonging, and personal identity. School-based programs can increase access to resources and home-based programs facilitate strengthening of family cohesion; recovery of lost culture and meaning can be advanced through narrative therapy and creativity. These young people are rewriting their life stories. When they are able to access the strengths of cultural traditions and healthy models, they can resist the disorganizing effects of exposure to dominant American culture and community violence. Group counseling and structural family therapy afford modalities for reclaiming cultural and family strengths while increasing resilience (see Minuchin, Colapinto, & Minuchin, 1998).

SUMMARY AND RECOMMENDATIONS

Latino adolescents present problems in four life domains: academic and vocational adjustment, delinquency and substance abuse, pregnancy and sexually transmitted diseases, and violence. The literature on academic and vocational adjustment indicated that completion of high school and postsecondary education prepares youth for meaningful careers rather than poverty-bound service and labor occupations. In order to help Latino adolescents complete education, well-integrated, school-based counseling and development programs should be available. Service providers should speak Spanish and be culturally empathic. Peer counselors can help with school-to-work transitions.

The literature on delinquency and substance abuse introduced concepts related to family and community disorganization. Evidence-based programs addressed relevant cultural issues by taking family counseling and parenting training efforts to the home setting. Understanding delinquency and substance abuse among Latino adolescents revealed the lack of structures, norms, and guidance practices. Treating these problems requires strengthening family cohesiveness and traditional Latino family values.

The problem of violence demands an integrative, multisystem approach. Breaking the cycle of violence involves group work and structural family therapy. Boundary setting defines the rich developmental and cultural experiences that should be included in one's life while identifying the toxic and shameful life experiences that should be excluded. Similar to treating the problem of sexuality, effective counseling for reducing violence will involve reexamination of exaggerated gender role stereotypes and behavioral expectations. Stories, folk tales, biographies, and family photos represent excellent resources for reclaiming lost identities and building coping and problem-solving skills. Counseling Latino adolescents is a process of helping lost children find their way to rewarding adult lives.

REFERENCES

Acosta, O. M., Weist, M. D., Lopez, F. A., Shafer, M. E., & Pizarro, L. J. (2004). Assessing the psychosocial and academic needs of Latino youth to inform the development of school-based programs. *Behavior Modification, 28,* 579–595.

Arbona, C. (1989). Hispanic employment and the Holland typology of work. *Career Development Quarterly, 37,* 257–268.

Arcaya, J. (1999). Hispanic American boys and adolescent males. In A. M. Horne & M. S. Kiselica (Eds.), *Handbook of counseling boys and adolescent males: A practitioner's guide* (pp. 101–116). Thousand Oaks, CA: Sage Publications.

Arfaniarromo, A. (2001). Toward a psychosocial and sociocultural understanding of achievement motivation among Latino gang members in U.S. schools. *Journal of Instructional Psychology, 28,* 123–136.

Atkinson, D. R., Jennings, R. G., & Liongson, L. (1990). Minority students' reasons for not seeking counseling and suggestions for improving services. *Journal of College Student Development, 31,* 342–350.

Bacigalupe, G. (2000). El Latino: Transgressing the macho. In M. T. Flores & G. Carey (Eds.) *Family therapy with Hispanics: Toward appreciating diversity* (pp. 29–57). Boston: Allyn and Bacon.

Baptiste, D. A. (1987). Family therapy with Spanish-heritage immigrant families in cultural transition. *Contemporary Family Therapy: An International Journal, 9*, 229–251.

Baruth, L. G., & Manning, M.L. (1992). Understanding and counseling Hispanic-American children. *Elementary School Guidance & Counseling, 27*, 113–122.

Becker, H. K., Felkenes, G. T., Magana, L., & Huntley, J. (1997). A socioeconomic comparison of drug sales By Mexican-American and Mexican immigrant male gang members. *Journal of Gang Research, 4*, 37–47.

Black, C., Paz, H., & DeBlassie, R. R. (1991). Counseling the Hispanic male adolescent. *Adolescence, 26*, 223–232.

Brook, J., Whiteman, M., Balka, E., Win, P., & Gursen, M. (1998). Drug use among Puerto Ricans: Ethnic identity as a protective factor. *Hispanic Journal of Behavioral Sciences, 20*, 241–254.

Chiang, L., Hunter, C. D., & Yeh, C. J. (2004). Coping attitudes, sources, and practices among black and Latino college students. *Adolescence, 39*, 793–815.

Constantino, G., Malgady, R. G., & Cardalda, E. (2005). TEMAS narrative treatment: An evidence-based culturally competent therapy modality. In E. D. Hibbs & P. S. Jensen (Eds.), *Psychosocial treatments for child and adolescent disorders: Empirically based strategies for clinical practice* (pp. 717–742). Washington, D.C.: American Psychological Association.

Crean, H. F., & Arvey, H. (1992). A declaration of beliefs and visions: Houston's school of the future. In W. H. Holtzman (Ed.), *School of the future* (pp. 97–114). Washington, D.C.: American Psychological Association.

De Leon, B. (1996). Career development of Hispanic adolescent girls. In B. J. R. Leadbeater & N. Way (Eds.), *Urban girls: Resisting stereotypes, creating identities* (pp. 380–398). New York: New York University Press.

Dembo, R., Dudell, G., Livingstone, S., & Schmeidler, J. (2001). Family empowerment intervention: Conceptual foundations and clinical practices. *Journal of Offender Rehabilitation, 33*, 1–31.

Dembo, R., Pacheco, K., Schmeidler, J., Fisher, L., & Cooper, S. (1997). Drug use and delinquent behavior among high-risk youths. *Journal of Child & Adolescent Substance Abuse, 6*, 1–25.

Dembo, R., Ramirez-Garnica, G., Schmeidler, J., Rollie, M., Livingstone, S., & Hartfield, A. (2001). Long-term impact of a family empowerment intervention on juvenile offender recidivism. *Journal of Offender Rehabilitation, 33*, 33–57.

Dembo, R., Schmeidler, J., Nini-Gough, B., Sue, C.C., Borden, P., & Manning, D. (1998). Predictors of recidivism to a juvenile assessment center: A three year study. *Journal of Child & Adolescent Substance Abuse, 7*, 57–77.

Dembo, R., Schmeidler, J., & Wothke, W. (2003). Impact of a family empowerment intervention on delinquent behavior: A latent growth model analysis. *Journal of Offender Rehabilitation, 37*, 17–41.

Dennis, M., Titus, J. C., Diamond, G., Donaldson, J., Godley, S. H., Tims, F. M., Webb, C., Kaminer, Y., Babor, T., Roebuck, M. C., Godley, M. D., Hamilton, N., Liddle, H., & Scott, C. K. (2002). The cannabis youth treatment (CYT) experiment: Rationale, study design and analysis plans. *Addiction, 97*, 16–34.

Dulmus, C. N. (2003). Approaches to preventing the psychological impact of community violence exposure in children. *Crisis Intervention & Time Limited Treatment, 6*, 185–201.

Ehrensaft, M. K., Cohen, P., Brown, J., Smailes, E., Chen, H., & Johnson, J. G. (2003). Intergenerational transmission of partner violence: A 20-year prospective study. *Journal of Consulting & Clinical Psychology, 71*, 741–753.

Funk, R. R., McDermeit, M., Godley, S. H., & Adams, L. (2003). Maltreatment issues by level of adolescent substance abuse treatment: The extent of problem at intake and relationship to early outcomes. *Child Maltreatment, 8*, 36–45.

Gil, A., Vega, W., & Biafora, F. (1998). Temporal influences of family structure and family risk factors on drug use initiation in a multiethnic sample of adolescent boys. *Journal of Youth and Adolescence, 27*, 373–393.

Gorman-Smith, D., Henry, D. B., & Tolan, P. H. (2004). Exposure to community violence and violence perpetration: The protective effects of family functioning. *Journal of Clinical Child & Adolescent Psychology, 33*, 439–449.

Gorman-Smith, D., Tolan, P. H., Sheidow, A. J., & Henry, D. B. (2001). Partner violence and street violence among urban adolescents: Do the same family factors relate? *Journal of Research on Adolescence, 11*, 273–295.

Griffin, K., Botvin, G., Scheier, L., Diaz, T., & Miller, N. (2000). Parenting practices as predictors of substance use, delinquency, and aggression among urban minority youth: Moderating effects of family structure and gender. *Psychology of Addictive Behaviors, 14*, 174–184.

Guzman, M. R., Santiago-Rivera, A. L., & Hasse, R. F. (2005). Understanding academic attitudes and achievement in Mexican-American youths: Ethnic identity, other-group orientation, and fatalism. *Cultural Diversity & Ethnic Minority Psychology, 11*, 3–15.

Hammond, W. R. (2003). Public health and child maltreatment prevention: The role of the Center for Disease Control and Prevention. *Child Maltreatment, 8*, 81–83.

Hogue, A., Liddle, H., Becker, D., & Johnson-Leckrone, J. (2002). Family-based prevention counseling for high-risk young adolescents: Immediate outcomes. *Journal of Community Psychology, 30*, 1–22.

Kataoka, S. H., Stein, B. D., Jaycox, L. H., Wong, M., Escudera, P., Tu, W., Zaragoza, C., & Fink, A. (2003). A school-based mental health program for traumatized Latino immigrant children. *Journal of the American Academy of Child & Adolescent Psychiatry, 42*, 311–318.

Kazdin, A. E. (2002). Psychosocial treatments for conduct disorder in children and adolescents. In P. E. Nathan & J. M. Gorman (Eds.), *A guide to treatments that work* (2nd ed.) (pp. 57–85). London: Oxford University Press.

Kenny, M. E., Gallagher, L. A., Alvarez-Salvat, R., & Silsby, J. (2002). Sources of support and psychological distress among academically successful inner-city youth. *Adolescence, 37*, 161–182.

Landgarten, H. B. (1993). Magazine photo collage: A multicultural assessment and treatment technique. Philadelphia, PA: Brunner/Mazel.

Liddle, H. (1996). Family-based treatment for adolescent problem behaviors: Overview of contemporary developments and introduction to the special section. *Journal of Family Psychology, 10*, 3–11.

Liddle, H.A., Dakof, G.A., Parker, K., Diamond, G.S., Barrett, K., & Tejeda, M. (2001). Multidimensional family therapy for adolescent drug abuse: Results of a randomized clinical trial. *American Journal of Drug & Alcohol Abuse, 27*, 651–688.

Liddle, H. A., & Hogue, A. (2000). A family-based, developmental–ecological preventive intervention for high-risk adolescents. *Journal of Marital & Family Therapy*, *26*, 265–279.

Liddle, H., Rowe, C., Dakof, G., Ungaro, R. & Henderson, C. (2004). Early intervention for adolescent substance abuse: Pretreatment to post treatment outcomes of a randomized clinical trial comparing multidimensional family therapy and peer group treatment. *Journal of Psychoactive Drugs*, *36*, 49–63.

Lopez, D. A., & Brummett, P. O. (2003). Gang membership and acculturation: ARSMA-II and choloization. *Crime & Delinquency*, *49*, 627–642.

MacMillan, R. (2001). Violence and the life course: The consequences of victimization for personal and social development. *Annual Review of Sociology*, *27*, 1–22.

Marsiglia, F., Kulius, S., Hecht, M., & Sills, S. (2004). Ethnicity and ethnic identity as predictors of drug norms and drug use among preadolescents in the U.S. Southwest. *Substance Use & Misuse*, *39*, 1061–1094.

Marsiglia, F., Miles, B., Dustman, P., & Sills, S. (2002). Ties that protect: An ecological perspective on Latino/a urban preadolescent drug use. *Journal of Ethnic & Cultural Diversity in Social Work*, *11*, 191–220.

Merali, N. (2002). Perceived vs. actual parent–adolescent assimilation disparity among Hispanic refugee families. *International Journal for the Advancement of Counseling*, *24*, 57–68.

McGurk, S. R., Cardenas, J., & Adelman, H. S. (1993). Utilization of a school-based clinic for identification and treatment of adolescent sexual abuse. *Journal of Adolescent Health*, *14*, 196–201.

Minuchin, P., Colapinto, J., & Minuchin, S. (1998). *Working with families of the poor.* New York: Guilford Press.

Morales, G. (2003). Chicano music and Latino rap and its influence on gang violence and culture. *Journal of Gang Research*, *10*, 55–63.

National Center for Victims of Crime. (2002). *Teenagers at greatest risk for crime victimization.* Washington, D.C.: National Center for Victims of Crime.

Newcomb, M. D., & Félix-Ortiz, M. (1992). Multiple protective and risk factors for drug use and abuse: Cross-sectional and prospective findings. *Journal of Personality & Social Psychology*, *63*, 280–296.

Newcomb, M. D., Locke, T. F., & Goodyear, R. G. (2003). Childhood experiences and psychosocial influences on HIV risk among adolescent Latinas in Southern California. *Cultural Diversity & Ethnic Minority Psychology*, *9*, 219–235.

O'Farrell, T. and Feehan, M. (1999). Alcoholism treatment and the family: Do family and individual treatments for alcoholic adults have preventive effects for children? *Journal of Studies on Alcohol*, *13*, 125–129.

O'Hearn, T., & Gatz, M. (2002). Going for the goal: Improving youths' problem-solving skills through a school-based intervention. *Journal of Community Psychology*, *30*, 281–303.

Peters, R. D., McMahon, R. J., & Quinsey, V. L. (Eds.) (1992). *Aggression and violence throughout the life span.* Newbury Park, CA: Sage Publications.

Pilgrim, C., Abbey, A., Hendrickson, P., & Lorenz, S. (1998). Implementation and impact of a family based substance abuse prevention program in rural communities. *Journal of Primary Prevention*, *18*, 341–346.

Rennison, C. M. (2002). *Hispanic victims of violent crime: 1993–2000*. Washington, D.C.: U.S. Department of Justice, Bureau of Justice Statistics.

Rubenstein, A. K. (2003). Adolescent psychotherapy: An introduction. *Journal of Clinical Psychology, 59,* 1169–1175.

Sheidow, A. J., Gorman-Smith, D., Tolan, P. H., & Henry, D. B. (2001). Family and community characteristics: Risk factors for violence exposure in inner-city youth. *Journal of Community Psychology, 29,* 345–360.

Stanard, R. P. (2003). High school graduation rates in the United States: Implications for the counseling profession. *Journal of Counseling & Development, 81,* 217–221.

Talbot, D., & Kuehn, P. (2002). The postsecondary preparation of San Joachin Valley Hispanic rural high school students. *Journal of Hispanic Higher Education, 1,* 111–124.

Tashakkori, A., Ochoa, S. H., & Kemper. E. A. (1999). Push and pull factors in the educational attainment of Hispanics: Current realities and future directions. In A. Tashakkori & S. H. Ochoa (Eds.), *Readings on equal education: Education of Hispanics in the United States: Politics, policies and outcomes* (pp. 249–268). New York: AMS Press.

Taylor, J., & Carey, G. (1998). Antisocial behavior, substance use and somatization in families of adolescent drug abusers and adolescent controls. *American Journal of Drug & Alcohol Abuse, 24,* 635–646.

Ulloa, E. C., Jaycox, L. H., Marshall, G. N., & Collins, R. L. (2004). Acculturation, gender stereotypes, and attitudes about dating violence among Latino youth. *Violence & Victims, 19,* 273–287.

Wills, T. A., Yaeger, A. M., & Sandy, J. M. (2003). Buffering effect of religiosity for adolescent substance use. *Psychology of Addictive Behaviors, 17,* 24–31.

Wilson, J. Q., & Herrnstein, R. J. (1986). *Crime and human nature: The definitive study of the causes of crime.* New York: Touchstone Books.

CHAPTER 8

Couple Counseling With Latinos

MARIO ZUMAYA

Methods of couple conceptualization are covered from a constructivist's perspective, followed by a suggested couple counseling approach that includes specific phases of counseling. This chapter concludes with a case.

REASONS AND INDICATIONS FOR PRACTICING COUPLES COUNSELING

Counseling must assist consultees or clients in the development of their personal capacities to become what they want to be as partners. The word "couples" is used to emphasize that the concept of an ideal couple does not exist: people may live as a couple, relating with each other well or badly, in particular and distinct manners. Thus, the counseling process should be flexible enough to adapt and accommodate the uniqueness of each couple.

Couples difficulties can be defined as being those experiences arising from differences, friction or arguments that are part of living as a couple. Moreover, the term refers to the inevitable adjustment or adaptation to a person of a different or same sex who comes from a family structure and organization that is unfamiliar. People come into a relationship with expectations, behaviors, and emotional states that are sometime incomprehensible or classified as inadequate by the other.

Couples difficulties become a problem when repetitive interaction causes suffering for those involved, the couple themselves, and anyone who has a close affective relationship with them, especially the children, if there are any. Solutions for these problematic interactions have been tried without much success,and could suggest an inherent attitude and pattern within couples that might contribute to maintaining the problem.

Repetitive interaction refers to a model or pattern of conduct that takes place between members of a couple regarding limits, power, and intimacy. Repetitive interaction also includes levels of verbal and nonverbal interaction that require "mutual collaboration." Couples with problems do not experience these interactions as mutual collaboration but as friction or struggle that has nothing to do with collaboration. The couple is not aware that they are reacting to each other automatically and without control over what they consider to be mistaken, unfair, stupid, and illogical or simply "bad faith" behavior by their partner. They are establishing a repetitive interaction that causes suffering. They are also unaware that the problems and pain caused contribute negatively to their identities as individuals and as partners.

The term "suffering" identifies a wide range and intensity of psychic pain in the diverse combinations of suffering's "basic colors": anxiety, sadness, anger. These emotions always are present in the couple, which leads the couple to implement diverse "solutions," which were learned in each partner's family of origin. In general terms, what each tries to do is to pressure the other into stopping what is regarded as mistaken. "Solutions" consist of various actions and inactions, such as shouting, keeping quiet, cutting oneself off, threatening, hurting, withdrawing and complaining to friends or family of origin, working compulsively, being unfaithful, and thereby maintaining the problem by becoming an insoluble part of it.

It is important for the counselor to identify particular problem areas in which the couple is experiencing unresolved difficulties. Counseling is especially helpful when the reason for the consultation becomes clear and is directly a consequence of the couple's ineffective interactions. Ineffective interactions may arise from:

1. power struggles: the issue of who rules and in what capacity
2. transgressing the partner's limits: the issue of what or who intervenes in the partner's life
3. diminished intimacy: the issue of how close or distant the partners feel emotionally, which translates into an unsatisfactory erotic life

These problematic interactions are intertwined and influence each other. For example, a problem with limits regarding intimacy and power dynamics can negatively influence the relationship if one partner spends more time with family of origin than with the other partner.

Couples counseling is clearly indicated as the specific and indispensable form of help under the following conditions:

1. The couple agrees to seek help to improve their relationship. Seeking help is infrequent, generally due to ignorance about therapy. Partners seek help when critical or intensely painful situations could lead to separation, such as when unfaithfulness is discovered, domestic violence occurs, or one or both partners experience substance addictions, compulsive behavior, and/or affective or psychotic disorders.
2. The couple is in the formation stage and seeks help as a preventive measure. Couples are increasingly seeking counseling before living together, when encountering some problems, or after becoming afraid of potential difficulties. Partners are especially more likely to seek counseling when they have been previously married or in relationships, an increasingly frequent situation in Latino/Latina cultures.
3. The couple is terminating through divorce proceedings already under way. The couple's habitual problems can take on extraordinary and even tragic dimensions, as clearly illustrated in the movie, *The War of the Roses*. The divorce may be signed, the marriage legally dissolved, and the now former spouses may continue as a couple united by resentment and hate.

Couples counseling under these conditions may provide a means for the couple to understand the subjective mechanisms that led to the breakup in less destructive ways. The couple may then be able to separate with less suffering for them and those they love.

Clinicians should take the time to reflect on the delivery of the counseling services they provide. Ecker and Hulley (1995) argue that the effectiveness of psychotherapy is more limited by the theoretical constructions of the psychotherapist than by the psychological organization of the persons seeking help. In counseling couples, a constructivist perspective of counseling seems to be appropriate as it concentrates on understanding the human existence rather than on the set of techniques. The counseling relationship within this conceptual framework is one in which the therapist seeks to understand the significance construction process of the clients. Thus, each individual is considered as a bearer of a meaning that allows him or her to recognize and to reference each immediate experience in terms of him/herself and the world (Granvold, 1999).

The ongoing narrative process of explaining the experience performs a crucial role in giving consistence to the experience of living. The human living event and the organization of experience can be consequently considered as a dual and circular process between an *I* that undergoes the experience based on emotions and feelings and a *Me* that observes and evaluates the language, narration and articulation of a meaning that guarantees a sense of continuity

and individual uniqueness. Social life is a sphere in which the individual constructs and articulates the "organization of significance" itself. The feeling held
by an adult about the self always relates to the knowledge of others about him
or her. Living in an intersubjective reality permits an individual to recognize
him/herself only in reference to the relations established with others.

CONCEPTUALIZATION OF THE COUPLE

Species must solve two fundamental problems to be successful: ensuring
security and effective reproduction. These are two central elements of adaptive functioning. Consequently, the human brain has evolved to organize
sensorial information in ways that promote both protection and reproduction. Nevertheless, a fundamental clarification is made here: human nature
is not just biological but social. "Natural" is anything not touched by culture,
and nothing human escapes culture. The basis of a culture lies within being
emotionally attached to one another within the relationship. The attachment
processes were studied and described by Bowlby (1969; 1973; 1980) and pro-
vocatively updated by Crittenden (1997).

Attachments represent successive phases of life, the space in which personal
significance emerges and is articulated. Intimate ties and sentimental relations
acquire the function of confirming, stabilizing and later articulating the pattern
of coherence of personal significance structured up to that moment (Guidano,
1991). Attachment reflects the relational history of the child (Karen, 1998),
it codes the behavior possessed by the intimate relations and defines how to
feel about one's self when emotionally involved with another. Care providers
teach small children how to use mentally accessible affective and cognitive
information when they modify their pattern of responses to match the child's
affective signals (Vygotsky, 1987).

Attachments may be categorized into three patterns that form a schema
that promotes future individual attachment:

1. Security: an example is when a predictable and sensitive response is
   given to child's needs. Children learn to use both affective and cognitive
   information (Ainsworth, 1979)
2. Avoidance: small children whose affective signals are punished learn
   that their cognitive predictions may be reliable but that their affective
   predictions are erroneous. Consequently, these small children discard
   information about their own feelings as they organize behavior
3. Consistency: children of inconsistent care providers learn that affection
   is not consistently strengthened or punished.

Consequently, such children are incapable of organizing their behavior around
affection or cognition. They are the ones who come from an ambivalent,

insecure, or ambivalent/avoidance attachment pattern (Crittenden, 1985a, 1985b, 1988).

METHODOLOGY IN COUPLES COUNSELING

Psychotherapy and consequently counseling have been called "the cure through the word through conversation." The nature of this conversation has changed. It used to consist of talking about feelings, relationships, the past, or any other subject that the client wanted to talk about. Counseling was thus like any other kind of talk: a conversational method. Doing it this way—talking about oneself and one's experience—is useful. Sharing painful memories helps. However, it can also be a long, slow, and useless method (Kurtz, 1990). It does not always touch on deep issues and, especially, it does not focus directly on experiences in the present.

The change of approach based on the methods developed in psychodrama and Gestalt therapy towards experience was also a change towards the present, where experience is. In the 1980s, therapies took a further step: they went from not only dealing with experience but also, more importantly, to focusing on the organization of the experience. The goal of these therapies is to contact and understand the events that create and maintain the slowing of experience in the self. We do it with the intention to transform the way in which we organize experiences.

The therapist's conviction that the constructs organizing and generating the client's problems are immediately accessible and modifiable from the commencement of the therapy is an indispensable condition for counseling. That is, the elements that make up the client's world of significance and generate his or her problems are in the therapist's office, at hand and immediately accessible, and therefore transformable. The elements present may, of course, include representations of past experiences, but these representations exist in a subjective present and should not be confused with an objective past.

The fundamental characteristic of constructivism is the creation of new significances and its emphasis on the plasticity of the experiential reality. The constructivists' position, however, is not that "anything goes" or that people are free to configure any reality that we want. We do not have the ability or the ethical license to create any reality arbitrarily. Instead, the constructivist vision stresses that people are more adept *than they realize* at modifying the reality that they currently inhabit.

Within its strategy for solving problems in counseling, constructivism coordinates and integrates the use of a variety of techniques taken from different psychotherapeutic traditions without falling into arbitrary eclecticism. It is claimed that it the therapeutic design must be served by the technique and not the technique that constitutes the constructivist dimension of the work.

The therapist focuses on finding and enticing the client to experience what is called the "emotional truth" (Ecker and Hulley, 1996) of the symptom or problem, a kind of significance that the patient has lost in his or her world of experiences. The emotional truth of the symptom may be understood as one of the most influential formations with a person's world of meanings. This formation of significance may be conceptualized in terms of what is called "posture" (Ecker and Hulley, 1996), which essentially is a constructed version of reality to which a strategy to respond to this reality is added. It consists of either conscious or unconscious display of emotions, cognitions, and sensations and/or movements that

- constitute the construction of significance for certain kinds of sensations, creating an experiential reality
- are activated when the current perception of a situation or event seems somehow compatible or analogous with a stored representation of this kind of situation
- distinctively predispose the person to respond to such a situation with specific protective actions designed to ensure security and well-being or to avoid harm and suffering

Couples counseling tries to explore and understand the position triggered in the members of the couple concerning the individual experiential version of the problem that has arisen. This means that it may be possible to focus the intervention on an analysis of the interaction of the two individual organizations of significance in the creation of the couple system and to be able to acknowledge and/or reformulate a shared significance.

This crisis is defined by the inability to narrate the common experience by referring to a shared significance, but only to individual significances in the crisis situation that lead to counseling. By reformulating an issue of life in common, they may stay together; this can only happen if the image of each other is still considered as valuable, not disappointing.

In reference to the basic method used to make the client aware of the rules of organization of his or her experience and the attribution of significance to this experience, Vittorio Guidano (1995) has called this the self-observation method in which the clients must be trained from the first sessions. It consists of working in the interphase, which may be understood as an intermediate position between the narration of the experience under way and the explanation given to it—that is, reconstructing what a person feels and how this feeling is expressed. This is always done with the two members of the couple present.

In terms of the technique to be used, the problematic events of the week that are meaningful for the clients are selected; these have been recorded in their self-observation task, and they are reconstructed; that is, the events are taken and then reordered in a sequence of scenes as if they were part of a movie script. By going back and forth through the scenes training the client to focus on individual images, we try to reconstruct simultaneously the immediate experience of the client or clients in that sequence of scenes and the way in which they are explained and reordered. It is as if the therapist and clients were in a movie production room, in an action replay device (film editing machine), going back and forth, zooming in and out of scenes, paying attention to details that could be significant. The same scene must be perceived in two ways: from the subjective viewpoint—that is, from a point in which one is acting directly as an actor—and from the exterior, as an external observer who looks on after having acted. Different things are seen: when looking from "within," one is more interested in seeing the motivation behind the act. When one looks from the "outside," however, there is more interest in seeing the consequences of the act.

Mixing the two points of view, that is, consequence and motivation, it is possible to reconstruct the immediate experience (what the client feels) and then the explanation can be seen (how it is referred to). Thus, the clients can see the part that is beyond their awareness and to which they cannot even refer because the objective of the reconstruction is to make them recognize the part of the immediate experience that they do not see or have problems in recognizing, and to lead them to recognizing and referring to such as a person.

Once the preceding has been carried out relating to the problems presented by the couple, work is started on the experience under way (in the same counseling session) regarding each other by narrating events lived in the week or weeks prior to the current session. The objective is not to return to the ideal or correct level of living, but to get the "patient system," the couple, to assimilate the experiences under way and to integrate them in the individual and shared narrative. Thus, the problem is worked on at two levels simultaneously: (1) how the narrative coherence of the couple system is made up, which is inseparable from (2) how the narrative coherence of the individual system is made up.

WORK CONTRACT AND COUPLES COUNSELING PHASES

The work contract in this kind of counseling is established under the following rules:

- The counselor will always have both members of the couple present at the same time.
- The number of sessions is agreed upon in blocks of four, at the end of which progress or difficulties in reaching the goals agreed upon are evaluated. No fewer than 12 and no more than 20 sessions take place, with the possibility of recontracting once the sessions agreed upon have been covered. The reasons for doing this are as follows:
  - to transmit to the clients and impose on the therapist a feeling of "pressure" to solve the problem

- to create an expectation in the clients that a solution is possible in the short term
- to establish a time direction for the process—that is, it must be clear that there is a limit for all of these things
- in general, the clients' time and money availability is limited
- It must be made clear that neither one should feel obliged to raise subjects that he or she does not want to express in front of the partner.
- When discussing a subject, each one will make an effort to express his or her point of view and not comment on or criticize what the partner has expressed. The purpose of this parameter is to modify the tone of communication—that is, to progress from all kinds of complaints, which give rise to sterile arguments, to focusing attention on the self.

COUNSELING PHASES

First Evaluation

This evaluation takes place in the first four sessions. It starts with a presentation of the problem that covers the statement of the reason that led the clients, at this particular point, to resort to counseling and the personal viewpoint concerning the problem presented and the experiences associated with it. It terminates with the therapist's restatement of the problem and the proposal of a treatment plan in accordance with the couple's desires. If the crisis is terminal, the strategy is different and focuses on how to better structure the separation process. This process, as we have seen, can be very prolonged and painful.

The following points are very clearly explained to the couple in this initial session:

- Each member is the one who constructs the reality that he or she lives as a problematic and not what the other "makes them live."
- The counselor does not favor either of the two, but is not against anybody.
- The purpose of the work to be done is not to keep the couple together, but to orient the process of understanding their unhappiness and problems to enable them to make the most adequate choices, whatever they are.
- The rules of counseling are explained, together with how exceptions are handled (cancelled appointments, fees, extra appointments).

The evaluation terminates with the first restatement that emphasizes the existence of two intertwined levels (systemic bowtie; Procter, 1981, 1987) in the couple's interaction: the level of action lived (organized) as problematic by one of them and the level at which this one interprets (organizes) this action. This in turn produces an action that will be experienced by the other as problematic and be interpreted in such a way that it produces an action that is interpreted…in an intertwining that is anticipated or produces feedback by or for one or the other. This process emphasizes the centrality of the couple's relationship dynamic and communication to facilitate a commitment by regarding a subject or "knot"—the "need" that both have of the problem, which determines a system coherence that starts to emerge.

Second Evaluation

This is a reformulation of the crisis situations concerning the patterns emerging from the organization of the self. The affective history of both members is explored in the 5th to the 12th sessions to try to sketch a linking style that furnishes the base to understand the "organization of personal significance" (Guidano, 1987, 1991). The work will consist of analyzing the acknowledged crises that took place in the week between two successive sessions; their reformulation will lead to the recognition of the dynamic belonging to one's organization of significance and that of the partner, and to its assembly through the expression or inhibition of the personal demands. They will always be very explicative, even the ritualized situations in which the areas of emotive complicity of the relationship are reaffirmed (Guidano and Dodet, 1994).

The work done in this second phase is similar to individual therapy through the self-observation method. The situations of conflict are reconstructed. The first reconstruction concerns how they are experienced by one of the members of the couple and how this person gave it significance and made the experience coherent. Then the same situation may be reconstructed in the other member, or there may be a review, together with the other partner, on how the disturbance generated by the other's reconstruction was organized.

The discrepant situations may be reformulated in this phase based on understanding how each situation turns into a personal reality, according to each member of the couple's organization of significance, and how this represents interference in sharing a common code. In other words, each one knows his or her restrictions in giving significance to a situation that is interpreted in the characteristic way of the other. The emergence of two different and equally valid points of view permits flexibility in the couple system and generates the opportunity to create a new common significance.

This procedure makes it possible to comply with the essential focus of the couple: modify each one's perception of the other by modifying or reviewing the feeling of oneself, thus connecting personal development with each member in the couple system. In other words, connect aspects of personal significance that were not previously recognizable. These phases are not rigid in terms of compliance, as if they were a technique. The sequence is more of a reference for the counselor about how to help the couple system become more abstract and flexible and, on the other hand, help each member in the couple achieve greater self-awareness and autonomy.

Before presenting a clinical example, I would like to quote Rafael Manrique (1994):

> A psychotherapy or *consejería* [my italics] must be one of the non-trivial forms of knowledge; that is, a system of knowledge in which it is accepted that the experience of the world is what the world creates. A system of thought that accepts we are responsible for our actions. And when because of situations of violence and exploitation we cannot be, it trains us to maintain a critical, personal, active and responsible position, in spite of everything, when faced with these personal, family or social situations.

CLINICAL EXAMPLE

The couple. María and José, both 40 years of age, have a 19-year relationship: 3 years of courting and 16 married. They are middle class, primary and secondary school teachers, respectively. They have three children: one teenage daughter aged 14 and two sons aged 10 and 6.

Reason for consultation. The daughter is in counseling because of behavioral problems and low grades at the institution where I give the course on couple counseling training. She had mentioned to her therapist that her parents' continued quarreling affected her very much, and they were channeled to couple counseling.

The context. The couple is counseled at the Instituto de Salud Mental de Nuevo León (a state in the northeast of México) in Monterrey (2 hours from the U.S. border). All the counseling sessions were held in a classroom before a group of students taking my course. The reason for doing it like this, instead of the traditional room with a one-way mirror, is that in this way what is taking place is shown on the other side of the mirror. The therapist, with his patients, seem to appear on a TV screen or theater stage—a scene in which one is not physically there and therefore does not participate emotionally but through the impact received from the scene. Such TV or theater scene would very markedly exemplify the so-called "scientific" objectivity in that there is no interference with what's happening; it is "only" observed. Such objectivity is impossible; consequently, I prefer to feel and have the entire group—patients, therapist, and students—feel the counseling session, in and from the creation of a learning process for all those involved from which there is bound to be a difference or substantial change concerning what was experienced before the session.

First Evaluation

Presentation of the Problem

Mario Zumaya (MZ): It seems that your daughter finally got you to come to counseling. I would like to listen to you about the problem you're facing that made you seek counseling at this point.

María (Ma.): For some time, for 2 or 3 years, I've been trying to convince José that we should come to couple counseling. Now that our daughter is older and doing poorly at school, he's decided.

MZ: But that's her problem, doing poorly at school. What do you think your problem is? José?

José (J) (motionless, looking at the floor, very low voice): We fight a lot…have been for years…5 or 6….We're different; she's at me all the time, for any reason and she thinks the only thing I can do is always make mistakes.

Ma. (crying, choking voice): Right, but he doesn't participate in anything; he cuts himself off, he's always in a bad mood and only talks to the children to scold them. He hardly talks to me during the week and on the weekends it's only sarcastic jibes. Also, he's always complaining about some pain, his back, his legs. He doesn't sleep well and he's always tired.

J: She shouts, cries, and complains all the time.

MZ: María and José, I want to be sure that I understand what's happening. How do you interpret this? What does what each one said make you think? María, about what José's just said, what's wrong with him? José, what do you make of María's reacting this way?

Ma.: I think he's depressed, always has been—perhaps because he married me without loving me enough. He only cares about the kids, and then not much. He's selfish and doesn't share anything.

José: She's very cruel. She thinks I make everything up…my backaches, insomnia, that I'm worried about our kids' future. She doesn't understand me. I'm just a paycheck for her.

MZ (drawing on a sheet of paper the actions that make up the complaints about each other and the interpretation or construction that they put on such actions; see Figure 8.1): I'll show you the diagram and check that the information in it is correct.

Comment. According to Neimeyer (1993),

> As illustrated graphically, the behaviors of each spouse were consistent with his or her interpretation of the marital situation and in turn provided apparent validation for the (problem-maintaining) constructions of the partner and so on in a seamless pattern of mutual validation with no clear beginning or end. The "bowtie" also provided a potential "road map" for future interventions, suggesting four potential targets for change corresponding to the constructions and actions of both spouses.

As you can see, you do things in a certain way in order to understand, interpret, or construct what the other one has done or is doing. María criticizes José all the time; she cries and says that he's cruel. José thinks that María

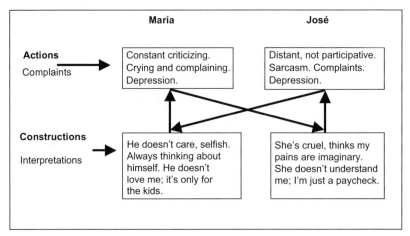

Figure 8.1   Actions and constructions of Mária and José

doesn't understand him and that he's just a paycheck for her. Consequently, José cuts himself off and he's sarcastic because he's selfish and doesn't love her and is still with her just for the kids. What we need to understand, and then later modify, is what they do in order to feel and interpret their problems as they are doing it.

Comment. Up to this point I am using and will continue to use in all the sessions two essential elements that function as skills and tasks (Kurtz, 1990):

- *Tracking* is the ability to follow the present experience flow of the other. This implies two tasks for the interviewer: being in the client's world and, at the same time, being outside that world and able to look at it with a broader perspective. It is a way of being with someone in an attitude of interest and curiosity. It is not about the content of the other's story. It is not solving problems or supposing who the other person is. It is much simpler and translates in the production of declarations and comments by the interviewer who, with the verbal and nonverbal acquiescence of the client, shows that he or she is being "tracked" adequately. The feeling of boredom in the interview is a sign that the interviewer has lost track of what is really interesting for him and the other party.
- *Contact* is the activity and ability to create a connection and keep it; at a technical level, it is making a declaration of contact. In order to make contact, the therapist shows understanding through tracking; he offers a brief, simple comment showing that he is following the client's present experience, what is happening from one moment to another. The comments are not indispensable; however, establishing and maintaining contact are. Therefore, it is not necessary that the interviewer understand everything he is told; it is sufficient to understand just a

part. The contact allows the interviewer to focus on the parts of the experience on the limit of the consciousness, which are not necessarily related to verbalizations.

MZ: What would you like to be different after the sessions we're going to have? What the other one does or how to understand it?

J and Ma. (alternatively and agreeing): Yes...and we also need better communication.

Comment. The crisis that took them to counseling is not considered to be terminal, but rather part of a cycle that has to do with the experience, in both of them, of not being able to love each other. This leads them to withdraw or fight and feel anger or despair because of the feeling of rejection and abandonment and, getting closer, to reinitiate the cycle. The rules of the counseling were explained and they were told that the work scheme would cover 11 more sessions.

Conceptualization of the problem. Over the next two sessions, the history of each one was explored in the presence of the other. José is the son of alcoholics. He had been physically and psychologically abused since he was a child. He has always been withdrawn, always a good student whose most important gratification has always been academic accomplishment to cover his family needs. The courting and marriage were at María's initiative; she was his only girlfriend after high school.

María is the oldest child of eight; she was an alternative mother for her siblings (her mother is chronically depressed) and had worked since she was a teenager. To date, she is the central figure in her family of origin. José was her only boyfriend and, a few days before the wedding, she was the victim of an attempted rape, which radically changed her attitude towards sexual life. José was told about this 2 or 3 years after the marriage because of his insistence on having more frequent and passionate sexual relations.

Both make up depressive-type personal meaning organizations. Consequently, counseling work is focused on the reconstruction of situations of conflict between them that are made into "evidence" of the inability to be loved, the threat of a loss of the relationship, and a feeling in both that ranges between rage and depression due to the nonsatisfaction of affective needs and the perpetuation of a self-devalued identity.

A reformulation of the problem is arrived at in the fourth session— particularly the communication defect, which is redefined as attention focused on nonverbal messages from the other and an inexistent acknowledgment of their own emotional demands in the relationship. There is the proposal and discussion about the concept of "feeling about one's self" (basic affective tone that is triggered in terms of typical difficulties) awakened by the attitude of the other and the possibility that this feeling of the self could be the consequence of:

- the perception of the partner
- the perception of being in a couple that, in the case of these two, is focused on a feeling of mutual distrust
- disappointment in themselves because of the feeling of impotence to modify the relationship and therefore the self-perception of being unworthy of love

Work is started on the analysis of the bad feeling in everyday situations, seeking the personal meanings involved in them. It is stressed that the purpose of the therapy is to understand the personal and couple dynamics and not to seek success in terms of maintaining or dissolving the couple.

The sessions after the first four are characterized by a serious problem in facing crisis situations. The initial subject is always proposed by María about vaguely defined issues. José then intervenes; he tends to contradict her in principal conceptual questions. In the fifth session, the issue of distrust, blame, and disappointment in themselves and in the other are defined:

María describes that she has had problems in "giving" herself sexually to José, especially if the approaches follow a fight or a "small misunderstanding." Her perception of "tension" triggers an emotional reaction that could make her cold later—all of which is together with a feeling of guilt concerning José's behavior. José, on the other hand, turns to María in his desire to make love with explicit attitudes, without considering her demands for affective foreplay. When José perceives a feeling of loneliness caused by María's rejection, it creates a painful indefinition of himself that drives him to be sarcastic with her—an external definition even though it is negative.

Ma.: José always seeks me sexually on weekends. He's always rough and does not try to seduce me.

MZ: Could you tell me what happened?

Ma.: We were going up the stairs and he touched my butt...

MZ: What did you feel?

Ma.: Rage, anger...How dare he, if we've quarreled over the kids?

MZ: And what did you think?

Ma.: That, as usual, he thinks I'm an object...a thing. And the truth is that I also think so. I'm just here to please everybody.

MZ (touching her shoulder): María, stop, please. Close your eyes. Reconstruct the scene in your head and focus on it. Tell me, when you felt the rage, did you have any other feelings?

Ma. (taking a long pause and crying quietly): Yes, I felt and feel something else...shame...sadness, disappointment in him and me: how could I put up with all this?

MZ: María, go back to the scene in your head. When did you feel anger? When José touched you, before or after?

Ma. (concentrating hard): It was before…when he let me pass to go up
the stairs and he looked at me strangely…like with scorn and lust…
when he touched my butt, it was like confirming that I'm an object…

MZ: And when did you feel shame?

Ma.: Before going up, when we were in the living room, quiet, bored
as always.

MZ: Could you reconstruct the entire scene from the living room to the
bedroom?

Ma.: Yes, shame about the silence between us in the living room…anger
at seeing his look…disappointment, later.

MZ: María, open you eyes. Look at José (motionless and staring at the
floor). Tell me, what were your feelings for José at that moment?

Ma. (with a sad smile): Shame. I know he will ask me to forgive him and
I surely will. But I don't trust him, or myself, and I don't think things
will change for the better. I'm to blame, because I'm dumb and frigid,
for what's happening to us.

MZ: And you José, what do you feel about what María says? Don't tell me
what you think, tell me what do you feel?

J (still staring at the floor): The same as her…sadness and anger…I'm
shit and I know that I can't or don't want to change. We're trapped
(he raises his head and his face expresses a mixture of pain and
anger). Naturally (sarcastically), her frigidity doesn't help.

MZ (addressing both): And, at this moment, how do you think each one
will react?

J: María will stiffen up…rigid and she won't talk to me.

Ma.: He will cut himself off as usual. When we leave, he'll give me the
car keys and take a taxi home and block himself off for hours.

Comment. José and María relate the feeling of distrust in each other with
the fear of breaking the tie. They have deep feelings of anguish and impotence
about the likelihood of a break, which they attribute to traits inherent to their
characters. For them, the feeling of distrust is felt as threat of either one of the
couple of leaving, together with an inevitable sense of loss; consequently, the
perception of their selves is manifested as a feeling of impotence.

María's rigidity is reformulated in terms of behavior that tends to prevent
the feeling of loss felt during an argument, as well as the internal search to
maintain a stable sense of identity. It also tends to be derived in rigid emotions
of despair and rage at the perceived loss when José cuts himself off. Of the
subjects brought up in the next six sessions, the subject of disappointment in
the relationship is defined in terms of Jose's image and her own. María expresses sadness and despair, which is always accompanied by a feeling of disappointment and is associated with situations in which "José seems to be distant,
absent." A new reformulation is reached: in María, the disappointment is seen

as a feeling of exclusion and loss, which she acknowledges through the affective activation of despair; the cause of the loss is self-referred and the feeling of herself is derived from this, which leads to the rigid and cold attitude.

José, however, sees the same disappointment as a threat of loss that creates the basis of behavior dictated by the need to prevent it and turns into being distant and blocking all dealings with her. This behavior will then be reformulated in terms of expressing anger and the search in himself for the capacity to react to eventual abandonment.

Throughout the sessions, the ability to make self-observations is stimulated concerning the forms of expression and acknowledging the emotion of rage and its meaning—that is, anger as the only controlling instrument, at a bearable level, in a feeling of defenselessness.

On the other hand, given their social isolation (they have practically no friends), their couple relationship has been the most relevant context for the creation and stable maintenance of the feeling of personal identity; it has blocked, to a certain extent, the structuring of a more adult, therefore autonomous, self, with less dependence on each other. From the beginning, each situation that could have been perceived as a crisis in the relationship, however small, was seen as an attack on the feeling of personal identity, giving rise to emotive reactions difficult to elaborate.

The nonexpression of their feelings, needs, and demands was for both a condition not to provoke situations in which a break would have meant a moment of unbearable indefinition; additionally, it was a cause for subsequent situations of possible rejection and loss outside the couple (family, friends, work). Only acknowledgment and elaboration of a feeling of loss and shame consequent with the change of image (disappointment) in both made it possible to reformulate new rules within the couple relationship. These rules included establishing given situations of discrepancy and emotionally painful activation, individualized spaces and times to carry out Moviola (action replay) exercises that allow them to be more self-aware and differentiated—less reactive, more reflexive.

By analyzing the concrete situations present through the Moviola technique, it was possible to reach greater individualizing in both. Only by becoming autonomous and aware of their form of constructing their experiences—and therefore less dependent on each other—have they been able to express their demands and make a choice that they could more faithfully interpret. That choice is an increase in intimacy resulting in deciding what to take from the relationship and what to discard, clarifying and being responsible for the mutual constructions of each one's image and identity.

REFERENCES

Ainsworth, M. D. S. (1979). Infant–mother attachment. *American Psychologist, 34,* 932–937.

Bowlby, J. (1969). *Attachment and loss*. Vol 1. New York: Basic Books.

Bowlby, J. (1973). *Attachment and loss*. Vol 2. New York: Basic Books.

Bowlby, J. (1980). *Attachment and loss*. Vol 3. New York: Basic Books.

Burr, V. (1995). *An introduction to social constructionism*. London: Routledge.

Crittenden, P. M. (1985a). Maltreated infants: Vulnerability and resilience. *Journal of Child Psychology and Psychiatry*, *26*, 85–96.

Crittenden, P. M. (1985b). Social networks, quality of parenting, and child development. *Child Development*, *56*, 1299–1313.

Crittenden, P. M. (1988). Relationships at risk. In J. Belsky & T. Nezworski (Eds.). *Clinical implications of attachment* (pp. 136–174). Hillsdale, NJ: Erlbaum.

Crittenden, P. M (1997). Patterns of attachment and sexual behavior: Risk of dysfunction vs. opportunity for creative integration. In L. Atkinson & K. J. Zucker, *Attachment and psychopathology* (pp. 47–95). New York: Guilford.

Ecker, B., & Hulley, L. (1995). *Deep-oriented brief therapy*. San Francisco: Jossey, Bass.

Ecker, B. & Hulley, L. (1996). *Depth-oriented brief therapy: How to be brief when you were trained to be deep and vice-versa*. Jossey-Bass Publishers, San Francisco.

Granvold, D. (1999). Constructivist theory and practice. In P. Lehmann & N. Coady (Eds.) *Theoretical perspectives in direct social work practice: An eclectic-generalist approach*. New York: Springer.

Guidano, V. F. (1987). *Complexity of the self*. New York: The Guilford Press.

Guidano, V. F. (1991). *The self on process*. New York: The Guilford Press.

Guidano, V. F., & Dodet, M. (1994) Terapia cognitiva sistémico procesal de la pareja. *Revista Argentina de Clínica Psicológica*, *III*, 1. 17–31.

Guidano, V. F. (1995). Constructivist psychotherapy: A theoretical framework. In, Neimeyer, R. A. & Mahoney, M. J. (Eds.), *Constructivism in psychotherapy* (pp. 93–108). Washington, D.C.: American Psychological Association.

Karen, R. (1998). *Becoming attached*. Oxford University Press: New York.

Kurtz, R. (1990). Body-centered psychotherapy: The Hakomi method: The integrated use of mindfulness, nonviolence and the body. San Francisco: Life Rhythm.

Manrique, R. (1994). *La Psicoterapia como Conversación Crítica*. Madrid: Libertarias Proudhufi.

Neimeyer, R. A. (1993). Constructivist approaches to the measurement of meaning. In Neimeyer, G. J. (Ed.), *Constructivist assessment. A casebook*. Newbury Park, CA: Sage.

Procter, H. G. (1981). Family construct psychology. In S. Waltrond-Skinner (Ed.), *Developments in family therapy* (pp. 35–366). London: Routledge.

Procter, H. G. (1987). Change in the family construct system. In R. A. Neimeyer & G. J. Neimeyer (Eds.), *Personal constuct therapy casebook* (pp. 153–171). New York: Springer.

Vygotsky, L. S. (1987). *The collected works of L. S. Vygotsky* (R. W. Rieber & A. S. Carlton, Eds.; N. Minick, Trans.) New York: Plenum Press.

CHAPTER 9

Group Counseling With Latino Populations

NORMA S. GUERRA

Group counseling is a strategy that is believed to be effective across cultures. Despite very few empirical studies demonstrating the efficacy of this approach, the benefits of appropriate and well-organized group programs seem to be evident (Yalom, 1995). This chapter presents a case of a 7-year-old Latino boy who benefited from a group counseling program. A number of group counseling approaches are discussed, including person centered, rational-emotive behavior therapy, and an integrated problem-solving model.

INTRODUCTION

Beto Dominguez, a 7-year-old Latino boy, has just been diagnosed with type I diabetes. Rosa Dominguez, Beto's mother, is overwhelmed by the news and is having difficulty accepting the doctor's diagnosis. The doctor explains the seriousness of Beto's condition and the need for immediate action. Rosa tries to listen to the doctor, but her level of anxiety is so high that she is unable to process what he is telling her.

Rosa is a single mother who moved away from her family 2 years ago to attend community college. Rosa was awarded a small scholarship and a part-time work–study position on campus. This has enabled Rosa to work during the day while Beto is in school. The two have been living in this small town for 2 years. Initially, moving away from family and friends was difficult; however, Rosa and Beto have adjusted fairly well.

As Rosa tries to comprehend her son's condition, she wonders whether she is being punished for leaving home, for not having married Beto's father, or for wanting a better life for her child. Upon first hearing the news Rosa immediately thought about quitting school, returning home, and asking her parents to forgive her and help her cope with the situation. The thought of asking her parents for help is not easy for Rosa, but she is not sure where else to turn.

Upon hearing the news, Rosa's mother is upset, "Why are you trying to make him sick? There is nothing wrong with him." As they continue to talk, her mother begins to blame Beto's biological father for the disease. After the long and disappointing conversation, Rosa hangs up the phone and decides that returning home would just cause additional complications. Unable to sleep that night, Rosa thought about where she could go to get the support that she needed to get through this difficult situation. Finally, after much thought and consideration, Rosa decided to speak with the school counselor, even though she knew the woman was not a Latina.

CULTURAL CONSIDERATIONS

Cultural sensitivity is a commonly used term within multicultural counseling literature. Padilla (2001) explains it as a series of open-ended substantive adjustments, methodological inclusions, and adaptations used to facilitate and assess culture. The purpose is to identify levels of cultural affiliation. An evaluative element is involved in understanding cultural characteristics. This information can be used to improve the counselor's effectiveness when communicating with the client. This approach suggests that the more skilled the counselor is in understanding the client's culture, the greater is the likelihood for success within the counseling exchange. This orientation is only one side of the counseling communication; equally important is the client's cultural perceptions toward counseling.

Cultural engagement is not a commonly used construct in the counseling literature. Adapting from literature addressing effects of perceived control, Skinner, Wellborn, and Connell (1990) suggest that engagement is an underlying self-regulated involvement, an active component in successful learning. The willingness to change involves sustainable individual engagement and belief that success is possible. Lee and Liu (2001) used a stress-coping framework to identify distinct interpersonal patterns among Hispanic, Asian American and European college students. The results of their study indicated that Hispanics tend to assume a passive (tolerant; less engaged) response to the psychological distress introduced with as intergenerational family conflict. In order to have meaningful communication, there must be a shared commitment to participate in the exchange among the individuals. Inasmuch as Latino individual/group counseling involvement may vary, culturally perceived levels of control and response to distress within the activity becomes an important consideration.

Past experiences with individuals from different cultural backgrounds may affect the degree of open communication a Latino client uses when engaging with the counselor. Success of the interaction may not be solely found in counselor capability, skill, or culturally identified background assessments; rather, it *may* be in the willingness of the Latino client to invest in the exchange. If the client perceives the counseling session as a threat, with limited possibility for success due to differing cultural views, the counselor may be at a loss to understand the dynamics. The counselor's skill is truly effective only after the establishment of a trusting therapeutic relationship in which the counselor is able to monitor self in relationship to the client and the client's level of cultural engagement. It may be useful to the counselor to view the client's motivational interest as a reflection of self-regulated beliefs, perceived control, and beliefs of success—all of which may be observed as cultural engagement.

It is not unrealistic to link client cultural engagement and expectancy with counselor competence. Constantine, Juby, and Liang (2001) address the limited empirical information that examines perceived levels of multicultural competence, suggesting that information about potential associations may facilitate overall effectiveness. A study by Heppner, Cook, Wright, and Johnson (1995) examined multidimensional coping styles by focusing on individuals' willingness to engage in problem solving. The results suggested that behavioral, cognitive, and affective activities can inhibit or facilitate a predictive impact on problem-solving competency. Finally, in a study by Hanson and Mintz (1997), the researchers found that as problem-solving self-appraisal became more favorable, confidence, control, and willingness to engage in problem solving increased.

It is important to note that, from a Latino perspective, the diagnosis of diabetes is not an individual counseling challenge involving only medical intervention, but rather warrants a group or family intervention. Any change that occurs through this process has the potential to affect others involved in Rosa's and Beto's lives. Family is highly valued in the Latino culture and in this case the family unit includes not only Rosa and Beto but also Rosa's parents. Additional background information will be important for the counselor to better understand the family system, which may include aunts, uncles, cousins, and close family friends. Although the counselor working on this case comes from a different cultural background, based on her conversation with Rosa, she is aware that the family's involvement in this process will be imperative for a successful outcome. After talking with Rosa, the counselor learns that "family" in this case involves Beto's grandparents (Saul and Carmen Dominguez) and Rosa's older sister (Cecilia Dominguez).

GROUP COUNSELING MODELS

Person-centered rational-emotive behavior therapy (REBT) and problem-solving therapies appear to be well suited for counseling Latinos. The counseling models presented are general resources in response to the identified needs related to the presented case. The following sections briefly discuss person-centered therapy and REBT approaches to group counseling. The final model presents a problem-solving model known as LIBRE and will be discussed in greater detail and used to discuss the case of Rosa and Beto Dominguez.

The person-centered approach (Rogers, 1957) views the client as the authority figure and allows the client to process his or her experience, thereby fulfilling his or her growth potential. Carl Rogers believed that individuals experience incongruence when their self-concept does not match their experiences. Rogers believed that the individual's awareness of incongruence results in feelings of anxiety.

The goal of person-centered counseling is to provide unconditional positive regard, empathy, and congruence to help clients grow to their full capacity (Rogers, 1957). Unconditional positive regard means that the individuals are nonjudgmentally accepted regardless of their behavior (Rogers). Empathic understanding translates into hearing the individual's thoughts and feelings accurately from the client's perspective (Rogers). Congruence relates to the authenticity of the professional providing the assistance with the problem-solving technique (Rogers). Together, these three conditions are believed to enable an individual to develop and grow in his or her special way.

In person-centered group counseling, the goal is to encourage the individual group members, and the group as a whole, to work to their full capacity (Rogers, 1970). The role of the group leader is to facilitate this process by providing a safe and nurturing environment that demonstrates acceptance of everyone involved in the process, including the leader's self-acceptance (Rogers). Typically, person-centered groups comprise approximately 10 individuals who meet for a couple of hours a week (Corey, 1990). The group leader works with all of the members to determine the number of sessions in which they will meet, rules to which members will adhere, and expectations (Corey).

Corey (1990) suggests that when the group leader is working with individuals from different cultural backgrounds, he or she needs to be cognizant of the manner in which the core conditions are communicated. Specifically, group leaders can "enhance the group process by making appropriate interventions and by taking an active part in leading (as well as facilitating). They can also design structured groups that are theme oriented and that have both a therapeutic and an educational focus" (Corey, p. 308). Person-centered group counseling, when used appropriately, can be an effective means of producing positive change in clients from a variety of backgrounds. However this approach does not account for different levels of engagement that may arise within the group process.

Another effective approach for producing client change, particularly with Latino clients, is REBT. This approach focuses on uncovering irrational beliefs leading to unhealthy negative emotions and replacing them with more productive and reasonable alternatives (Ellis & Dryden, 1997). REBT utilizes cognitive and behavioral approaches when working with clients. Emphasis is placed on the client's willingness to take action and work to produce change (Ellis, 1982).

The goal of REBT groups is to encourage members to learn how to identify irrational beliefs and make adjustments in their thoughts and behaviors to live more fulfilling lives (Ellis, 1982). The role of the group leader is to challenge members' irrational thinking and teach them how to think logically about their problems (Ellis). REBT groups can be large or small and can be used to work with a wide range of client problems (Corey, 1990). This approach is educational and more directive than other approaches and utilizes a variety of techniques, including imagery, role-playing, and homework assignments (Corey).

REBT can be an effective approach when working with individuals from a variety of cultural backgrounds, particularly those who prefer a direct approach to counseling. Corey (1990) notes that the group leader should exercise caution when challenging irrational thinking from clients with different cultural backgrounds. The group leader needs to encourage members to examine their belief system in a way that still allows them to retain "respect for their cultural heritage" (Corey, p. 443). It is important to remember that each member is unique and has his or her preferences for and expectations of therapy. It is the responsibility of the group leader to ensure that the group's goals and structure are appropriate for each group member.

The final counseling approach offered is the LIBRE model (Guerra, 2004), an integrated engagement and problem-solving approach designed to offer individuals a structured, goal-oriented, self-regulated, solution-oriented dialogue. LIBRE, the Spanish word for free, is an acronym listing the steps of the program. The steps are

Listen to the person's narrative.
Identify the presenting issue.
Brainstorm possible solutions.
Reality check all possible solutions.
Encourage the person to develop a personalized best plan and incentives
    to facilitate personal investment.

The LIBRE stick figure tool, developed as a visual guide for the LIBRE dialogue, offers a user-friendly aid in processing identified concerns. The external prompt allows the client to focus on his or her own personal needs without external intrusion by the counselor. This approach incorporates the client freedom to assume a direct or an indirect coping style. The client is in control of the process and may pause to disengage to better process the identified concern.

The role of the counselor is to facilitate the process and to teach the client problem-solving skills while encouraging the client to take the lead in managing the situation. The client controls the regulation of content and pace of the session. Through this process, he or she selects a problem, invests in developing a personalized plan, and ultimately resolves the selected problem. Clients using LIBRE have reported feeling a sense of accomplishment as a result of being able to identify a solution to their problem and see it work, even in a myriad of conditions beyond their control (Guerra, 2003).

The LIBRE model can be used when working with individuals, families, and groups. This model serves to empower clients by teaching them a problem-solving strategy that they can use in their daily lives. If this approach is used in a group setting, the group members can decide to complete the stick figure as individual members or as a team. The decision to use this model as individual members or as a group will depend partly on the problem-solving ability and ages of the group members.

If each member of the group completes the LIBRE stick figure tool, the counselor will facilitate the dialogue by asking them to share common concerns (themes) as the Listening step. Once the group determined focal concern is Identified, the Brainstorming and Reality Testing steps provide an opportunity for the group to begin sharing their thoughts in the development of a plan. Group members discuss their feelings and roles regarding their plan and Encourage each other as they finalize their (group and individual) steps. The LIBRE model in group therapy may vary in the number of sessions.

When the LIBRE model is used in group therapy, the number of sessions will vary depending on client's ability to problem-solve, age of the group members, and willingness of the members to engage in the activity. Because this model places emphasis on the client's cognitive and problem-solving functions, it is not well suited for individuals who have impaired cognitive capacities (Guerra, 2003).

Possible setbacks when using this approach may include the counselor's lack of cultural awareness and sensitivity, lack of rapport between counselor and client, and an inability of the counselor to handle client resistance effectively. As found with preliminary feedback, clients report increased levels of self-efficacy after learning how to use this model to handle a crisis.

After talking with Rosa, the counselor decides to organize a group to help the Dominguez family cope with the situation. Due to Beto's age, the counselor decides to form two groups: one for the adults and one for the children. The adult group will comprise eight members: the Dominguez family and another Latino family, the Garza's, whose 10-year old daughter was recently diagnosed with diabetes. The children's group will comprise three elementary age children who have recently been diagnosed as diabetic. The school counselor will lead the adult group and a local community counselor, who has several years' experience working with children who have been diagnosed with diabetes, will work with the children's group. The two groups will meet at the same time, but in separate rooms. The adult's group will focus on problem solving and the children's group will focus on educating the children about diabetes and teaching them coping strategies to deal with the disease.

CASE ILLUSTRATION OF THE LIBRE MODEL

The process of determining the goals, structure, and expectations of the adult's group begins prior to the initial session with a pregroup questionnaire. This allows the counselor to gain a great deal of useful information from the group members and helps make the initial session more efficient and productive. Based on the responses from the questionnaire, the counselor learns that the group members would prefer only a few counseling sessions that are fairly structured and focused on finding solutions that will help the families cope with their children's condition. The counselor's goals for the first group session include establishing rapport with each of the members and clarifying the goals and purpose of the group.

The initial session begins with group and group leader introductions and background about their group processing goals. The next half hour is spent exchanging information about why they are compelled to participate in this group. Throughout this process, the counselor learns important information about each of the members' backgrounds and worldviews. Once the counselor is confident that a foundation of trust and openness has been laid, she facilitates a discussion about the purpose and goals of the group. As the counselor listens to each of the members, she is aware that they would all like to find ways to deal with their children's diagnosis as quickly as possible. Based on this information, the counselor suggests using the LIBRE model to achieve the group's goals. The counselor explains the model and shows them the LIBRE stick figure worksheet that will be used throughout the process (see Figure 9.1) and encourages the group to discuss what they think about using this approach.

After a decision is made to use this model, the counselor works with the group to determine whether each group member would like to complete the model individually or with the family. As each of the members shares thoughts about how he or she would like to use the model, the counselor makes a list of the pros and cons. Once each of the members has had an opportunity to share, the group reviews the list and decides to fill out the LIBRE model with their family. The group decides that they would like to move through the steps together. An agreement is made that, if one of the families becomes stuck on one of the steps, the other family will offer support and suggestions.

Because the group has stated that they think only a few group sessions will be necessary, the counselor decides to end the first session by reviewing

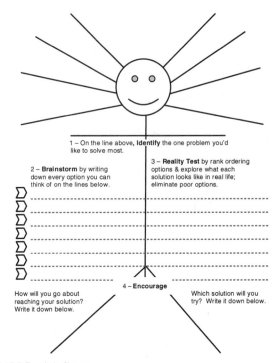

Figure 9.1 LIBRE stick figure.

the ground rules for LIBRE so that the majority of the second session can focus on using the model. The counselor begins by stating that the purpose of the ground rules is to provide parameters for developing discussion that will lead to solutions. The counselor lets the group know that the counselor's role will be to function as a neutral outsider who facilitates the process and that each member will play an active role as he or she identifies solutions. The basic ground rules for using the LIBRE model are listed in Table 9.1.

After introducing and facilitating a discussion about the ground rules, the counselor closes the group by encouraging each member to think about specific concerns regarding their children's condition. The counselor also suggests that the group meet two more times—once the next week to work through the LIBRE model and then the following week to discuss progress and any concerns that the family might have.

It is important to remember that the counselor assumes a reflective facilitating role when using this model and structures the session to accommodate the group members. The group members take an active role in describing the stress and challenges that they are facing, and the counselor guides the process through active listening. Throughout this process, the counselor is careful to adjust the intervention and her interactions so that culturally sensitive practices are used in an effort to maximize each member's level of engagement

Table 9.1   LIBRE Ground Rules

Respect all persons involved with the LIBRE activity. Maintain goodwill in assisting the individual(s) in a manner that neither demeans nor embarrasses anyone involved with the process.

Safety/safe environment is deliberately extended to the individual seeking assistance. The counselor should afford the individual a relaxed, secure environment.

Confidentiality is paramount to the success of the model. Confidentiality allows the opportunity to process through difficult feelings without losing face and without fear of others knowing what has been shared. The counselor champions confidentiality as much as possible. The only breach in confidentiality should occur if safety, abuse, and breaking the law/other stated parameters are violated.

Independence is modeled and encouraged as the client regulates the problem-solving process. The LIBRE processing activity is designed to be instructional to empower the individual to use the problem-solving dialoguing steps to help him/her with future problem solving.

during the session. LIBRE success is linked to the client's willingness to remain engaged as the counselor listens and provides support. Through this process, the client should feel accepted and valued; the counselor's inability to communicate these conditions will most likely result in the client's lowered level of engagement. A culturally competent counselor will possess the ability to identify and effectively apply strategies and techniques that will convey a sense of acceptance and safety in which the client can openly communicate thoughts and feelings.

As stated previously, the counselor structures the sessions to fit the needs of the group members. Thus, if one of the families begins to withdraw, the counselor should follow the family's need to stop and summarize the steps that they have completed in an effort to encourage them to continue the process if they wish. As the families move through each of the steps, the counselor should mirror their speech and language usage. However, it is recommended that the counselor rephrase strong language that may be maintaining or exacerbating any debilitating thoughts to more neutral words that still reflect the members' intent.

The following week the group begins with a discussion about what was decided during the previous session and reviews the LIBRE ground rules. The counselor begins the LIBRE dialogue by placing two stick figure worksheets on the table and asking each family member to take turns sharing his or her concerns about the children's condition. The following prompt is suggested: "I am going to use this stick figure to list everything that is going on right now. We will start with the head and list each concern that you have as hair on the stick figure's head." As the counselor listens to each family's narrative, she restates any concerns and records the information on the worksheets.

Occasionally, the counselor might ask an open-ended question to facilitate exploration of the problem. After listening to each family's concerns, the counselor will encourage him or her to identify the most pressing concern. The concern is then restated as a question, which is used to identify the second step: identifying the presenting issue.

In this step, the counselor restates the identified issue and writes it across the shoulders of the LIBRE stick figure. In this case, the Dominguez family wants to know how they can help Beto handle all of the changes that will take place as a result of his condition. The counselor facilitates a group discussion, encouraging each member to share thoughts and feelings about the situation. After some discussion and clarification, the group is invited to begin the next step in the process: brainstorming.

In this step the counselor explains that *all* solutions should be considered, regardless of how impossible they may seem. The counselor begins by modeling the process and suggests two solutions for each of the families. She then encourages each family to generate anywhere from eight to ten solutions. Throughout this process, the counselor reminds the families to identify real and "nonsense" options, emphasizing that the development of a logical and well-examined plan of action will come later. Each family's willingness to explore as many options as possible reflects its commitment to solving the problem. Once several options have been listed, the group is ready to proceed to the next step: reality testing.

The goal of this step is for the group to identify what they think will be the best solution for the identified problem. The counselor's role is to guide each family's critical thinking by helping them explore what steps they will need to take for this solution to work, as well as to identify possible consequences of each solution. Each family's problem-solving ability will dictate how much assistance the counselor offers during this process. It is important for the counselor to keep in mind that cultural variables may play a role in the degree to which individuals engage in and have experience with problem solving. The counselor's knowledge of and sensitivity to the client's cultural background may be useful in understanding how the client approaches this task.

The counselor may facilitate this process by saying, "As we begin considering all of the solutions that you have identified, I want you to think about which one of these solutions would be the most beneficial for you and your family." The counselor guides the group through this process and helps them identify possible consequences of each solution. Once the group has identified a suitable solution, the counselor summarizes the decisions made during the session and reviews the possible consequences and the actions that each member will need to take.

The final step in the LIBRE process, encouragement, requires that the group engage in self-reflection and continue to develop the personalized plan of action. The counselor invites the group to share their thoughts and feelings regarding the choices that they have made using the LIBRE model. It is important that each group member (those most closely involved in the child's life) feels confident and comfortable with the final plan of action. Through this process, each group member learns to recognize aspects of the situation that are within his or her control.

In this case, the group would like to normalize many of the changes that the family will face. For example, part of the Dominguez family's plan is for everyone to develop healthier eating habits. Through this process, the group has become aware that by educating themselves about their child's condition, they can help monitor their children's physical needs in an effort to keep them healthy. As the session comes to an end, the counselor encourages each group member to process his or her experience. Finally, the counselor thanks each of the members for the hard work. The group closes with a discussion about their goals for and expectations of next week's session.

CONCLUSION

Group counseling is a complex process that has the potential to help clients from a wide variety of backgrounds. A culturally competent counselor will invest a great deal of thought in the planning process to ensure that the group is culturally appropriate and geared towards the specific needs of the members. The group leader needs to have a clear idea of the purpose of the group and whom it will serve because this will help in determining the structure, size, and length of time of the group and the role of the leader and its members (Corey, 1990). A pregroup interview during the selection process can provide important information for the group leader that will help in making these decisions. This also allows the potential group member a chance to meet the group leader and ask questions that will help him or her decide whether participation in the group would be helpful.

Once the group is established, the leader will need to remain aware of how culture may be affecting the developmental stages and needs of the group. The manner in which the leader handles resistance, conflict, communication of empathy and respect, cohesion, and termination needs to be consistent with the cultural values and beliefs of the group members (Corey, 1990). Although this task may seem daunting, the impact that a well-planned and skillfully run group can have on its members is invaluable.

REFERENCES

Constantine, M. G., Juby, H. L. & Liang, J. C. (2001). Examining multicultural counseling competence and race-related attitudes among white marital and family therapists. *Journal of Marital and Family Therapy*, 27(3), 353–362.

Corey, G. (1990). *Theory and practice of group counseling* (3rd ed.). Pacific Grove, CA: Brooks/Cole Publishing Company.

Ellis, A. (1982). Rational–emotive group therapy. In G. Gazda (Ed.), *Basic approaches to group psychotherapy and group counseling* (3rd ed.). Springfield, IL: Charles C. Thomas.

Ellis, A., & Dryden, W. (1997). *The practice of rational–emotive behavior therapy.* New York: Springer Publishing Company, Inc.

Guerra, N. S. (2003). *LIBRE model: Technical report to the Alamo Area Counsel of Governments.* Unpublished report.

Guerra, N. S. (2004). *LIBRE problem solving handbook.* Academy of Teacher Excellence. University of Texas at San Antonio, TX.

Hanson, K. M., & Mintz, L. B. (1997). Psychological health and problem-solving self-appraisal in older adults. *Journal of Counseling Psychology, 44*(4), 433–441.

Heppner, P. P., Cook, S. W., Wright, D. M. & Johnson, W. C. (1995). Progress in resolving problems. *Journal of Counseling Psychology, 42*(3), 279–293.

Lee, R. M., & Lui, H. T. (2001). Coping with integrational family conflict: Comparison of Asian American, Hispanic, and European American college students. *Journal of Counseling Psychology, 48*(4), 410–419.

Padilla, A. M. (2001). Issues in culturally appropriate assessment. In L. A. Suzuki, J. G. Ponterotto, & P. J. Meller (Eds.) *Handbook of multicultural assessment* (pp. 5–27). Thousand Oaks, CA: Sage Publications.

Rogers, C. (1957). The necessary and sufficient conditions of therapeutic personality change. *Journal of Consulting Psychology, 21*, 95–103.

Rogers, C. (1970). *Carl Rogers on encounter groups.* New York: Harper & Row.

Skinner, E. A., Wellborn, J. G., & Connell, J. P. (1990). What it takes to do well in school and whether I've got it: A process model of perceived control and children's engagement and achievement in school. *Journal of Educational Psychology, 82*(1), 2232.

Yalom, I. (1995). *The theory and practice of group psychotherapy* (4th ed.). New York: Basic Books.

CHAPTER 10

Parenting in Latino Families

HOMER A. BAIN

Diana (Latina mother): "I don't like Marcia's (age 28) attitude toward boys. I think we should talk to her. Until she's married, she's our responsibility. We have to guide her."

George (Anglo father): "Wow, I gave that up when she went off to college."

This quote from a client couple is drawn from "Imago Therapy With Hispanic Couples" (Luquet & Hannah, 1998). It offers a "slice of life" look at parenting in an American semi-Latino household. The Latino mother's first point is that parenting lasts a long time. "Until she's married, she's our responsibility." She adds later, "They [are] always our family." Also, the parents' role is a large one. It includes an expectation of authority: "We have to guide her." Latino parents in their earlier as well as later years are always entitled to *respeto* (respect). This implies obedience from younger children and at least a thoughtful hearing from others. This chapter examines concepts such as authority versus permissiveness that are salient to all families, including Latinos. A number of parenting models are discussed, followed by a case presentation.

INTRODUCTION

Part of the background for helping Latino parents today is that professional and public concern has grown over decades about problems of American children at home and school. The increase in medications and therapies for diagnoses like ADHD (attention deficit hyperactivity disorder) is stimulating research that includes cultural environments and parenting styles affecting these phenomena. Daniel Siegel's (1999) *The Developing Mind* is a recent pioneering synthesis and advancement of some of these studies relating neurobiological and interpersonal influences on child development and behavior. This chapter relies partly on the latter kind of "anecdotal" research as illustrative of more general conclusions. It also, however, references other qualitative and quantitative studies as applicable and gives some attention to underlying philosophical assumptions.

AUTHORITY VS. PERMISSIVENESS

For George in the example of George and Diana, as further conversation would show, children's autonomy is emphasized over conformity to parental expectations from the beginning, and children are to differentiate, replacing parents with peers at least after high school. To his wife's appeal, "We have to guide her," George replies, "Wow; I gave that up when she went off to college." This is continuous with other conflicts on authority discussed in the same conversation. Diana says, "I just get tired of waiting for you to do or say something. I end up being the bad guy and you're the good guy."

Today, the relation of children's early and later problems to the lack of parental authority is a great concern in professional and popular literature. Much research confirms a preference for some version of "authoritative" parenting (Kaufman et al., 2000) and, in most cases, entails a critique of present American styles as too permissive. The need for parental confidence to provide structure and set limits for children is one way in which this is expressed (Doherty, 2000).

Latino cultures are known for their emphasis on parental authority, on *respeto*. Diana in the previous conversation is critical of her Anglo husband George for not taking charge and for leaving her with the "bad guy" role. Although the male in Latino settings is normally in the forefront of family authority, some type of partnership is typical. George's individual personality plays a part; however, different cultural emphases are evident in this family's conflicts over parenting authority in general.

The authority issue often comes to the fore in terms of parental styles of discipline. Discipline usually means setting limits, although its broader meaning should be to provide structure and proactively offer guidance that would prevent much misbehavior

As an Anglo parent and now grandparent, I am sometimes at a loss to be proactive and imaginative in this kind of discipline. For example, when I was assisting in a recent fourth-grade Bible school children's group, the normally full curriculum of activities stalled momentarily, leaving the children waiting for the next phase. I was reduced to "shushing" the restless children, until another assistant (a Caribbean Latina) providentially came up with some songs to sing and games to play.

In the case of parental styles emphasizing authority and discipline, Latino sources have begun in some instances to borrow from more permissive Anglo models while they retain their special stress on parental firmness. Latino cherishing of children (Rodriguez, 1999) has always led to emphasis on the empathic bond with parents as the context of respect and obedience. Possibly for this reason, I have found Latino couples, including parents, responsive to my imago relationship therapy, drawn from the work of Harville Hendrix and Helen Hunt. The imago approach would be called permissive by some standards, emphasizing as it does the mirroring of feelings by partners and between parents and children in the tradition of Carl Rogers, Robert Carkhuff, Thomas Gordon, Haim Ginott, and others.

However, the highly structured and directive process provided for couples and parents has an authoritative appeal for Latinos. Hendrix and Hunt's book on parenting (1997) comes out of their rearing six children and deepening through their experience—the imago theme that I call taking turns at empathic listening. With adults or children, problems occur when both parties want to be heard at once: "I hate this." "Well, I hate that." "You did this." "Well, you did that." "I want this." "Well, I want that."

I was trying one night to get a bouncy, "wound up" child to stay in bed and go to sleep; as I struggled to assert my Latino authority, by some grace I decided to pause and ask, "Why are you doing this?" The question, which was essentially "taking turns" at showing *respeto*, instead of just demanding it, led the child to share some realistic fears and conflicts and then settle down to sleep.

"Whose turn is it?" is a question consciously or unconsciously decided every moment or at least after every impasse. Who is going to listen first? Who will listen next? This process is systematized in the intentional dialogue of imago therapy—to agree up front that each party will take turns listening to understand and will paraphrase back what is said (with feeling) to be sure that he or she "got it," thus saving disagreements for "my turn" when the other has heard and is willing to listen in the same way. This has been practiced effectively by children in home and school settings across cultures. I recently watched a video in which Israeli children vigorously engaged in the exercise.

The empathic bond aimed at here could be called the foundation of all relationships. I am understood; my position (usually my deepest fear, realistic or not) is cared for and valued, whether agreed with or not. I can then hear that the other is in a different place and can more likely respect that. I can more likely agree on limits to be accepted by either or both of us.

Asking and giving, variations of Piaget's (1972) "assimilation" and "accommodation," or the "differentiation and union" of development, are a tandem, with each motion valid. At times, they merge naturally. At other times, there is a special value in separating them rigorously. This is brought home by the current negative psychological term, "codependence." Although this term can express an exaggerated self-sufficiency that denies persons' legitimate need for each other, its true meaning is "overdependence." The nature of overdependence is precisely mixing asking and giving too much, thus making each too dependent, too conditional, on the other. If I give while I'm supposedly asking, I am bribing or buying a response. I need to ask more unconditionally: "Do it, if you do, not because I've done or will do something for you or because you fear my disapproval, but as a free gift, just because you think I need it and you care about me." This is trusting in the other's love, beyond our control.

Conversely, to ask while I'm supposedly giving, is deceitfully to pretend to focus on your interests while exploiting you (however unconsciously) for mine. The Latino *dicho* (saying) captures it: *Dar por recibir no es dar sino pedir.* (To give in order to receive is not to give but to ask.) I need to give more unconditionally, not because you have done or will do something for me or because I fear your disapproval, but as a free gift, just because I think you need it and I care about you. We may underestimate children's motivation to give a free gift out of love—granted that any gift may involve a mixture of motives, as with all of us.

Therefore, the "secular" term "codependence" opens our eyes to the fact that *respeto* is a two-way street. In a sense, as Latino models stress, parental authority is unconditionally given. In another sense, it must be earned. If Latino cultures' immense valuing of children is to be honored, "parents themselves must first behave with respect" (Nava, 2000, p. 38). To take priority, their judgments must be realistic, not projections of their anxieties. The child is entitled to have his or her needs be the primary focus.

In this proactive provision of structure and when we come to the limit-setting phase of discipline, many parenting skills that apply in the family could also have the broader adaptation to community and international life to which Latino commitment also extends. An example is Don Dinkmeyer's STEP program (systematic training for effective parenting; Dinkmeyer, 1984; Dinkmeyer, McKay, & Dinkmeyer, 1997). STEP and another syndicated program, "active parenting," developed by Michael Popkin (1993) are available in Spanish and claim a strong research base. They derive from the psychology of Alfred Adler (1927, 1951), who parted with Freud and predated object relations theories by seeing human motivation as based on relational power.

Adler's concept of power was not that of aggression as venting, power to defeat, but power to belong to the social group. It was contrasted with inferiority, another concept native to Adler. In this view (elaborated by Rudolph Dreikurs, 1964, before the Dinkmeyers), children's or anyone's level of encouragement or discouragement with respect to the power to belong determines health or pathology. In the STEP assessment, children feeling slightly discouraged tend to try (1) to get attention. If they are more discouraged, they engage in (2) a power struggle. If they are severely discouraged, they opt as a last resort for (3) revenge or, alternatively, (4) a display of inadequacy, a kind of passive revenge.

This is a kind of mini-*DSM* (*Diagnostic and Statistical Manual*) for child pathology. It is also a treatment. The constructive parental response to (1) attention-getting is to give more attention—not on demand, but unpredictably, when not expected. The response to (2) a power struggle is to enlist the child proactively in a cooperative enterprise. Response to (3) revenge or (4) inadequacy is, again, positive unpredictability, not retaliation in kind.

At all levels, the effort is to give positive and negative reinforcement in a way that clarifies as much as possible the inherent goals and consequences of the child's action, not the personal disposition of the caregiver. The words "encouragement" and "discouragement" are used in STEP instead of "reward" and "punishment" to highlight this distinction. Natural consequences are events that flow automatically from the behavior, such as no more food to replace what is thrown on the floor. Logical consequences are imaginative constructions by the parent that accord as closely as possible with the behavior, such as nonuse of the car for a period after returning home late.

Concepts of empathy through paraphrasing feelings are also used in this program, partly drawn as in imago therapy from the psychologist Carl Rogers (1961), in STEP via Thomas Gordon's PET, parent effectiveness training (1970). The goal is to create a relationship bond within which the more cognitive–behavioral reinforcement process can proceed. What is added to PET in STEP is the notion of consequence: the last resort "or else," the coercive sanction if the parent's needs and feelings are totally disregarded. Even when consequences are in force, listening to feelings is important and often defuses conflict along with, or when possible without, the sanctions.

Although one research group endorses punishment, including corporal punishment, and classifies STEP, along with PET as purely permissive (McPheters & Robinson, 2002), other research and practice supports some notion of "consequences" in distinction from "punishment."

One instructive point in STEP, for families and for other social groups, is to note how the misdirected positive human motivation to belong is the root of much conflict. Although human self-defeating tendencies distort this motivation into excesses of greed and power over others, it still behooves parents and anyone to search for and affirm all positive motivation in the child or any other friend or enemy.

Furthermore, it is also instructive to note that, even though revenge ("getting even") is one of the most widespread human reactions as a posture of power, it is *the most impotent of positions*—a function of the lowest level of discouragement, the level of greatest hopelessness: "I can't get what I really want from you; I can only hurt you." In some ways, we recognize this truth more clearly among children than between parents and children, and even less among other social groups, including nations.

All the strategies of discipline described earlier are based on the original meaning of discipline: discipling, provision of alternatives, proactive imagination. *Violence and revenge are a failure of imagination.* This failure is self-perpetuating because it begets fear, which further stifles imagination and provokes the escalation of retaliation in kind, each time with the justification of previous hurts. This is expressed in the Latino *dicho*, "*haz mal, espera otro tal*" (Do wrong, expect another wrong). Rodriguez (1999, pp. 246–250) discourages parental spanking in similar terms to these as provocative of the spiral of violence. She adds guidelines to minimize these effects if spanking is used as a last resort.

Violence may be other than physical. There are the verbal put-downs, whether of children or between other family members. The plaintive children's saying reveals the truth of its opposite: "Sticks and stones may break my bones, but names will never hurt me."

When consequences are used for limit-setting, personal feelings of care-givers can still be expressed through "I-messages," contrasted with the shame-and-blame, name calling, and sarcasm of criticism starting with "You are…" or "That is…." In my marriage counseling, one client initially frustrated my efforts to teach "I-messages" in the terms, "When you _____ (behavior), I feel _____ (emotional word), because _____ (interpretation). He told his wife, "When you…act like a b…, I feel…that you are a b… because…you really are a b…." Progress came later!

In a similar vein, a health agency director in Mexico told of a 4-year-old walking alone for 12 blocks to the clinic for treatment of a facial bruise, clearly the result of abuse. Asked his name, he replied matter of factly, "*Cabron*" (son of a b----).

ENJOYMENT

The treatment of authority and discipline has been extensive, as the concern is extensive in parenting. The hardships and privations of Latinos in particular, often under conditions of poverty and discrimination, have required discipline of children as well as adults. The Latino experience has required virtues like "*trabajo duro, lealtad, y fortaleza*" (hard work, loyalty, and fortitude; Nava, 2000).

Another gift of Latino cultures is that, in the midst of strenuous challenges, the ultimate goal—that of making a world in which it is "safe to play"—has not been lost. The Latino theme of enjoyment and festivity has at times been disparaged and caricatured in its emphasis on "*fiesta, siesta y manana.*" This may have led in turn to a defensiveness in which Latinos have sometimes felt it necessary to defend their work ethic. In reality, Gloria Rodriguez's portrayal of children playing in the midst of a family festivity highlights a less recognized but even more fundamental "grace ethic": enjoyment of the gifts of life.

> In the Hispanic world, life is celebrated with music and brilliant colors. Like the bright paper flowers and colorful ribbons at our celebrations, a child's imagination and creativity abound through our rituals and folklore. Singing, dancing, clapping and shouting, "*Gritos*"…energize us and keep us happy and healthy….Although Hispanics are known to have a powerful work ethic, we also believe in enjoying life (1999, p. 21).

Humorist Garrison Keillor gently satirizes his overly serious Lake Wobegon Scandinavian culture: "Today was a bad day. It was a bad day because yesterday was such a good day. Pleasure just makes the rest of life worse." Fun and pleasure, including the deepest pleasure of love, are gifts not completely in our control. In mundane terms, they require letting our parasympathetic nervous system take over from our more crisis-oriented sympathetic nervous system. They do require that the other beat in the rhythm of seriousness, caution, and discipline, to maintain conditions in which it is "safe to play."

This returns to the original function of discipline: provision of resources, protection, guidance, and structure in advance so that children can, to the extent possible, have fun and stay out of trouble. The extent to which children have been able to do this, even under conditions of serious danger, has been amazing. It has been documented by narratives like the *Diary of Anne Frank* (1993) during the holocaust and, more recently, in Deborah Ellis's (2004) *Three Wishes: Palestinian and Israeli Children Speak*.

SELF-PARENTING

For this safety to play to be a natural outcome of parenting, we as parents must stay connected to our inner child. The therapy of transactional analysis (Berne, 1961) provided the now well-known concepts of parent, adult, and child. I call them "oughts, thoughts, and wants." "Child" is wants and feelings. Latino cultures have a laudable appreciation of children and thus of feelings. Though not to be followed uncritically ("If it feels good, do it"), feelings are clues to the depths of our real, "gut" values and commitments. They may be partly distorted and unreliable due to the mixed bag of our childhood histories. Thus, part of our parenting job is to seek ongoing parenting to heal the wounds and build on the joys of our personal and cultural pasts.

One of the more playful ways of doing this, for children or adults, is an exercise that I have devised in which persons recall happy and unhappy early memories that yield clues to present issues. I have defined these in terms of what, in the way we remember being treated as children, always helped and hurt the most. Chances are that those main satisfactions and frustrations are still what helps and hurts the most in the way in which we are treated today.

Persons or groups discuss these stories and help each other sort out recurrent themes. Each one then formulates a succinct T-shirt slogan that interprets to intimates and to the world, "How I most need and do not need (front and back, respectively) to be treated." My T-shirt says on the back, "Don't Scare Me" and on the front, "Encourage My Courage." This comes out of mixed childhood experiences as the oldest of three, of being highly valued and encouraged to perform, while having fears of engagement partly borrowed from parents. My wife, Irma, the youngest of eight in a close Mexican family, was also greatly loved, but the last to have la palabra, to get a word in around the dining table. Her T-shirt slogan became "Don't Discount Me" and "Take Me Seriously!"

The most effective thing about the T-shirt is that it enshrines the I-message concept of relationship over the "you are…" message that provokes self-defense. Even a third option, the authoritative "you ought…" message, also can arouse resistance to perceived domination. Certainly any authoritative parental system, including the Latino, has its "oughts" that go beyond a parent's personal preference. Still, a judicious parental use of "I need" can keep a parent humble about having the high moral ground. It may also give the child an option to bestow a gift rather than submit to a demand.

Another truly risky aspect of the T-shirt slogan is that it has an aspect of personal confession. I may be seen acting in a way that provokes the opposite of what I say I want or I may be projecting as my need what I am actually insensitive to in others. I may not be planning to get what I want and be satisfied, but to continue to suffer and feel self-justified. It is important not to use these insights as occasions for "shame and blame" of ourselves or others. In religious terms, it is not healthy to be too great an expert on sin.

We may derive some consolation from recognizing that, in all of us, along with the famous "Serenity Prayer" of Reinhold Niebuhr that defines sainthood: "Grant me the serenity to accept the things I cannot change, courage to change the things I can, and wisdom to know the difference," there is in our nature what I have called an antiserenity prayer: "Grant me the anxiety to continue battling the things I cannot change, the timidity to avoid changing the things I can, and the commitment to stay miserable (sufrido in Latino terms) in any case." We are okay as long as we see and accept this gracefully in ourselves first.

PARENTS ORGANIZING FOR CHANGE

All family models of whatever style can be seen, as previously suggested, to reflect larger societal values and goals. Though Latinos espouse the values of family and community, there are always tensions between the two. Throughout history, parents have been encouraged to "take back your kids" from a larger society that partly opposed their agendas. As is the case today, subcultural groups have typically had differences and contradictions as to which values of the dominant culture to embrace or oppose.

For example, one issue dividing parents and the larger society today might be consumerism and the media promotion of children's greed, along with that of adults. United voices are raised against this trend, as they are against others. At the same time, the dominant culture's web or system is so strong that united action is hard to effect, particularly action that can affect public policy. Paradoxically, many people who suffer the most vote for leaders who promote consumer buying as economic policy. This is similar to the many who suffer from lack of child health insurance while voting for leaders who abolish it.

Latinos have typically suffered discrimination in mainly Anglo society or even by their own leaders in Latino societies. Sometimes, out of loyalty or realism, they have allowed themselves to be recruited to support the status quo against natural allies (other groups seeking change). There is certainly a risk for "underdogs" to take on "top dogs." It may seem safer to use Freud's defense mechanism of "identification with the aggressor" (1952). This also can lead to transferring anger internally within one's ethnic, economic, and family circles.

Some Latino leaders help refocus the anger at injustice in directions where it belongs and with constructive goals. Ernesto Cortes (1996) is a major figure in the Industrial Areas Foundation (IAF), a network of community organizations. The IAF has 60 affiliates nationwide. They fight (*luchan*) through democratic procedures for basic family needs of jobs, education, and similar concerns of members.

These members are institutions: churches, schools, unions, and other groups composed of families, on the premise that institutional power (organized people) is needed to deal with institutional power (organized money). Cortes and the IAF have extended the pioneering work of earlier Latino advocates like Cesar Chavez (Nava, 2000, p. 161f) for a role in public decision-making. The southwest region of the IAF, from Louisiana to California, has about 30 of the nonpartisan groups, which are serious "players" in their cities and states and unite Latino with other cultural groups at all economic levels. A recent convention in Los Angeles drew 15,000 people to reorganize the city's IAF group. Families, many of them Latino, in 15 IAF organizations across Texas are presently lobbying the state legislature for children's health insurance, child protective services, and public education funding.

Related efforts on a smaller scale involve parent or family advocacy groups such as those pioneered by family therapist William Doherty. Together with J. S. Carroll, he has launched the Families and Democracy Project (2002) and also, with Barbara Carlson, a movement called Putting Family First (2002). These are projects to resource parents who want to protect family priorities by uniting for mutual support through democratic action in their communities. The assumption is that individual families are too isolated to reverse trends alone and that civic participation is essential to modifying the cultural pressures that threaten them.

The Families and Democracy Project goes further. "The producer–consumer model that dominates work with families does not engage the capacity of families to be producers and contributors to the common good and not just consumers of services." The project's goal is to "renew and transform family science and practice as work by, for and with citizens" (workshop handout at conference of American Association of Pastoral Counselors, 2004). This in some ways answers Goolishian & Anderson's (1987) comment about professionals becoming the new extended family. In this model, other families with common problems and visions instead of kinship become part of the extended family. More than this, they help to "reweave the fabric" (Cortes, 1996) of community—the wider system so much in need of this renewal and so much a traditional commitment of Latino cultures.

This approach may be problematic for professional caregivers. As providers, we have to some extent been socialized into the "consumer–provider" orientation and tend to organize our lives around "billable hours." There are positive benefits to this. One is cost-effectiveness. It is also one way to invite clients' investment in their treatment. There is a legitimacy to clients having a setting in which their remedial needs and not those of others can be the focus. Furthermore, there is a legitimacy in Latinos having access to the specialized, by-appointment care, with cultural sensitivity, that typifies the "consumer–provider" relationship at its best. Also, therapeutic orientations as well as client needs may call for a more interior or limited interpersonal focus.

At the same time, I can still remember how alien in some ways the rhetoric of "health care delivery" struck me when it came into vogue, seeming at least to imply a transaction that might be commercial while not holistic and collaborative. Discerning judgment will always be needed as to how one's healing can have all these dimensions, including reaching out to others as healers, an important feature in many helping traditions.

Looking for ways in which children can give to the family and the community is an important frontier. This is especially true because their obvious economic value in earlier agricultural settings has been eroded. Adding to the easier projects of direct service to individuals, the concept of advocacy, learning with their parents to meet with business and government leaders for public policies, is a more difficult yet rewarding step. A 12-year-old in a Latino San Antonio *barrio* (neighborhood) proudly boasted, "I got my street!" She was referring to having participated in parents' discussions with city officials about needed renovations on the block.

The importance of children contributing to the family mirrors the need for citizen participation in a democratic society. I have said hopefully that professional caregivers could learn this kind of democratic advocacy through lobbying for their professional interests, an increasing necessity, and then could transfer the skills to coaching their clients to do the same. This does not happen automatically. It requires the truly professional attitude that, in exchange for clients' payment (however that is arranged), therapists will devote themselves to clients' interests, within the bounds of their expertise and agreements.

Part of this expertise may well be that of referral and collaboration with other caregivers and larger systems as with clients. To return to the specific question of culture, perhaps the first collaboration with clients of another culture is to invite them to help us understand that culture. As a pastoral counselor, I have regarded every culture as some blend of incarnation and idolatry—a new creative variation in human life, with its own bias and need for correction. From moment to moment in our work, we will always make our best call about which is which. We are wise if we first become aware of our bias, by an appreciation of others' qualities, whether personal, cultural, or the usual uncertain blend of both. May Latino parents benefit from our intentions and our actions, for them and with them, to the end that all the families of the Earth may be blessed.

CASE CONCLUDED

What kinds of outcomes may we hope to achieve if we counsel parents according to the principles of respecting communality with some ratio of individualism, and authority with a degree of permissiveness; respecting the emphasis on the feeling life of persons and, especially, the playfulness of children; and building on the commitment to community, as well as family, and to the legacies of spirituality encompassing all?

Mario, a 9-year-old Latino boy, loves spiders and snakes, to the chagrin of the girls in his class; he loves tigers and superheroes even more and, even more than that, he loves video games and active sports in which he can exercise his physical and mental energy. His family recently moved into a new neighborhood, requiring the children to attend a different school. In the new school, Mario is for the first time having behavior problems leading him to be sent repeatedly to the principal's office. He mainly follows misbehaving friends in difficulties of inappropriate talking, horseplay, practical jokes (like putting an insect down the back of a classmate's shirt), and neglect of assignments, in spite of obvious academic ability.

Mario's parents, Jaime and Delphia, have high school educations and technical training. Both work outside the home, Jaime as an auto mechanic and Delphia as a dental hygienist. They require day care for a 4-year-old daughter and rely on a city-sponsored after-school program with tutoring and recreation for Mario and his 7-year-old brother. They are strict with the children, who have chores, and they expect them to make at least "B" grades in school. Discipline is mainly in the form of privileges granted or withheld; spanking is avoided. They are active Catholics with Sundays devoted to mass and to biweekly Sunday afternoon extended-family gatherings (backyard barbecue type), usually at the home of Delphia's parents. They make an effort to have family meals most nights, bedtime prayers, and family vacations.

Jaime's and Delphia's parents came from Mexico, leaving their own parents there, who are deceased except for Delphia's grandmother, age 75, who occasionally visits and is visited. Jaime's parents are divorced and his father is remarried; both parents live some distance away. Jaime has three brothers, two older and one younger. The older brothers, one single and one divorced with no children, live in the community. The younger brother lives with the mother out of town. Some family vacations aim at reconnecting with Jaime's more dispersed family.

Delphia's parents still reside in the community. She has two younger brothers and three younger sisters; three of her five siblings are married and also have children. Two of her siblings are out of the state and three are within driving distance for the Sunday and other gatherings.

This is a proud Mexican American family, and although they have had divorces and other child behavior problems throughout the clan, Jaime and Delphia are particularly distressed over Mario's situation. Mario is one of the more talented of the children; he is popular with his cousins at the family gatherings, shows an occasional spiritual interest, and is expected to go to college and "do well" in life. After consultation among the adults at family gatherings, the parents decided to go to a professional counselor on Delphia's health insurance provider's list.

After an evaluation that included a psychiatric consultation, Mario was diagnosed with "adjustment disorder with mixed disturbance of emotions and conduct," 309.4 (*DSM-IV*). He was not medicated. His therapist, a non-Latino with multicultural interest and experience, focused on getting to know the family in two conjoint sessions with Mario and the nuclear family and once in a larger grouping of family members. He then met with Mario alone for four biweekly sessions, interspersed with two sessions with Jaime and Delphia as a couple.

In the family sessions, Mario appeared to be closer to his mother. He expressed a yearning, as did Delphia, for more time talking and doing things with Jaime. Jaime described work pressures as limiting his time and energy for companionship with his wife and children. Also, he showed some awkwardness in communication with both. Mario's siblings agreed that school was pressured. Though the weekend family gatherings were appreciated by all, including the extended family members, the children missed having more time with both parents.

In Mario's private sessions, he spoke of worrying about his parents' coldness to each other, especially about his mother, whom he had seen crying at times. He also expressed the wish that his father would let him help fix the family car and also let him join a neighborhood swim team and attend his swim meets.

In their joint sessions, Jaime and Delphia practiced paraphrasing back each other's feelings, taking turns. Beyond frustrations, both recalled fun times together "before the kids." Encouraged by the counselor, they came up with some plans for how these might be recovered, as in a few weekends away each year as a couple and a "date night" at least once a month. They thought that extended family could take some responsibility for the children during these times, in return for trading off at other times, because Jaime's and Delphia's parents and siblings had their own work and family pressures. At the counselor's suggestion, they also agreed to talk to each other for at least 5 minutes every day after coming from work about how their day went before turning to TV or home chores.

Jaime alluded to Mario's asking to help work on the car, which he said he would consider, and also to Mario's expressed wish to join the swim team, which both parents agreed would depend on his grades. The counselor concurred, affirming the parents' limit-setting and Mario's need to have quality time with dad—even if his "help" made the car work take longer.

Delphia and Jaime also reported an incident on a weekend, when they had taken the children with some cousins to a playground. Delphia heard Mario shout a vulgar phrase and immediately, with Jaime's support, called him and his principal playmate for a 5-minute "time out" at opposite ends of the picnic table at which they sat. The 5 minutes was started over due to the boys' fidgeting. After 5 minutes of quiet, Delphia kissed both boys and sent them back to play. They ran off cheerfully and eagerly.

On another occasion during this time, Jaime and Delphia took Mario to a rally at the city council. This rally was organized by a group of cooperating churches. Its purpose was to appeal for continued funding for the city's after-school program, which provided the tutoring and recreation for Mario and his brother. The grandparents watched the younger siblings for the evening. In individual counseling sessions, Mario said that he liked the event and felt more grown up as part of a family team, dealing with powerful institutions that could help or hurt them all.

Mario reported toward the end of his sessions, confirmed by his parents, that the incidents of getting in trouble in school had diminished and that his grades were slightly improved. The counselor complimented him and invited him to return if needed in the future. He wrote in a concluding evaluation,

> Parents are bonding more and teaming to show real gifts for limit-setting with affirmation. This allows Mario to "be a kid" as well as perform, without undue concern for "parenting the parents." His getting in trouble is seen as partly due to the stress of moving and changing schools. It also seems partly to be the "cry for family help" of the "identified patient," alerting parents to their unmet needs with each other.

It is clear that the initial strengths of this family are unique for Latino or non-Latino cultures. This highlights goals of therapy as related to the larger society: to co-create family models and to enhance family development across the board, along with symptomatic treatment. Again, with imagination, such goals can at least be approximated, especially with therapists' appreciation of and collaboration with families of all cultures.

REFERENCES

Adler, A. (1927). *Understanding human nature.* Oxford: Oneworld Publications.

Adler, A. (1951). *The practice and theory of individual psychology.* New York: Humanities Press, American Psychiatric Association.

Berne, E. (1961). *Transactional analysis in psychotherapy.* New York: Grove Press.

Cortes, E. (1996). Reweaving the social fabric. *Boston Review, 21*(6), x

Dinkmeyer, D., Sr. (1984). *Systematic training for effective parenting.* Atascadero, CA: Impact Publishers.

Dinkmeyer, D., Sr., McKay, G. & Dinkmeyer, Jr., D. (1997). *The parents' handbook: Systematic training for effective parenting (STEP).* Atascadero, CA: Impact Publishers, Inc.

Dreikurs, R. (1964). *Children: The challenge.* New York: Hawthorne Books.

Doherty, W. (2000). *Take back your kids.* Notre Dame: Sorin Books.

Doherty, W., & Carlson, C. (2002). *Putting family first.* New York: Henry Holt.

Doherty, W., & Carroll, J. S. (2002). The families and democracy model. *Family Process, 41,* 579–589.

Ellis, D. (2004). *Three wishes: Palestinian and Israeli children speak.* Toronto: Douglas & McIntyre.

Frank, A. (1993). *The diary of a young girl* (1947). New York, NY: Bantam Books.

Freud, S. (1952). *The major works of Sigmund Freud.* In Hutchins, R. M. (Ed.), *Great books of the Western world.* Chicago: Encyclopedia Britannica.

Goolishian, H. & Anderson, H. (1987). Language systems and therapy: an evolving idea. *Journal of Psychotherapy, 24,* 529–535.

Gordon, T. (1970). *P.E.T. (parent effectiveness training).* New York: New American Library.

Hendrix, H., & Hunt, H. (1997). *Giving the love that heals: A guide for parents.* New York: Simon & Schuster.

Kaufman, D., Goften, E., Santa Lucia, R., Salcedo, O., Rendina-Gobioff, G., & Gadd, R. (2000). The relationship between parenting style and children's adjustment. *Journal of Child and Family Studies, 9*(2), 231–245.

Luquet, W. & Hannah, M. T., Eds. (1998). *Healing in the relational paradigm: The imago relationship therapy casebook.* Washington, D.C., London: Taylor & Francis.

McPheters, J. and Robinson, P. (2002). *Systematic training for effective parenting: An empirical review.* Paper presented at the American Association of Behavioral and Social Sciences, Las Vegas, Nevada, 2002.

Nava, Y. (2000). *It's all in the frijoles.* New York: Simon & Schuster.

Piaget, J. (1972). *Genetic epistemology.* (and writings from 1929 to 1977) New York: Columbia University Press.

Popkin, M. (1993). *Active parenting now—the basics.* Kennesaw, GA: Active Parenting Publishers.

Rodriguez, G. (1999). *Raising nuestros ninos. Bringing up Latino children in a bicultural world.* Forest City, NC: Fireside Books..

Rogers, C. (1961). *On becoming a person.* Boston: Houghton Mifflin.

Siegel, D. (1999). *The developing mind.* New York: Guilford Press.

CHAPTER 11

Sexual Counseling With Latino Couples

STEPHEN SOUTHERN

"Sex is a natural function" was the cornerstone of the Masters and Johnson model for treating sexual dysfunction and dissatisfaction (Masters & Johnson, 1966, 1970). Through the pioneering efforts of William Masters and Virginia Johnson, their students took the message of sexual health around the world. With the introduction of Viagra (sildenafil citrate) and effective medical procedures to treat erectile dysfunction and other sexual difficulties, some "overmedicalization" of sexual treatment has occurred (Bancroft, 2002; Sigusch, 1998; Tiefer, 2001). However, cases of sexual healing point to the significance of the couple's relationship and the promises of genuine intimacy. Sexual counseling involves combining the techniques of sex therapy with selected methods of marital or couples counseling. Although a generic sexual counseling approach can facilitate sexual health across cultures, outcomes for Latino couples may be improved by attending to specific strengths and needs associated with Hispanic or Latino relationships.

D. H. Lawrence, the English author, captures the heart of a "new" sexual health model for couples in his poem "Wedlock" (de Sola Pinto & Roberts, 1978, p. 245). Lawrence described the passion experienced in the depths of intimacy:

How I love all of you! Do you feel me wrap you
Up with myself and my warmth, like a flame round the wick?
…I spread over you! How lovely your round head, your arms,
Your breasts, your knees and feet! I feel that we
Are a bonfire of oneness, me flame flung leaping round you,
You the core of the fire crept into me.

Intimacy is the core component of the love experience in pair bonding. The word "intimacy" was derived originally from the Latin *intimus* meaning "inner" or "inmost." The French *intime* signifies "deep, fervent, and ardent." In Italian and Spanish, *intimo* indicates closeness or "innermost." The Spanish word, *intimidad*, captures the essence of the special private life shared by the couple apart from the demands of the world. The derivation of intimacy reflects the intense emotional experience by which each loving partner is drawn to the other. At the heart of intimacy is the existential encounter of "I and thou" (see Buber, 1923/1970). Intimacy reflects a "loving struggle" of two individuals attracted to one another precisely for the goal of establishing "we," an abiding mutuality that will endure and produce beneficial outcomes. Sexual intercourse is a powerful symbol of the loving embrace of intimacy.

When individuals experience problems in sexual functioning, they tend to withdraw and avoid opportunities for physical and emotional closeness (McCarthy, 1997; Moret, Glaser, Page, & Bargeron, 1998). As they break their psychological bond, the couple loses shared meaning and identity. Either partner may experience loss and grief, frustration and anger, or fear and worry. Unhappy couples tend to focus on negative attributes and exchanges, eroding the rewards associated with being committed to the relationship (see Jacobson & Christensen, 1996). Although many unhappy couples remain married for religious, family, and material reasons, they express their alienation in myriad ways, including abandoning their sexual relationship.

Sex therapy techniques can be used to remove roadblocks linked to specific sexual disorders. As roadblocks are removed, opportunities for intimacy enhancement increase. Classic models of sex therapy (Kaplan, 1979; Masters & Johnson, 1970), as well as more contemporary approaches (Barbach, 1997; McCarthy, 2001; Rosen & Leiblum, 1995; Schnarch, 1997; Schwartz & Masters, 1988), focus on the "marital unit" or couple dyad. Positive sex therapy outcomes have been associated with improvement in dyadic communication, expression of affection, and partner support (Hawton, Catalan, & Fagg, 1992).

The purpose of this chapter is to provide an overview of sexual counseling, including an integration of sex therapy and relational counseling, as applied to the strengths and needs of the Latino heterosexual couple. There is an emphasis upon the marital sexual relationship within the contexts of Latino family values and cultural considerations. In particular, special gender-related and religious issues were incorporated in the sexual counseling model. Case studies explore applications of the generic model with selected types of sexual dysfunction.

SEX THERAPY:
THE FOUNDATION FOR INTIMACY ENHANCEMENT

Sexual counseling affords opportunities for enhancing intimacy while facilitating sexual health. Although there has been a proliferation of sex therapy techniques, the classic work of Masters and Johnson Institute established the fundamentals for the field. Before 1970, sexual dysfunction was treated typically by psychiatrists and psychologists as symptoms of underlying mental and emotional problems. In 1959, Masters and Johnson (1966, 1970) began their revolutionary approach to resolving sexual problems. They worked with couples (originally called "the marital unit") because each case of sexual dysfunction was considered relational in origin. In the pioneering model, the male and female cotherapy team helped couples overcome relational and emotional roadblocks to intimacy. Masters and Johnson offered specific homework exercises to address particular roadblocks in the sexual response cycle.

The Masters and Johnson (1970) model for sex therapy involved intensive treatment of couples experiencing sexual dysfunction. Frequently, the couple had complementary sexual dysfunctions. For example, the man presented rapid ejaculation, while the woman complained of anorgasmia (inability or difficulty with orgasm). Masters and Johnson observed that untreated sexual problems tend to get worse. There is a syndrome or negative feedback loop in which more focus or preoccupation with a sexual concern produces greater "spectatoring" and resulting performance pressure.

As a partner becomes preoccupied with constructing a solution to the sexual problem, the natural sexual response is overwhelmed with anxiety and self-doubt. With increasing anxiety and sense of failure, the dysfunctional person withdraws and the couple loses opportunities for corrective experiences. Because sex is a taboo topic, partners are reluctant to discuss their sexual concerns and vulnerabilities. They suffer in silence or look outside the relationship for a "quick fix." Eventually, the relationship erodes and partners may blame or attack one another for sexual dissatisfaction.

The intensive treatment model of Masters and Johnson (1970) is organized to produce rapid results and engender hope. Ideally, treatment is offered daily by the dual gender, cotherapy team for a period of 2 weeks. Daily continuity and removal from typical work and family distractions prepare the couple for optimal progress. Variations on the basic model include "weekend intensives" or even once weekly outpatient visits. Beneficial changes can take place; however, the efficacy of sex therapy decreases with deviations from the original intensive model (Masters & Johnson; Schwartz & Masters, 1988).

Although Masters and Johnson (1970) prescribed homework ("touching opportunities" or touching exercises) for particular types of sexual dysfunction, there are several core interventions in sex therapy. Initially, the couple is asked to refrain from sexual outlet. This "authoritative pronouncement" (Masters & Johnson, pp. 287–290) enabled the couple to focus on intimacy without the demand to be sexual. This intervention disrupts the pattern of negative feedback loops and creates the possibility of change. Now, the couple could enjoy a beautiful sunset while walking leisurely in Forest Park. They could discuss their enthusiasm for new discoveries or reclaiming of former avocations and pleasurable life experiences. The naturally healing couple can move toward sexual fulfillment by experiencing intimate communication, sensuality, and romance.

Another common intervention involves a "roundtable" (Masters & Johnson, 1970, pp. 57–78) discussion of the results of assessment. Although the marital unit is the primary level of analysis, the male cotherapist interviews the husband (or male client) at length, while the female cotherapist conducts an assessment with the wife. The couple and cotherapy team return to the table to make meaning of the initial evaluation and provide sex education and guidance. The success of the roundtable intervention is based on removing the secrecy and mystery surrounding the sexual concerns. The experience desensitizes anxiety through helpful discussion and solutions are framed in positive terms to capitalize upon natural resources of the couple. Dr. Masters was an excellent listener and storyteller who could help the couple understand the dyadic nature of the sexual concerns. The successful roundtable discussion introduced the couple to the process of sex therapy homework exercises.

The next step in the generic model of sex therapy involved one of the most famous interventions: "sensate focus" (Masters & Johnson, 1970, pp. 66–85). Sensate focus encouraged concentration on the here-and-now sensations involved in intimate, nonsexual contact. Initially, each member of the couple engaged in "selfish touching," in which touch is guided by one's genuine interests rather than trying to do anything to or for one's partner. If the partner feels any discomfort or wishes to redirect the one doing the touching, the person places her or his hand on top of the partner's hand. This practice, like other techniques in the Masters and Johnson model, establishes the foundation for sexual self-responsibility. Components of the sensate focus homework address roadblocks associated with sexual withdrawal, spectatoring, and performance pressure. In this manner, the dissatisfied or dysfunctional individual becomes a participant in ongoing sexual intimacy, rather than an anxious observer or a dehumanized sex object.

Masters and Johnson (1970, pp. 342–360) reported success rates as high as 97% for rapid ejaculation and 80% across all male and female sexual dysfunctions. However, their model and research have been criticized for errors in data gathering, heterosexist bias, and male-centered conceptualization of the sexual response cycle (Reynolds, 1977; Tiefer, 1991; Zilbergeld & Evans, 1980). The evolution of the Masters and Johnson Institute model was influenced by basic assumptions regarding the pathogenesis or evolution of sexual dysfunctions.

In the past, 90% of sexual dysfunction cases were treated as psychogenic in origin (Kaplan, 1983; Masters & Johnson, 1966, 1970; Wincze & Carey, 1991). Today, the etiology of most cases, especially among men, is determined to be organic, primarily because technological advances permit the identification of subtle anatomical and physiological factors. It is likely that almost all cases of sexual dysfunction involve mixed etiology with psychogenic and organic contributing factors (Burvat, Burvat-Herbaut, Lemaire, Marcolin, & Quittelier, 1990; Kaplan, 1983; Kellett, 1995). Even Pfizer (1998, pp. 9–11), the pharmaceutical company responsible for developing Viagra, included with their drug some educational materials regarding intimacy enhancement. Dr. Gerald R. Weeks, a marital and sex therapist, recommended removing some relational roadblocks in conjunction with medication regimen. Dr. Weeks observed that "…no treatment for ED will make these barriers magically disappear" and that "your relationship needs to be a priority at times" (Pfizer, p. 11).

Technological advances from the 1990s to the present have facilitated accurate assessment and reliable treatment of sexual dysfunction. Although sex therapy lacks definitive research findings (Reynolds, 1977; Rosen & Leiblum, 1995; Weis, 1998), the classic Masters and Johnson Institute model (Masters & Johnson, 1970; Schwartz & Masters, 1988) has provided the guiding conceptual and clinical paradigm in sex therapy for decades. The core components of sex therapy, including sensate focus and nondemand pleasuring, have been supported in several studies (Hawton et al., 1992; Hirst & Watson, 1997; Rosen & Leiblum; Sarwer & Durlak, 1997; Wylie, 1997).

Effective sex therapy involves intensive (ideally daily) sessions conducted by a dual gender, cotherapy team. The dissatisfied or dysfunctional couple reclaims the natural sexual function through shifting the focus from the sexual symptoms, refraining from intercourse for a time, receiving accurate sexual information and encouragement, practicing nondemand sensual touching, and implementing communication techniques and touching exercises through systematic homework assignments. The homework includes specific interventions for particular types of sexual dysfunction.

TYPES OF SEXUAL DYSFUNCTION

According to the sexual health model, there are two major domains of assessment: the individual and the relationship (McCabe & Cobain, 1998). Some cases of sexual dysfunction seem to be related primarily to individual, mostly organic factors (e.g., vascular erectile dysfunction). Other cares are clearly relational in nature, such as sexual desire discrepancy. Comprehensive

Table 11.1   Types of Dysfunction by Sexual Response Cycle Phase

Phase	Type of Dysfunction	
	Male	Female
Desire	Hypoactive sexual desire	Hypoactive sexual desire[a]
	Sexual aversion	Sexual aversion
	Sexual desire discrepancy	Sexual desire discrepancy
	Sexual compulsion[a]	Sexual compulsion
	Paraphilia	Paraphilia
Arousal	Erectile dysfunction[a]	Sexual arousal disorder
Orgasm	Delayed ejaculation	Anorgasmia[a]
	Rapid ejaculation[a]	
Resolution	Pain	Pain[a]
	Sexual compulsion	Sexual compulsion
	Sexual dissatisfaction	Sexual dissatisfaction

[a] Common or typical presenting problem.

evaluation of sexual dysfunction should be tailored to the particular presenting problem while examining the functions of the symptom and effects of the problem upon the marriage or committed couple. Particular disorders for men and women exist in each phase of the sexual response cycle, which consists of desire, arousal, orgasm, and resolution. The types of sexual dysfunction are presented in Table 11.1.

The types included in the table have diagnostic criteria (American Psychiatric Association, 2000, pp. 535–582) or represent classifications recognized in sex therapy practice (see Kaplan, 1983; Masters & Johnson, 1970; Wincze & Carey, 1991). Dysfunctions may be considered primary, if they have been experienced lifelong, or secondary, reflecting an acquired condition often caused by another problem. In addition, a sexual dysfunction may be generalized, occurring across sexual encounters or partners, or situational, applying only to certain settings or partners. Each of the types can be briefly described:

- *Hypoactive sexual desire* refers to persistent or recurrent lack of fantasy, positive self-talk, or interest in sexual activity.
- *Sexual aversion* involves persistent or recurrent avoidance of sexual outlet or repulsion due to distress associated with potentially sexual stimuli.
- *Sexual desire discrepancy*, frequently encountered among unhappy couples, refers to a significant difference in desire for sexual outlet, leading to frustration or dissatisfaction for one or both partners.

- *Sexual compulsion* refers to preoccupation with sex and hyperactive sexual behavior that leads to negative consequences (Carnes, 1996; Schwartz, 1996).
- *Paraphilias* are conditions in which sexual interest and preferred or exclusive sexual outlet are associated with variant or atypical objects, partners, or activities (Abel & Osborn, 1992; Moser, 1992).

Desire phase disorders are encountered often in clinical practice and interfere with the pursuit of partner-oriented, intimate sexual expression (Lobitz & Lobitz, 1996; MacPhee, Johnson, & van der Veer, 1995).

The next class of disorders or dysfunctions occurs during the arousal phase of the sexual response cycle. *Erectile dysfunction* refers to difficulty attaining or maintaining sufficient erection for penetration. The rigidity of erection varies significantly over time and situation and may be affected by many different chronic and situational factors. Therefore, it is useful to discuss erectile dysfunction in terms of whether or not the man presents difficulty or inability to complete satisfying intercourse. Erectile dysfunction has been called "impotence," a term with many negative and shameful connotations, especially for masculine men.

Similarly, *female sexual arousal disorder* has been called "frigidity," a term that is seldom used in professional settings, but continues to be encountered in the general public. Female sexual arousal disorder occurs when there is difficulty with vaginal lubrication or vasocongestion of the labia or clitoris. Although arousal phase disorders can be linked to many organic impairments of the vascular or neurological systems (e.g., secondary to diabetes), physiological excitement can be affected by individual anxiety or relational stress. The arousal phase progresses in the Masters and Johnson (1970) model until the person reaches a plateau, which heralds the near-future onset of orgasm.

Orgasm phase disorders may be secondary to chronic illness or side effects of certain medications, especially the selective serotonin reuptake inhibitors such as Prozac (fluoxetine hydrochrloride) (Seagraves, 1998). However, disorders of orgasm can be related to difficulty in "letting go" or facilitating the mental and physical stimulation sufficient to evoke the reflex. Individuals who try to have excessive control in their lives may experience problems with orgasm (Anderson & Cyranowski, 1995; Heiman & LoPiccolo, 1988). In the relational or dyad conceptualization, withholding ejaculation or orgasm can be related to passive–aggressive maneuvers to deny or manipulate one's partner.

Only 40 to 50% of women are regularly orgasmic during sexual intercourse (Masters & Johnson, 1970). The "male superior" or "missionary" position may not provide adequate physical stimulation for some women. Many women are at least situationally anorgasmic due to certain setting factors and partner variables. If a woman has never experienced orgasm by any means, then she may present *inhibited female orgasm*. The popular term for the condition is "preorgasmic" because every woman has the right to enjoy and make meaning from the natural sexual function (Heiman & LoPiccolo, 1988).

Men also present problems with orgasm. In *delayed ejaculation*, the man has difficulty in attaining an orgasm, especially in the context of partner-oriented sexual activity (Apfelbaum, 1989). Some men have never been able to experience a climax (i.e., ejaculatory incompetence). Other men experience orgasm too quickly. The diagnosis of *rapid ejaculation* (usually called "premature ejaculation") involves subjective estimates from the man and his partner about the desired duration of intercourse. Relational factors play a critical role in the assessment and treatment of rapid ejaculation (McCarthy, 1994; Spector & Carey, 1990).

Few classification systems include resolution phase disorders, perhaps because the resolution phase is one of the controversial aspects of the "male-centered" Masters and Johnson model (Masters & Johnson, 1970). Yet, it is clinically useful to think of concerns that arise whenever orgasm has occurred or the sexual outlet has been terminated before orgasmic release.

Table 11.1 makes reference to pain, which could be considered a separate category of dysfunction. Pain may occur in men who maintain an erection too long without the vascular changes associated with orgasm. Similarly, women can experience genital pain when the vasocongestion is not resolved. Men may experience pain at ejaculation secondary to prostate infection. Women may have infection, inflammation, or adhesion that contributes to pain during intromission (i.e., insertion of the penis into the vagina), intercourse, or orgasmic contractions. Pain is a signal from the body that sexual outlet is unwanted or should cease.

Pain in women is rather commonplace. Dyspareunia, associated with discomfort or pain in the genitals, is incompatible with pleasure and intimacy in the sexual experience (Meana & Binik, 1994; Steege & Ling, 1993). Yet, many couples continue sexual outlet, even when pain is excruciating, thus contributing to other sexual dysfunctions or syndromes, including anorgasmia. Vaginismus is another form of pain in women in which involuntary contraction of the circumvaginal musculature makes penetration difficult or impossible (Read, 1995). Vaginismus is encountered among survivors of sexual abuse (Leiblum, Pervin, & Campbell, 1989). In fact, much sexual dissatisfaction and avoidance in men and women can be attributed to the long-term effects of neglect or abuse in childhood, including lack of sex information; negative attitudes towards sex; punishment of natural sexual development; and poor family boundaries (Kinzl, Mangwerth, Traweger, & Biebl, 1996; Sarwer & Durlak, 1996; Wilsnack, Vogeltanz, Klassen, & Harris, 1997).

In the relational context, unexpressed and unfulfilled sexual needs can lead to situational and chronic forms of *sexual dissatisfaction*. Either member of the couple or both may rate the sexual relationship as uninteresting, burdensome, or intrusive. When certain sexual acts are forced upon a partner, even one's spouse, then there are violations of the natural sexual function, integrity, and intimacy. Infrequency in sexual outlet leads to sexual dissatisfaction in couples. Successful resolution of any given sexual experience should include pleasure, sense of satisfaction, relaxation, and sharing of meaning.

Sexual outlet can become compulsive or addictive for some men and women. *Sexual compulsion*, a desire and a resolution phase dysfunction, indicates that sexual outlet is not satisfying the natural sexual function, tending to interfere with intimacy and meaning making and producing negative consequences for the couple (Schwartz, 1996). Although more men seem to present sexual compulsion or addiction, women may be drawn increasingly into cybersex addiction, involving pornography, chatting, and matchmaking. Sexual compulsion is associated with hypersexual interests and behaviors, which could lead some individuals away from a commitment to one's partner toward involvement in extramarital sexual relations or affairs.

By examining the types of sexual dysfunction depicted in Table 11.1, it is possible to discern the high risk that most couples will encounter sexual dissatisfaction or disorder. The sexual problem has in the typical case a mixed etiology with organic and psychogenic factors. Although organic etiology is associated with individual contributing factors, every sexual dysfunction represents a dyadic problem. The sexual difficulty may reflect underlying emotional and relational issues or contribute to emerging marital problems in a couple formerly satisfied with their relationship. Specific sexual dysfunctions are grouped according to phase in the sexual response cycle: desire, arousal, orgasm, and resolution. Before addressing counseling interventions for specific sexual dysfunctions, it is helpful to consider known characteristics of Latino couples because unique resources and needs can be taken into consideration in treatment.

STRENGTHS AND NEEDS OF LATINO COUPLES

Professional literature and clinical experience, especially the cases of Masters and Johnson Institute, indicate some special considerations concerning sexual counseling with Latino couples. Certain characteristics are related to participation of Latino or Hispanic men and women in counseling and psychotherapy. Other considerations reflect the influence of Latino cultural values upon sexuality and intimacy. Individual and couple factors contribute to the identification of Latino strengths and needs in sexual counseling.

Sexual counselors will need to attend to general cultural considerations in offering services to Latino couples. *Familismo* refers to the valuing of close family ties because many Latinos come from very cohesive families with multigenerational connections (Dingfelder, 2005, p. 59). Based on a couple's experience with *familismo*, discussing family problems with a stranger could be considered disloyal. However, close family ties can provide a strong support system and motivation to use available help. Dingfelder (pp. 58–61) has described some other cultural considerations.

Simpatia is related to a desire for interpersonal harmony or smooth relations. Unlike mainstream American culture, Latinos may view assertion and confrontation as negative or disrespectful. *Respeto* involves deference and respect to individuals in positions of authority. *Respeto* could contribute to accepting expert opinion and implementing changes recommended by the sexual counselor. Complementing the potential benefits of expert power in treatment is the relational power of disclosure. In *personalismo*, close and friendly relationships require sharing from one another's lives. Sexual counseling process and outcome can be facilitated through counselor self-disclosure of small details from his or her life (Dingfelder, 2005, p. 59). In this manner, the counselor is able to join with the Latino couple, opening the channel of communication, securing necessary data, and making effective treatment recommendations.

Specific cultural considerations relate to Latino strengths and needs in sexual counseling. Many of the specific characteristics are associated with the tendency to adhere to gender roles as portrayed within the traditionally patriarchal Latino culture. Latino couples who may be dealing with financial demands and other family adjustments tend to be pragmatic about love and less idealistic about sex (Contreras, Hendrick, & Hendrick 1996).

Traditional and religious couples may receive scripts from their parents and the church that marriage is a sacrament, sexuality is reserved for marriage, and marital sexuality is intended to produce children. Sex outside marriage and procreation is bound to guilt and unsafe sexual practices. Guilt associated with premarital and extramarital sexual contacts contributes to resistance to birth control and condom use. Consequently, Latinos have HIV/AIDS rates three times higher than non-Hispanic White men; Latinas have 6.5 times higher rates than non-Hispanic White women (Zambrana, Cornelius, Boykin, & Lopez, 2004, p. 1152). Two thirds of the cases were caused by heterosexual intercourse. In addition, Latina adolescents now present adolescent pregnancy rates higher than those of African American and Anglo American teens (Erickson, 2003). Erickson noted that the scripting of gender roles contributed to lack of planning and protection in initial sexual experiences, leading to high rates of teen pregnancy and STDs.

Latino boys described sex as a powerful, irresistible experience in which abstinence is a threat to self-image and sex with prostitutes is acceptable because there is no responsibility (Morales, 2003). Single and married immigrants, especially when they were separated from their families, engaged in frequent extramarital sex and contacts with prostitutes (Guilamo-Ramos, Jaccard, Pena, & Goldberg, 2005; Viadro & Earp, 2000). For many Latino adolescents and adults, sexual outlet is inevitable and risky for themselves and their partners.

Latina girls felt pressured by their boyfriends, peers, and older siblings to have sex in early adolescence, typically by 15 years of age (Aarons & Jenkins,

2002). Latinas had difficulty discussing safe sex practices because of power imbalances with their partners (Harvey, Beckman, & Bird, 2003; Harvey, Beckman, Browner, & Sherman, 2002). Latinas were unlikely to label coercive sexual experiences, including sexual harassment and rape, as abusive (Cortina, 2004; Lira, Koss, & Russo, 1999; Iturrioz, 2000). They did not disclose sexual abuse because of the importance of remaining a virgin, the taboo nature of sex, and self-blame or guilt (Iterrioz).

Traditional (less acculturated) Latinas favored large families (Unger & Molina, 2000). They were primarily involved in decision making about household matters and children (Harvey et al., 2002). Adolescent girls who talked with their mothers about dating and sexual experiences reported good maternal relationships and conservative attitudes about premarital sex (Romo, Lefkowitz, Sigman, & Au, 2001, 2002). Traditional teens, with higher levels of religiosity, were likely to delay sexual involvement (Hardy & Raffaelli, 2003). Similarly, family connectedness, as measured by knowledge of family stories, predicted less sexual risk taking (Landau, Cole, Tuttle, Clements, & Stanton, 2000). Traditional Latino family values produce benefits and risks with respect to sexuality.

Latinas may feel compelled to be sexual with their boyfriends or husbands because of the power imbalances in the relationship. They are vulnerable to STDs, HIV/AIDS, teenage pregnancy, sexual harassment, and sexual abuse. Due to exaggerated gender role expectations, Hispanic girls and women may not disclose their concerns, fearing judgment or experiencing guilt for not being virginal. Traditional Latinas are encouraged to be oriented to family and children. When girls enjoy open communication with their mothers about dating, marriage, and sexuality, they tend to resist pressures to become sexual and delay first intercourse. Teens who are religious and connected closely to their families may be protected from the disorganizing aspects of majority society: maintaining abstinence or avoiding risky sexual practices.

Latino boys and men receive very different sex role socialization and conditioning. They may be encouraged by peers and older males to express their manhood through sexual outlet. They exert control over decision making about sexual outlet in their relationships. Some Latinos may not perceive sex with prostitutes or extramarital sexual relations as unacceptable. In fact, sex outside the context of an intimate or committed relationship may be desirable because of the reduced burden of responsibility. Recent immigrants, including married men separated from their wives and families, may engage in risky sexual contacts. Failure to use condoms contributes to relatively high rates of STDs, HIV/AIDS, and teenage pregnancy. Partners of Latino men who engage in risky behavior are vulnerable to infection.

Some of the promises and pitfalls of Latino cultural values extend to the gender role scripts of *machismo* and *marianismo* (i.e., model of Mary). *Marianismo* reflects the close ties between Latino cultural values and Catholicism. Latinas who follow the model of Mary express piety, purity, and self-sacrifice (Cofresi, 2002; Koss, 1997). *Marianismo* provides the traditional code for sexual behavior of Latinas, specifying chastity before marriage, sexual passivity in the marriage, and deference to the husband (Cofresi).

Machismo is a robust, multidimensional construct (Torres, Solberg, & Carlstrom, 2002). Although some emphasize the recent confusion of "macho" with *machismo*, emphasizing the dominating and aggressive connotations of the label, machismo actually has beneficial and humanitarian aspects (Bacigalupe, 2000, pp. 39–44). Machismo is rooted in the desire of the Latino to support and protect his family. A truly masculine man is responsible and honorable. He wishes to maintain *"dignidad"* (dignity) in his relations with others. He values the community or network of support among men (*"compadrazco"*), although this sense of connection may be threatened by the individualism of dominant American society. Men who are operating under the influence of machismo may wish to maintain privacy, especially about family matters and deep emotions (Bacigalupe). However, it is possible to transcend the machismo and explore individual variations on the theme of masculinity (Beattie, 2002; Torres et al., 2002).

Bacigalupe (2000, pp. 47–49) recommended accepting the strengths of *machismo* in joining with the Latino man and, by implication, the couple. The counselor should not rush the interview or ask probing questions. It may be useful to communicate without clearly defined goals at the outset of counseling. Also, the counselor should be prepared to accept some loud or fervent speech and to accept the vigorous sharing of ideas in seeking communal, "familocentric" solutions to problems.

In order to avoid premature termination of counseling, a major risk in serving Latinos, it is important to be open and honest. Trust building is facilitated by counselor self-disclosure, as well as use of "*dichos*" (insightful sayings or slogans) and stories (Diaz-Martinez, 1999). Psychoeducational and cognitive–behavioral approaches may be preferred by Latino individuals and couples (Pastor, 2003; Tiago De Melo, 1998). Latinas will likely be the ones to disclose issues related to family issues, sexuality, and gender roles (Diaz-Martinez). Women may have some difficulty in reporting various sexual behaviors to an older man (Wilson, Brown, Meija, & Lavori, 2002). Men who are interviewed by women may minimize or deny the extent of extramarital sexual activities. However, Latinos are able to discuss visits to prostitutes and other sexual exploits openly with male counselors (Pastor).

Latino gender roles affect individual choices, marital dynamics, sexual interactions, and family issues. *Machismo* and *marianismo* also influence the extent to which the partners are engaged in the counseling process. The Latina may motivate the couple to come to sex counseling and she may introduce the problems to the counselor. However, it is likely that her husband or male partner, in a committed heterosexual relationship, will assume leadership:

guiding the communication process, perhaps arguing at times, and speaking for other family members with their best interests at heart.

SEXUAL COUNSELING INTERVENTIONS

Sexual counseling with Latino couples involves recognizing cultural preferences for communication and interaction, joining with the husband and wife (or man and woman in a committed relationship) in an appropriate manner, and addressing relevant relational and sexual concerns. The dual gender, cotherapy model of Masters and Johnson Institute would be ideal: the woman speaking with the female counselor and the man disclosing more freely to the male counselor. If only one counselor were available, then the process would be facilitated best by a man. Contrary to typical counseling practices, it would be acceptable for the husband or male partner to speak for his wife or family members. In addition, the respectful counselor would not direct the conversation toward rapid problem definition. Rather, the counselor would follow the lead of the male client, conversing in a friendly, familiar manner and making relevant self-disclosures (Bean, Perry, & Bedell, 2001).

There are several core components of sexual counseling in addition to the basic interventions of sexual therapy, which include authoritative pronouncement, roundtable, and sensate focus. Virginia Johnson of Masters and Johnson Institute contributed communication techniques to augment the touching exercises (Masters & Johnson, 1970). She advocated "I language" assertion so that women could express their thoughts and feelings. The sexual counselor must help the Latina express herself in a respectful, effective manner.

If the Latina embraces the traditions of self-sacrifice and duty, the couple may require help understanding that their sexual fulfillment will be based on the wife's ability to share with her husband in the safety of counseling and the privacy of their intimate relationship. Treatment of several female sexual dysfunctions, especially hypoactive sexual desire, involves assertion and sexual self-responsibility (Heiman, Epps, & Ellis, 1995; Schwartz & Masters, 1988).

She cannot say enthusiastically "Yes!" to sex because she is unable to say "No." The traditional Latina can be respectful to her husband and negotiate her sexual "duties" so that she does not feel coerced or used. Her husband can assist with her treatment by aligning with the counselor who gives the Latina permission to define aspects of her sexuality. If the female cotherapist is available, she can provide sex education and encouragement to explore eroticism. Negotiating inclusive and exclusive sexual boundaries (e.g., including various types of sexual outlets rather than relying only upon intercourse) affords opportunities for the couple to address the power imbalances in their traditional relationship indirectly.

Relationship contracting is another technique in sexual counseling that addresses power imbalances, repressed anger, and withdrawal or withholding.

According to the method described by Sager (1976), each partner individually prepares an ideal relationship contract, with at least three wants, needs, or preferences across 16 domains of married life. For example, the husband and wife will identify global and specific behaviors for themselves as well as for each other in various domains including finances, parenting, in-laws, friends, career, leisure, and religious life. Most couples present greatest differences in the domains of finances and sexuality. After completing the ideal contracts independently, the couple meets with the sexual counselor, who compares the "terms" and highlights areas of common interest. Then, the counselor helps the couple address expectations in each of the domains in the committed relationship. The couple negotiates the terms of a shared or joint relational contract—initially, through quid pro quo and later according to areas of individual strengths.

Relationship contracting adjusts boundaries so that the couple can enjoy greater intimacy. The shared relational contract is a guide for optimal functioning. The contract may be written, thus becoming a resource for conflict resolution and ongoing negotiation. Given the traditional Latino couple's preference for cognitive behavioral approaches, contracting should be an acceptable, relevant framework for conducting sexual counseling. Relationship contracting unearths some intrapsychic mechanisms based on early life experiences, as well as patterns of relational behavior that could represent reenactments of unfinished business or family-of-origin issues.

Although the sexual counselor may help the clients explore the underlying dynamics, it is generally not necessary. By encouraging homework, including written assignments, focused discussions, and touching exercises, the sexual counselor should be able to facilitate the change process without time-consuming exploration of individual issues. Depth-oriented counseling could lead to premature termination of counseling. The skillful counselor can neutralize roadblocks, even those based on unfinished business (e.g., neglect or abuse in childhood), through careful pacing and tailored homework.

The sexual counselor weaves a delicate fabric of ongoing diagnosis or problem specification with neutralizing roadblocks to intimacy through systematic homework. The counselor takes into account individual issues, patterns of relating, and shared resources. Sexual counseling is focused on a solution and enlists especially narrative approaches (see Freedman & Combs, 1996; White & Epston, 1990). The experienced counselor uses *dichos*, slogans, stories, and self-disclosures to overcome resistance and long-standing roadblocks to intimacy. Frequently, it is necessary to integrate sexual counseling with medical treatment for particular sexual dysfunctions.

Erectile dysfunction (ED) is the most common sexual problem presented in medical settings (Kellett, 1995). Several options are available for medical management of ED: Viagra (sildenafil citrate, a smooth muscle relaxer) or related medications, urethral suppository (MUSE or alprostadil), intracavernosal injection (Caverject), vascular microsurgery, and penile prosthesis (Ackerman & Carey, 1995; Morley & Kaiser, 1993). Some traditional Latinos have discovered herbal treatments, such as yohimbine (Guirguis, 1998), for erection problems. Sophisticated laboratory tests and imaging techniques can be used to diagnose organic erectile dysfunction. Yet, these procedures do not take into account the emotional reality of impotence.

The "impotent" man who has lost his masculine power becomes preoccupied with even slight changes in penile tumescence. Men are bombarded with advertisements in print and broadcast media, as well as the Internet, promising to restore manhood, sexual vigor, performance ability, and staying power. The adjectives used in advertising could easily describe the maintenance of a sports car. Masculine men, especially Latinos who have been influenced by modern versions of *machismo*, equate their gender role with sexual capacity. When a man focuses on losses of erection or rigidity, which may be temporary in nature, he anticipates "failure" and experiences irrational and self-defeating thoughts. The irrational thoughts and unrealistic expectations engender performance anxiety that steals blood flow to the penis. Although organic factors may contribute to ED, the syndrome of increasing performance pressure and anxious self-observation may maintain or exacerbate the problem (McCarthy, 1997; Masters & Johnson, 1970).

Interventions for ED typically include some attention to the cognitive distortions and negative self-evaluations that maintain sexual dysfunction. Zilbergeld (1978) delineated the "myths of male sexuality," which are based on a hypermasculine fantasy model of sex that constrains both partners. The myths that a man must orchestrate sex in which he is "hard as steel" and "lasts all night" contribute to erection problems and intimacy barriers. Treatment for ED involves examination of the gender role stereotypes and myths that interfere with sexual fulfillment (Barbach, 1997; McCarthy, 1994, 1997; Zilbergeld). Many men are surprised to discover that an erect penis is not a requirement for satisfying sex.

Sexual counseling for erectile dysfunction builds on the relaxing experience of sensate focus. By the third set of sensate focus homework exercises, the couple learns that a satisfying sexual outlet can occur through genital touching in an intimate, romantic context. Gradually, the focus of treatment is shifted to containment of the soft penis in the vagina, followed by gentle thrusting with the female astride. The therapeutic exercises are graduated to desensitize conditioned anxiety and promote sense of hope or accomplishment (Masters & Johnson, 1970).

Sexual counseling homework assignments are paradoxical and produce structural changes in marital systems. The natural sexual function is recovered by shifting the focus away from sex toward intimacy. The means for the man reclaiming his "sexual power" involves giving up control and letting his partner help him (e.g., initiating containment homework). The wife helps her husband and discovers her sexual options in the process. The hands-on nature of sexual counseling initiates a change process facilitated by examining irrational thoughts, exaggerated gender role expectations, and definitions of sexual success or fulfillment. Culturally sensitive counseling facilitates the couple enjoying their sexual relationship within the context of ongoing intimacy.

REFERENCES

Aarons, S. J., & Jenkins, R. R. (2002). Sex, pregnancy, and contraception-related motivators and barriers among Latino and African-American youth in Washington, D.C. *Sex Education*, 2, 5–30.

Abel, G. G., & Osborn, C. (1992). The paraphilias: The extent and nature of sexually deviant and criminal behavior. *Psychiatric Clinics of North America*, 15, 675–687.

Ackerman, M. D., & Carey, M. P. (1995). Psychology's role in the assessment of erectile dysfunction: Historical precedents, current knowledge, and methods. *Journal of Consulting & Clinical Psychology*, 63, 862–876.

American Psychiatric Association. (2000). *Diagnostic and statistical manual of mental disorders* (4th ed., text revision). Washington, D.C.: American Psychiatric Association.

Apfelbaum, B. (1989). Retarded ejaculation: A much misunderstood syndrome. In S. R. Leiblum & R. C. Rosen (Eds.), *Principles and practice of sex therapy: Update for the 1990s* (pp. 168–206). New York: Guilford Press.

Anderson, B. L., & Cyranowski, J. M. (1995). Women's sexuality: Behaviors, responses, and individual differences. *Journal of Consulting and Clinical Psychology*, 63, 891–906.

Bacigalupe, G. (2000). El Latino: Transgressing the macho. In M. T. Flores & G. Carey (Eds.) *Family therapy with Hispanics: Toward appreciating diversity* (pp. 29–57). Boston: Allyn & Bacon.

Bancroft, J. (2002). The medicalization of female sexual dysfunction: The need for caution. *Archives of Sexual Behavior*, 31, 451-455.

Barbach, L. (1997). *Loving together: Sexual enrichment program*. Bristol, PA: Brunner/Mazel.

Bean, R. A., Perry, B. J., & Bedell, T. M. (2001). Developing culturally competent marriage and family therapists: Guidelines for working with Hispanic families. *Journal of Marital & Family Therapy*, 27, 43–54.

Beattie, P. M. (2002). Beyond *machismos*: Recent examinations of masculinities in Latin America. *Men & Masculinities*, 4, 303–308.

Burvat, J., Burvat-Herbaut, M., Lemaire, A., Marcolin, G., & Quittelier, E. (1990). Recent developments in the clinical assessment and diagnosis of erectile dysfunction. *Annual Review of Sex Research*, 1, 265–308.

Buber, M. (1923/1970). *I and thou* (W. Kaufmann, Trans.). New York: Scribner's.

Carnes, P. J. (1996). Addiction or compulsion: Politics or illness? *Sexual Addiction & Compulsivity*, 3, 127–150.

Cofresi, N. I. (2002). The influence of *marianismo* on psychoanalytic work with Latinas: Transference and countertransference implications. *Psychoanalytic Study of the Child*, 57, 435–451.

Contreras, R., Hendrick, S. S., & Hendrick, C. (1996). Perspectives on marital love and satisfaction in Mexican-American and Anglo-American couples. *Journal of Counseling & Development*, 74, 408–415.

Cortina, L. M. (2004). Hispanic perspectives on sexual harassment and social support. *Personality & Social Psychology Bulletin, 30*, 570–584.

De Sola Pinto, V., & Roberts, F. W. (1978). *D. H. Lawrence: The complete poems.* New York: Penguin Books.

Diaz-Martinez, A. M. (1999). An exploratory study of Hispanic clinicians' perceptions of Hispanic women in therapy (doctoral dissertation, Rutgers University, 1999). *Dissertation Abstracts International: Section B, 59*, 4458.

Dingfelder, S. F. (2005). Closing the gap for Latino patients. *Monitor on Psychology, 36*, 58–61.

Erickson, P. I. (2003). Cultural factors affecting the negotiation of first sexual intercourse among Latina adolescent mothers. In M. I. Torres & G. P. Cernado (Eds.), *Sexual and reproductive health promotion in Latino populations: Parteras, promotos y poetas: Case studies across the Americas* (pp. 63–79). Amityville, NY: Baywood Publishing Co.

Freedman, J., & Combs, G. (1996). Narrative therapy: The social construction of preferred realities. New York: W. W. Norton.

Guilamo-Ramos, V., Jaccard, J., Pena, J., & Goldberg, V. (2005). Acculturation-related variables, sexual initiation, and subsequent sexual behavior among Puerto Rican, Mexican, and Cuban youth. *Health Psychology, 24*, 88–95.

Guirguis, W. (1998). Oral treatment of erectile dysfunction: From herbal remedies to designer drugs. *Journal of Sex and Marital Therapy, 24*, 69–73.

Hardy, S. A., & Raffaelli, M. (2003). Adolescent religiosity and sexuality: An investigation of reciprocal influences. *Journal of Adolescence, 26*, 731–739.

Harvey, S. M., Beckman, L. J., & Bird, S. T. (2003). Feeling powerful in heterosexual relationships: Cultural beliefs among couples of Mexican origin. *Culture, Health & Sexuality, 5*, 321–327.

Harvey, S. M., Beckman, L. J., Browner, C. H., & Sherman, C. A. (2002). Relationship power, decision making and sexual relations: An exploratory study with couples of Mexican origin. *Journal of Sex Research, 39*, 284–291.

Hawton, K., Catalan, J., & Fagg, J. (1992). Sex therapy for erectile dysfunction: Characteristics of couples, treatment outcome, and prognostic factors. *Archives of Sexual Behavior, 21*, 161–175.

Heiman, J. R., Epps, P. H., & Ellis, B. (1995). Treating sexual desire disorders in couples. In N. S. Jacobson & A. S. Gurman (Eds.), *Clinical handbook of couple therapy* (pp. 471–495). New York: Guilford.

Heiman, J. R., & LoPiccolo, L. (1988). *Becoming orgasmic: A sexual growth program for women.* New York: Prentice Hall.

Hirst, J. F., & Watson, J. P. (1997). Therapy for sexual and relationship problems: The effects on outcome of attending as an individual or as a couple. *Sexual and Marital Therapy, 12*, 321–337.

Iturrioz, M. V. (2000). Disclosure by Latinas of childhood sexual abuse (Doctoral dissertation, California School of Professional Psychology–Berkeley, 2000). *Dissertation Abstracts International: Section B, 61*, 2764.

Jacobson, N. S., & Christensen, A. (1996). *Integrative couple therapy: Promoting acceptance and change.* New York: W. W. Norton.

Kaplan, H. S. (1979). *Disorders of sexual desire.* New York: Brunner/Mazel.

Kaplan, H. S. (1983). *The evaluation of sexual disorders: Psychological and medical aspects.* New York: Brunner/Mazel.

Kellett, J.M. (1995). Functions of a sexual dysfunction clinic. *International Review of Psychiatry, 7*, 183–190.

Kinzl, J. F., Mangwerth, B., Traweger, C., & Biebl, W. (1996). Sexual dysfunctions in males: Significance of adverse childhood experiences. *Child Abuse and Neglect, 20*, 759–766.

Koss, J. D. (1997). The Maria paradox: How Latinas can merge old world traditions with new world self esteem. *Cultural Diversity & Mental Health, 3*, 156–157.

Landau, J., Cole, R. E., Tuttle, J., Clements, C. D., & Stanton, M. D. (2000). Family connectedness and women's sexual risk behaviors: Implications for the prevention/intervention of STD/HIV infection. *Family Process, 39*, 461–475.

Leiblum, S. R., Pervin, L. A., & Campbell, E. H. (1989). The treatment of vaginismus: Success and failure. In S. R. Leiblum & R. C. Rosen (Eds.), *Priniciples and practice of sex therapy: Update for the 1990s* (pp. 113–140). New York: Guilford Press.

Lira, L. R., Koss, M. P., & Russo, N. F. (1999). Mexican-American women's definitions of rape and sexual abuse. *Hispanic Journal of Behavioral Sciences, 21*, 236–265.

Lobitz, W. C., & Lobitz, G. K. (1996). Resolving the sexual intimacy paradox: A developmental model for the treatment of sexual desire disorders. *Journal of Sex and Marital Therapy, 22*, 71–84.

MacPhee, D. C., Johnson, S. M., & van der Veer, M. M. C. (1995). Low sexual desire in women: The effects of marital therapy. *Journal of Sex and Marital Therapy, 21*, 159–182.

Masters, W. H., & Johnson, V. E. (1966). *Human sexual response.* Boston: Little, Brown & Co.

Masters, W. H., & Johnson, V. E. (1970). *Human sexual inadequacy.* Boston: Little, Brown & Co.

McCabe, M. P., & Cobain, M. J. (1998). The impact of individual and relationship factors on sexual dysfunction among males and females. *Sexual and Marital Therapy, 13*, 133–143.

McCarthy, B. W. (1994). Etiology and treatment of early ejaculation. *Journal of Sex and Marital Therapy, 20*, 5–6.

McCarthy, B. W. (1997). Chronic sexual dysfunction: Assessment, intervention, and realistic expectations. *Journal of Sex Education & Therapy, 22*, 51–56.

McCarthy, B. W. (2001). Relapse prevention strategies and techniques with erectile dysfunction. *Journal of Sex & Marital Therapy, 27*, 1–8.

Meana, M., & Binik, Y. M. (1994). Painful coitus: A review of female dyspareunia. *Journal of Nervous and Mental Disease, 182*, 264–272.

Morales, (2003). Sex and sexuality among New York's Puerto Rican youth. *Journal of HIV/AIDS Prevention & Education for Adolescents & Children, 5*, 165–167.

Moret, L. B., Glaser, B. A., Page, R. C., Bargeron, E. F. (1998). Intimacy and sexual satisfaction in unmarried couple relationships: A pilot study. *The Family Journal: Counseling and Therapy for Couples and Families, 6*, 33–39.

Morley, J. E., & Kaiser, F. E. (1993). Impotence: The internist's approach to diagnosis and treatment. *Advances in Internal Medicine, 38*, 151–168.

Moser, C. (1992). Lust, lack of desire, and paraphilias: Some thoughts and possible connections. *Journal of Sex and Marital Therapy, 18*, 65–69.

Pastor, J. A. (2003). Latino clinicians' perceptions of Latino men in psychotherapy: An exploratory study (doctoral dissertation, Rutgers University, 2003). *Dissertation Abstracts International: Section B, 63*, 3933.

Pfizer (1998, May). *The new facts of life.* (Videotape and brochure, HX728F97). (Available from Pfizer U.S. Pharmaceuticals, 235 East 42nd Street, New York, NY 10017–5755).

Read, J. (1995). Female sexual dysfunction. *International Review of Psychiatry, 7,* 175–182.

Reynolds, B. S. (1977). Psychological treatment models and outcome results for erectile dysfunction. *Psychological Bulletin, 84,* 1218–1238.

Romo, L. F., Lefkowitz, E. S., Sigman, M., & Au, T. K. (2001). Determinants of mother–adolescent communication about sex in Latino families. *Adolescent & Family Health, 2,* 72–82.

Romo, L. F., Lefkowitz, E. S., Sigman, M., & Au, T. K. (2002). A longitudinal study of maternal messages about dating and sexuality and their influence on Latino adolescents. *Journal of Adolescent Health, 31,* 59–69.

Rosen, R. C., & Leiblum, S. R. (1995). Treatment of sexual disorders in the 1990s: An integrated approach. *Journal of Consulting and Clinical Psychology, 63,* 877–890.

Sager, C. J. (1976). Marriage contracts and couple therapy: Hidden forces in intimate relationships. Oxford, England: Brunner/Mazel.

Sarwer, D.B., & Durlak, J.A. (1996). Childhood sexual abuse as a predictor of adult female sexual dysfunction: A study of couples seeking sex therapy. *Child Abuse & Neglect, 20,* 963-972.

Sarwer, D. B., & Durlak, J. A. (1997). A field trial of the effectiveness of behavioral treatment for sexual dysfunction. *Journal of Sex and Marital Therapy, 23,* 87–97.

Schnarch, D. (1997). Passionate marriage: Sex, love, and intimacy in emotionally committed relationships. New York: W. W. Norton.

Schwartz, M. F. (1996). Reenactment related to bonding and hypersexuality. *Sexual Addiction and Compulsivity, 3,* 195–212.

Schwartz, M. F., & Masters, W. H. (1988). Inhibited sexual desire: The Masters and Johnson Institute treatment model. In S. R. Leiblum & R. C. Rosen (Eds.), *Sexual desire disorders* (pp. 229–242). New York: Guilford Press.

Seagraves, R. T. (1998). Antidepressant induced sexual dysfunction. *Journal of Clinical Psychiatry, 59,* 48–54.

Sigusch, V. (1998). The neosexual revolution. *Archives of Sexual Behavior, 27,* 331–359.

Spector, I. P., & Carey, M. P. (1990). Incidence and prevalence of the sexual dysfunctions: A critical review of the empirical literature. *Archives of Sexual Behavior, 19,* 389–408.

Steege, J. F., & Ling, F. W. (1993). Dyspareunia: A special type of chronic pelvic pain. *Obstetrics and Gynecology Clinics of North America, 20,* 779–793.

Tiago De Melo, J. A. (1998). Factors relating to Hispanic and non-Hispanic white Americans' willingness to seek psychotherapy (doctoral dissertation, Columbia University, 1998). *Dissertation Abstracts International: Section B, 59,* 2440.

Tiefer, L. (1991). Historical, scientific, clinical, and feminist criticisms of "the human sexual response cycle" model. *Annual Review of Sex Research, 2,* 1–23.

Tiefer, L. (2001). Arriving at the "new view" of women's sexual problems: Background, theory, and activism. *Women & Therapy, 24,* 63–98.

Torres, J. B., Solberg, S. H., & Carlstrom, A. H. (2002). The myth of sameness among Latin men and their machismo. *American Journal of Orthopsychiatry, 72,* 163–181.

Unger, J. B., & Molina, G. B. (2000). Acculturation and attitudes about contraceptive use among Latina women. *Health Care for Women International, 21,* 235–249.

Viadro, C. I., & Earp, J. A. L. (2000). The sexual behavior of married Mexican immigrant men in North Carolina. *Social Science & Medicine, 50,* 723–735.

Weis, D. L. (1998). Conclusion: The state of sexual theory. *Journal of Sex Research, 35,* 100–114.

White, M., & Epston, D. (1990). *Narrative means to therapeutic ends.* New York: W. W. Norton.

Wilsnack, S. C., Vogeltanz, N. D., Klassen, A. D., & Harris, T. R. (1997). Childhood sexual abuse and women's substance abuse: National survey findings. *Journal of studies on Alcoholism, 58,* 264–271.

Wilson, S. R., Brown, N. L., Meija, C., & Lavori, P. (2002). Effects of interviewer characteristics on reported sexual behavior of California Latino couples. *Hispanic Journal of Behavioral Sciences, 24,* 38–62.

Wincze, J. P., & Carey, M. P. (1991). *Sexual dysfunction: A guide for assessment and treatment.* New York: Guilford Press.

Wylie, K. R. (1997). Treatment outcome of a brief couple therapy in psychogenic male erectile dysfunction. *Archives of Sexual Behavior, 26,* 527–545.

Zambrana, R. E., Cornelius, L. J., Boykin, S. S., & Lopez, D. S. (2004). Latinas and HIV/AIDS risk factors: Implications for harm reduction strategies. *American Journal of Public Health, 94,* 1152–1158.

Zilbergeld, B. (1978). *Male sexuality: A guide to sexual fulfillment.* Boston: Little, Brown & Co.

Zilbergeld, B., & Evans, M. (1980). The inadequacy of Masters & Johnson. *Psychology Today,* June, 28–43.

PART III

Research and Conclusions

CHAPTER 12

Contemporary Issues and Research

ROBERT L. SMITH, NADIA BAKIR, AND RICHARD J. RICARD

INTRODUCTION

In the late 1980s and early 1990s, many popular publications were forecasting the time as the decade of the Latino in academic, economic, and political settings (Arredondo & Perez, 2003; Garcia-Preto, 1996). This did not occur, however, and Latinos were confronted with additional barriers, especially those who were immigrants. Legislation was imposed against bilingualism and affirmative action. This and other forms of exclusion served to worsen the troubling dropout rate of school-age Latino children at the time.

Structural changes in the contemporary U.S. economy (e.g., the movement of employment opportunities away from the states in which large Hispanic populations reside, community social disorganization, and the grave decline of public education) are serious challenges that threaten the well-being of countless Latino families (Vega, 1995). The repercussions are inducing a destabilization among low-income Latino families in various ways:

- Unemployment and underemployment are causing instability in income levels.
- Job seeking in other locations is causing the extended absence of family members.

- Employment conditions are leading to demoralization.
- Preoccupation about the well-being of children is prevalent as they are reluctantly left in unsafe environments lacking child care or suitable recreational amenities.
- Feelings of lack of opportunity, isolation, and racial enmity from non-Hispanics are increasing.

The need to better appreciate and address the mental health issues of Latino families is highlighted by the discrepancy between the pressing needs of Latinos for mental health services and the barriers keeping this group from access to such services (Kouyoumdjian, Zamboanga, & Hansen, 2003). At present, we know that effective therapy with Latino families requires consideration of the group's complex experiences in this country, including issues of race, gender, education, socioeconomic status, sociocultural history, acculturation, and more. However, reliable and consistent information within marriage and family therapy (MFT) literature for working exclusively with Latino families (Bean, Perry, & Bedell, 2001) is still lacking.

CONTEMPORARY ISSUES

Changing Patterns in American Family Structure

Over the last few decades, families have witnessed a dramatically changing world. Advances in technology, health, and other realms have allowed them more opportunities and choices than ever before (Sanchez, 2001). Along with these advances has come a change in the family composition. Whereas traditional nuclear families were once commonplace in society, families consisting of single individuals (especially women) and unwed couples are now increasing (Ortiz, 1995).

Latino and other minority families experience the same shifts as their majority counterparts, only with different results due to the added strains that arise from immigration, assimilation, and/or acculturation processes (Falicov, 1988; Sanchez, 2001; Sluzki, 1979; Szapocznik, Santisteban, Kurtines, Perez-Vidal, & Hervis, 1984). For example, being a Hispanic female and heading a family with children can have an impact on the economic security and status of the family because female-headed households have been shown to have lower income levels than families in general (Ortiz, 1995). Economic stressors may be contributing to the decrease of the two-parent Latino family and the augmenting feminization of poverty in certain areas of the Latino population, with grave implications for the welfare of Latino children (Vega, 1995).

Ethnic families are likely to confront stressful challenges as they attempt to survive and succeed in the majority culture (Falicov, 1988; Sanchez, 2001; Sluzki, 1979; Szapocznik et al., 1984). Nonetheless, Latino families and their extended networks have continuously demonstrated flexibility and adaptability in response to the poverty, immigrant adjustment, minority status, and acculturation stress inherent in their social history in the United States (Vega, 1995). The difference found in contemporary U.S. society is that American affluence is declining, the labor market for unskilled and semiskilled workers is decreasing, public education is deteriorating, and Latino population growth is contributing to existing resentment that many citizens harbor about immigration (Vega, 1995).

Vega contends that the relationship among disrupted families, economically strained environments with routine unemployment, and the rise in female-headed households are important trends to understand because changing family structures may represent the most important issue in the study of Latino family viability in the United States. She also suggests that current trends imply that this shift in the Latino family structure (from married to cohabitating partners, from nuclear to non-nuclear families, and toward female-headed households with children) may increase even more markedly in the near future. Also noteworthy is her postulation that changes in family structures, such as marital disruption (e.g., separation, divorce, or widowhood) and cohabitation, will have a significant impact on the efficiency of family-based socialization and the redefinition of Latino familism.

Changing Latino Demographics and Immigration

Legal as well as undocumented immigration has been the primary source of Latino population growth for decades; first generation presently (foreign-born) outnumbers the second and third-plus generations (Fry & Lowell, 2002; Suro & Passel, 2003). The majority of contemporary Latino migrants have been young adults in their child-bearing years (Pew, 2005; Suro & Passel, 2003). In 2000, the mean age of first-generation Latinos was 33.4 compared to 38.5 for non-Hispanic Whites. In addition, the fertility rate of Latinas was 3.51 births per woman, which greatly surpassed the 1.84 rate of their White counterparts, as well as that of any U.S. population segment. Many native-born Latinos today are the children of recent immigrants who, like their foreign-born parents, tend to be young and have high fertility rates (Acuña, 2003). This second generation of Latinos is expected to become the group's main source of growth over the next few decades, exceeding that of first-generation Hispanic immigrants. By 2020, the number of second-generation Latinos is expected to double in U.S. schools and triple in the U.S. labor force (Suro & Passel, 2003).

These facts have important implications for counselors, considering the significant differences between foreign-born and native-born (first-generation versus second-generation) Latinos in terms of English proficiency, education, income, and attitudes (Pew, 2005; Suro & Passel, 2003). This was recently confirmed through a series of national surveys, which found English- and Spanish-dominant Latinos to have markedly different attitudes toward controversial issues, including divorce, abortion, and homosexuality. English-dominant Latinos were found to have attitudes similar to those of the dominant U.S. culture, but the views of the Spanish-dominant group set them apart (Pew).

The rapid increase of Latino children in schools is also expected to continue. Fortunately, they seem to be fairing better, with increasing numbers finishing high school and moving on to college. Still, they continue to fall behind White students in all important educational domains. In high school, the curriculum assigned to Latino youth tends to be less demanding, which may account for their lower averages on national assessment tests and college entrance exams. Despite their significant academic improvements, the likelihood of Latino students completing college remains much lower than that of their White peers (Pew, 2005).

Latino Ethnic Identity

Ethnicity refers to a mutual heritage through which people have developed common values and customs, transmitted by virtue of its deep connection to the family (McGoldrick & Giordano, 1996). Ethnicity is a crucial determinant of ethnic identity because feelings of belonging and historical endurance are basic psychological necessities. The notion of a group's "peoplehood" stems from the combination of cultural history, race, and religion, which is sustained regardless of whether members are aware of their commonalities (McGoldrick & Giordano, 1996).

According to Vera and Quintana's (2004) meta-analysis of relevant empirical studies (Aboud, 1987; Bernal, Knight, Ocampo, & Cota, 1990; Bernal, Knight, Ocampo, Garza, & Cota 1993; Phinney & Chavira, 1995; Pizarro & Vera, 2001; Quintana, Ybarra, Gonzalez-Doupe, & De Baessa, 2000; Rotherman & Phinney, 1987), researchers seem to suggest that ethnic identity formation for Latinos involves a unique integration of self-identification, phenotypical features, primary and secondary cultural variables, interethnic and intraethnic interactions and attitudes, and a consciousness of one's ethnic group. According to the authors, each of the aforementioned variables lends itself to the psychological experience and expression of ethnicity by Latinos. Although contextual elements (e.g., family, community, and academic variables) are believed to have an impact on the relative significance of any one of these variables, the precise makeup of each may be influenced by two broad elements that affect identity development in Latinos: social cognitive maturation and ethnic socialization. These aspects, although interconnected, merit separate attention because each contributes to the ethnic identity of children.

Numerous studies concerning the self-identification of children contain implications about the development of Hispanic or Mexican American labels (e.g., Bernal et al., 1993; Hirschfeld, 1994; Matute-Bianchi, 1986; Quintana, 1994). Some believe that the ethnic term that young children initially pick up as a self-identifier may reveal the setting in which the label was learned. In particular, Quintana found that young children self-identified as Hispanic stated that they learned this term at school, and those self-identified as Mexican American said they had learned the term from their families. It is therefore clear, as Vera and Quintana assert, that early application of an ethnic label stems from the way in which children were taught or socialized by others to label themselves.

The nature of the Hispanic identity is further complicated by the *Mestizo* and *Criollo* ancestry of Latino subgroups (African, Asian, Native American, and European), which predisposes them to a range of phenotypical features (Arredondo & Perez, 2003; Vera & Quintana, 2004). The degree of discrimination experienced by Latinos is influenced to varying degrees by these physical features (Arredondo & Perez, 2003; Vera & Quintana, 2004) because those who look more Caucasian are likely to experience less discrimination than those appearing more indigenous (Arredondo & Perez, 2003; Vera & Quintana, 2004). Some of the literature examining ethnic and racial distinctions among Latinos has focused on the influence of racism on issues related to the quality of Latino life. Several have discovered correlations, along a continuum, among darker skin tone, lower income, lower educational level, and an overall low socioeconomic status (Arce, Murgia, & Frisbie, 1987; Relethford, Stern, Gaskill, & Hazuda, 1983).

An analysis of research has led Cervantes and Sweatt (2004) to conclude that the development of ethnic and racial identity among families is determined by several factors, including additional interethnic and interracial relations, as well as encounters characterized by racism and prejudice. They thereby state that addressing the significance of skin-tone variation and experiences of racism and prejudice within and outside families are crucial to understanding the contexts, beliefs, and values of Chicano families. Increased exposure to prejudice and discrimination increases the likelihood that Latinos will internalize negative sentiments regarding their ethnic identity (McGoldrick & Giordano, 1996). Vera and Quintana (2004) underscore the relevance of phenotype to this discussion, stating that physical appearance forms part of a person's self-concept, thereby affecting his or her ethnic and racial identity.

The next element in Latino ethnic identity consists of their primary cultural characteristics, which include culture-specific behaviors, values, and preferences that stem from their cultural or national origin (Bernal et al., 1993; Ogbu, 1994; Vera & Quintana, 2004). Primary cultural characteristics involve aspects such as language, food preferences, customs, and religious celebrations, among others (Bernal et al., 1993; Vera & Quintana, 2004). Furthermore, behavior of Latino families is guided by social norms and expectations (e.g., *personalismo, dignidad, familismo*) and gender-role socializations (Bernal et al., 1993; Vera & Quintana, 2004). Gender role expectations differ for men and women, and men have been found to adhere to their respective roles more than women do (Ocampo, Bernal, & Knight, 1993). The preservation of these primary cultural characteristics is connected to Latino ethnic identity.

Secondary cultural characteristics develop among Latino minorities in reaction to their exposure with the dominant culture (Ogbu, 1994). These include values, attitudes, and behaviors that arise from experiences of oppression and discrimination such as the national "English-only" movement currently under way (Hamann, Wortham, & Murillo, 2002). In fact, Vera and Quintana (2004) believe that recognition of such discrimination is the most consequential secondary cultural characteristic for this population. Quintana and Vera (1999) discovered elementary school-aged Mexican American children to be aware that they are discriminated against by parents, teachers, police, and government. Wortham (2002, p. 123) describes the "either/or" choice faced by many Latino children and adolescents as "either rejecting the Anglo values of the school and community as 'acting White,' or assimilating to those Anglo values and rejecting their Latino identities."

The awareness of ethnic identity differs widely from one group to another, and even within a single group, depending on individuals' experiences of prejudice and discrimination. In fact, discrimination is a form of interethnic interaction (Vera & Quintana, 2004), making it a significant component in Latino identity development. Minorities who have experienced the stigma of prejudice or discrimination might try to blend into the valued dominant culture (McGoldrick & Giordano, 1996). Many immigrant families feel obliged to reject their heritage, yet they lose a part of their identity in the process. This act of repressing their past makes Latinos increasingly vulnerable to social problems (Hamann et al., 2002; McGoldrick & Giordano, 1996).

Additional insight into the Latino group identity comes from the results of multiple national surveys conducted between 2002 and 2004 by the Pew Hispanic Center in partnership with the Henry J. Kaiser Family Foundation. Survey data revealed that two thirds of the Spanish-dominant, immigrant segment of Latino respondents identified with their countries of origins. It is rare that one's connection to one's native land dissipates completely. Still, a definite pattern exists whereby second- or third-generation Latinos speak more English than Spanish and prefer to identify as "American." The terms "Hispanic" and "Latino" were not found to be appreciated; however, a significant proportion of the project's population (regardless of generation and language preference) still chose to identify with them (Pew Hispanic Center/Kaiser Family Foundation [Pew/Kaiser], 2002). These elements of identity influence the manner in which Latinos relate to each other and to the dominant U.S. society (Pew/Kaiser, 2004).

Very little empirical research has concentrated on intervention strategies to foster positive ethnic identity development in children (Quintana & Vera, 1999; Vera & Quintana, 2004). Nonetheless, the existing studies suggest that family therapy is optimal as an intervention strategy when working with Latino children. Although individual counseling would likely assist Latino children struggling to develop positive ethnic identities, the powerful influence of family in Latino life cannot be denied. Latino parents face their issues of ethnic identity and socialization when deciding how they will approach matters relating to their children's race and ethnicity. Therefore, when assessing the child's identity development needs, helping professionals should explore the ethnic identities of the parents, their goals relating to the ethnic socialization of their children, and family rituals and traditions (Vera & Quintana, 2004).

Immigration

For decades, immigration has been the primary source of the U.S. population's impressive growth (Acuña, 2003; Fry & Lowell, 2002; Lee, Martin, & Fogel, 2005). The population increased by 32.5 million between the 1990 and 2000 censuses, with immigrants (or foreign born) accounting for 11.3 million of this growth (Lee, Martin, & Fogel, 2005). Foreign-born Latinos account for 22,381,207 (6.2%) of the nation's total population, and Mexicans form the largest subgroup (Pew Research Center, 2005). Latinos have come to the United States through legal and illegal immigration, through temporary labor programs, through conquest, and as refugees and asylum seekers. Modes of entrance have important implications regarding socioeconomic and acculturation issues, as well as resulting needs for services (Longres & Patterson, 2000). To work effectively with new Latino arrivals, counselors need an understanding of the challenges faced by these clients as they strive for social and economic security (Longres & Patterson, 2000).

The attitudes of native-born Americans (including Latinos) toward immigration vary greatly. Many welcome Latino culture as a contribution to the diversity of American society, celebrating it with parades, festivals, and other special events. Yet others have more negative attitudes toward immigrant Latinos, believing that their jobs will be stolen and their taxes raised as a result of immigrants (especially Latinos) overusing health, education, and welfare benefits (Balgopal, 2000). The hardships faced by Latino immigrants upon arrival are exacerbated by the resentment of certain hostile residents in the dominant society, due in part to stereotypical myths (Gibson, 2002). Reports reveal that Latino newcomers have been harassed at work, in stores and restaurants, and when walking down the street. They have been criticized for speaking Spanish and have been accused of being violent and dirty, of illegally entering the country, and of taking the jobs of citizens (Gibson; Wortham, Murillo, & Hamann, 2002). Anti-Latino sentiments have sparked initiatives to limit employment opportunities and the use of Spanish as well as access to social services and public schooling (Gibson, 2002).

For many Latinos, the experience of migration may be more markedly influenced by gender. Many married men come to the United States to generate income, leaving their families in their countries of origin. Men who migrate from areas with limited opportunities are often elevated in status by their families and communities because of the prospect of a regular income. However, researchers report that separation from their families leaves these men vulnerable to loneliness and depression (Guendelman & Perez-Itriago, 1987; Longres & Patterson, 2000). Without women undertaking traditional domestic chores for them in their host country, men must perform these tasks. Meanwhile, the families left behind learn to become more autonomous in the absence of the head of the household. Although a significant proportion of migrants are married women coming to join their husbands (Wilson, 1995), once these families reunite, their roles have changed significantly (Longres & Patterson, 2000). Altered gender roles are further amplified by the necessity for many Latina women to work in order to help support their families in the United States (Longres & Patterson, 2000).

Counselors and therapists working with Latino families will find these clients navigating through many of the same struggles as non-Hispanic families. Similarly, they may experience many of the same social problems as other immigrants in the United States, including alcohol and substance abuse, juvenile delinquency, family conflicts, and physical and mental health problems (Balgopal, 2000). However, professionals who have some understanding of these and other potential postmigration strains on Latino immigrant families may find that they are more competent in the delivery of appropriate mental health services.

Acculturation

Culture is the source through which families survive from generation to generation, using traditions and rituals as tools to pass down values, attitudes, and aspirations (Evenson & Evenson, 1991). This serves to reinforce family health by providing family members with a sense of stability, identity, and belonging (Sanchez, 2001). Losing one's culture is somewhat similar to losing one's sense of direction and results in cultural dissonance (Sanchez, 2001). This is particularly significant because cultural dissonance may become externalized in the form of dysfunctional behaviors that compromise the identity, stability, and security of the family (Sanchez, 2001).

The increasing diversity of the U.S. population requires that mental health professionals improve their understanding of the processes that take place when a person must master a new set of cultural norms, the effect of this learning on the person's traditional cultural norms, and how this effect relates to adjustment and well-being (Ponterotto, Costa, & Werner-Lin, 2002). Latino families are caught between at least two cultures and find themselves under continuous pressure to relinquish their values and adjust to the dominant culture (Garcia-Preto, 1996). The difficulty of predicting the effects of acculturation for Latinos is demonstrated by Cuéllar, Siles, & Bracamontes (2004) in their discussion of Chicano acculturation:

[Chicanos] experience different degrees of exposure to these two [Mexican and American] large complex cultural systems over time and integrate different aspects of these cultures throughout their lifespan. There are no fixed outcomes from acculturation processes: They are interdependent, transactional, and ecological and depend on numerous types of variables, including but not limited to environmental and contextual, individual personality, status, sociocultur[al], and political.

Research involving the effects of acculturation on Latino mental health is burgeoning and several themes have been presented. Research findings are presented and the need for additional research on this topic discussed later in this chapter.

Poverty, Unemployment, and Economic Mobility

Poverty is a common lifestyle for many Latinos who migrate to the United States. Even when they are willing to work for next to nothing, jobs are scarce as the economic decline continues for the working class (Longres & Patterson, 2000). Real wages have not increased since 1973 and jobs for skilled and unskilled labor are being eliminated by continuous downsizing and restructuring (Longres & Patterson, 2000).

Garcia-Preto (1996) states that limited access to resources traps Latinos in an oppressive and demoralizing cycle. Aside from the limited job opportunities, she indicates that housing is unaffordable and of substandard quality and that problems of speaking and understanding English additionally serve to retain Latinos on the periphery. She has demonstrated through a number of studies that this is especially the case for dark-skinned Latinos. According to research, dark-skinned Latinos were found to be more segregated from the non-Hispanic population than lighter skinned Latinos and, increasingly, darker skin was correlated with increased difficulty in finding housing and increased likelihood of earning lower wages. Garcia-Preto (1996) especially emphasizes the harmful effects caused by the absence of English-speaking abilities for all Latinos, explaining that, for those unable to speak English, this lowers their potential to earn higher salaries and attain higher paying jobs. However, she concludes by mentioning that the isolation possibly caused by the relegation of many to low-skill-level jobs can be ameliorated through emotional support of friends and family. Improving the prospects of recent immigrants and second- or third-generation Latinos may require very specifically targeted interventions.

RESEARCH

When research is conducted, consideration must be given to the diversity of Latino families. Consequently, assessing the strengths and vulnerabilities of individual Latino families could assist in the formulation of appropriate counseling interventions. Diversity is a subject of increasing importance in the counseling profession; thus, Vera and Quintana (2004) suggest that ethnic identity research and application will become increasingly significant in the examination of the mental health of Latinos and other ethnic minorities. To understand Latino clients, therapists must consider crucial identity issues, including race, gender, age, social class, immigration status, religion, sexual orientation, and disability (McGoldrick & Giordano, 1996). Four topics of research are discussed in this chapter: acculturation or the changing dynamic of the Latino family and cultures; empirical assessment of treatment approaches; methods to improve access for Latinos to mental health services; and training counselors and family therapists in Latino cultural competence.

Acculturation

Acculturation level is best defined as the extent to which an individual adopts the customs and values of a dominant culture (Flores & Heppner, 2002). Acculturation is often operationalized by behavior and thinking changes as a result of contact with a dominant culture as well as the degree to which a native culture's values beliefs, and traditions are retained (Sodowsky, Lai, & Plake, 1991). As discussed previously, studies on the impact of acculturation processes on individual and family variables have resulted in somewhat confusing conclusions (Magana, de la Rocha, Amsel, & Magana, 1996). However, there is a consensus from a number of studies that individuals from later generations tend to be more acculturated (Cuellar, Arnold, & Maldonado, 1995) into the dominant culture than individuals from earlier generations.

Part of the confusion is due to an oversimplification of the concept of acculturation by many researchers (Bean et al., 2001), who have almost uniformly viewed acculturation as a linear process by which immigrants progressively move toward assimilation of a mainstream culture (Portes, 1984). Recent efforts have addressed acculturation as a much more complex developmental process with a different trajectory and perhaps even a different endpoint—one, for example, characterized by various degrees of holding onto one's native culture—and yet accommodating many aspects of the new dominant culture. This more complex model of acculturation has been characterized as bicultural belongingness (Falicov, 1998). By establishing a degree of belongingness in two cultures, immigrant families can maintain a strong native ethnic identity despite the lessening of discrimination against them in the context of the dominant culture.

Therapists and researchers might focus their attention on different levels of acculturation within a single family. This focus might facilitate understanding of the cross pressures that are easily seen between family members who may be at different levels of acculturation, such as the conflict that might exist between parent and children (Gil & Vega, 1996; Szapocznik et al., 1994). For example, research as to how individuals and families negotiate such "contextual belongingness" might provide insight into therapeutic interventions that could be utilized when individuals experience tensions between these multiple functioning contexts. A literature addresses the typical cross pressures that minority adolescents experience between their peers and parents (Steinberg, Dornbusch, & Brown, 1992). This work seems generalizable to individuals at different levels of acculturation who, in their peer contacts, experience rejection from their native peers when they are perceived to be "selling out" to the dominant culture—that is, acting White (Ogbu, 1978).

Identification of normative processes of coping and adjustment of individuals from various degrees of immigrant status and "globally defined acculturation level" is a laudable initial research goal. This goal might be supported by quantitative studies addressing the extent to which factors such as time in the dominant culture and exposure to negative and/or positive pressures to change and assimilate.

In addition, qualitative inquiry into the perceptions of various Latino perspectives on such topics as alienation, perceptions of entrenchment/freedom, and how their native experiences continue to color their perceptions of how they fit in with the new/dominant cultural milieu are fruitful avenues of research that would add to the current body of literature. Finally, serious consideration should be given to how indices of cultural identity (e.g., racial classification, national origin, ethnic identity, language dominance, etc.) might moderate differences in the effectiveness of specific treatment modalities. The existing efforts, relevant issues, and limitations offered as barriers to this type of consideration are addressed in the next section.

Empirical Assessment of Treatment Approaches

Research into the efficacy of specific treatment interventions is perhaps the holy grail of current efforts to advance the fields of counseling, psychotherapy, and family therapy. Like the grail, the importance of this effort for counseling and family therapy practice is heralded almost universally; however, finding empirically sound work is very difficult (Bergin & Garfield, 1992).

There is a paucity of available research with Latino populations. Available results of outcome research—particularly that related to Latino populations—remain small (Bobo, Gilchrist, Cvetkovich, Trimble, & Schinke, 1988; Coatsworth, Santisteban, McBride, & Szapocznik, 2001; Muir, Schwartz, & Szapocznik, 2004; Navarro, 1993; Rosenthal, 2000). These results have allowed few empirically based unequivocal conclusions (Curtis, 1990; Rosenthal, 2000; Sue, Chun, & Gee, 1995). The critical need for additional research is only exacerbated by the almost universal call that therapeutic interventions be conducted and, if needed, adjusted according the culturally relevant dictates of the population for which they are meant to serve (Aguirre & Martinez, 1993).

The often cited meta-analytic reviews (Smith & Glass, 1977; Wampold, Mondin, Moody, Stich, Benson, & Ahn, 1997) conducted over the past three decades have illustrated convincingly that counseling and psychotherapy is effective (Wampold et al., 1997). However, these reviews have focused primarily on "bonafide" techniques and therefore have not addressed the relevance of cultural moderators or culturally specific approaches to treatment efficacy. Consequently, the existing efficacy research has proven to have very little localized impact on the practice and theoretical frameworks underlying current work with Latino populations (Helms, 1990; Sue et al., 1995). This has led many toward the rather pessimistic position that much contemporary thinking about Latinos is clearly grounded in stereotypes and often misinformation that has acquired "spurious validity through constant repetition in the literature" (Ruiz & Padilla, 1977, p. 403). The paucity of available research is in part due to the difficulty in the operationalization of research in ways that provide for valid conclusions (Garfield, 1992; Henry, Strupp, Schacht, & Gaston, 1994).

Challenges and difficulties of conducting research with Latino populations persist. Among issues specifically related to difficulties in conducting efficacy research with Latinos is a lack of appreciation of the true heterogeneity of characteristics possessed by individuals collectively referred to as Latino. The Latino label represents a vast array of individuals from a variety of national, ethnic, racial, and cultural backgrounds (Gilbert, 1989). Scholars state that caution should be exercised when using single labels to identify distinct cultural groups (Baruth & Manning, 1992). Research will continue to be limited and it may be difficult to reach conclusions that represent such a heterogeneous group of individuals.

For example, in a study on the family interaction patterns on engagement and retention in therapy, Santisteban and his colleagues (1996) found a large difference in the engagement and retention rates of clients depending upon their specific ethnic identity classification. The researchers concluded that patterns of interaction that prevent families from engaging in treatment are probably culturally specific. Further research should target specific patterns of interaction in each population and work to develop a theoretical framework for the development of specific therapeutic strategies for addressing these differences.

A concern regarding the generalizability of research with Latino populations is that they are disproportionately represented in the low-income status (Cortese, 1979). This situation has raised the concern that any results may not be so much about the Latino population, but about the population of poverty and would be the same among low-income non-Latino clientele. (See Helms, 1990, for a similar point.) Recent commentaries highlight the importance of maintaining a distinction between the culture of poverty issues from the Latino cultural values and perspective. This represents a formidable challenge for professionals conducting research with ethnic minority populations, who are generally represented disproportionally by low-income members.

What can be generalized from the current empirical base? Not withstanding these limitations, a corpus of research findings has begun to provide an evidence base for culturally specific interventions for Latino populations. These studies generally support the claim that Latinos benefit most when they show up and take full advantage of culturally sensitive family-based therapy (Rosenthal, 2000; Wells et al., 2001).

Treatment Modality

The results of recent research findings justify the historical investment in family-based interventions with Latino populations based on the cultural value of *familismo* (Muir et al., 2004). In one example of this, Szapocznik and his colleagues compared individual psychodynamic child therapy (IPCT) to a structured family therapy (SFT) approach for treatment of adolescent drug use within the family. Results showed that outcomes related to family functioning were much more positive after therapeutic intervention using SFT (Szapocznik et al., 1988). As a general systems theory approach, this family-centered approach illustrated the importance of connection between the therapeutic approach chosen and an important cultural normative belief.

The results seem less clear regarding the benefits of behavior therapy over any other particular modality. Although many interventions are based on the concept that Latinos will benefit more from behavioral or cognitive behavioral approaches than from psychodynamically oriented approaches, the results are mixed (Rosenthal, 2000). This conjecture is based on a number of generalized principles that behavioral techniques represent a better cultural match because they are concrete, focused on the present, and usually more effective in working with lower class clientele (Rosado, 1980). The valuable work by researchers focusing specifically on treatment parameters such as engagement and retention suggests that these might be the important outcome variables for future research endeavors.

Future research should focus on the sociocultural constraints that have limited the development of an adequate literature base in the area of efficacy of treatment with Latino populations. The moderating effect of social and/or linguistic acculturation is perhaps the most fundamental starting point for building an empirically sound research base. Questions need to be asked as to how issues of language use or social acculturation might moderate the effectiveness of previously documented treatment regimes. Recognizing the heterogeneity within the Latino culture, issues of ethnic identity may also play a moderating role in the effectiveness of a given treatment. Migrant status and socioeconomic status(es) are also potential moderating variables that merit research consideration.

Perhaps even more important is the inclusion of process-oriented research designs, which focus on specific components of the ongoing therapeutic environment, and how these affect outcomes. For example, the recognition of culturally specific reactions to counselor disclosure or confrontation within a therapeutic setting may moderate the impact of an intervention.

Improved Access to Mental Health Services

Latinos have very low rates of use of mental health services (Vega & Alegria, 2001). It seems paradoxical that the fastest growing and most highly visible minority group in the United States seems best suited for the epidemiological label of "hard to reach populations." Nonetheless, several major texts have discussed the vast underutilization of mental health of Latinos in the United States. This underutilization phenomenon is valid (Guarnaccia & Martinez, 2002). Studies concerning this topic have focused on barriers that limit the access of Latinos to mental health services.

The most robust finding of the underutilization of mental health services was documented among Mexican Americans from the Los Angeles Catchment Area Study and from the MAPPS (see Guarnaccia & Martinez, 2002). The MAPP results showed that non-Hispanic Whites were seven times more likely to use outpatient mental health service than Mexicans who spoke mostly Spanish. In addition, Mexicans who were less acculturated had very low use of any services that might address mental health problems. These findings are consistent with previous research findings indicating that, when Latinos seek help for mental health issues, they are more likely to seek help in general medical care settings than from specialty mental health care settings (Guarnaccia & Martinez).

Culturally rooted in the belief of *familismo*, families try to take care of themselves without inviting outsiders. Research has explored the help-seeking behaviors of Latinos who uniformly invest in family networks for support, particularly in "personal matters" (Pescosolido et al., 1998). For example, the label *locura* or madness carries an extremely negative connotation among Latinos. It is considered an incurable, severe mental illness. Consistent with the cultural value of *familismo*, a person who is *loco* is viewed as an embarrassment to the family and extended community (Jenkins, 1998).

As pointed out by several researchers (Pescosolido et al., 1998; Guarnaccia & Martinez, 2002), there is often an overinvestment in the family, which on occasion becomes a major barrier to access needed services. The client and family members have an unrealistic assessment as to the availability of helpful resources within the family (Guarnaccia & Martinez).

Although research on best practice for mental health treatment of Latinos is seriously lacking, the consensus is that Latinos benefit from therapy when they show up and take full advantage of it (Rosenthal, 2000; Wells et al., 2001). The key issue and research void appears to be getting Latinos into treatment and keeping them there. Getting them into treatment involves addressing the barriers discussed earlier. Providing bilingual/bicultural therapists to Latinos may keep them in care longer; this needs additional research to draw solid conclusions.

Szapocznik and his colleagues have documented over 30 years of efforts to define, implement, and refine family-based interventions for Latino populations living in Miami (Muir et al., 2004):

The success and longevity of this work is attributed to efforts to maximize collaboration with the Hispanic and African-American communities, implement culturally sensitive and clinically targeted interventions, conduct rigorous research to test the impact of interventions, and use clinical research findings as a foundation for continuous improvements and refinement.

Training Counselors in Latino Cultural Competence

In one of the most deliberate and thoughtful comprehensive reviews, Bean and his colleagues (2001) provided a content analysis of the Latino counseling literature that focused on the competencies and strategies appropriate for counseling Latino populations. These themes appeared to be consistent with the research-based information provided earlier in this chapter and in this volume as a whole. Efforts to develop competent counselors for working with Latino populations will benefit greatly from efficacy-based research, which will guide program development. These efforts might simultaneously be directed at improving training program effectiveness. The following guidelines are derived from Bean et al.:

- *Multiculturally competent therapists often use family therapy as the preferred treatment.* As suggested by the work of Szapocznik (reviewed previously), comprehensive and deliberate efforts to program culturally sensitive, family-based interventions have shown positive effects on Latino client engagement. Working within the family framework is conceptually consistent with the culturally valued attitude of *familismo.* Beginning therapists might invest in observing interaction dynamics and reflecting on common themes of how different culturally centered families "get things done." Therapists might also discover comparisons with their own family dynamics and develop a greater awareness.
- *Appreciate and accommodate culture-specific approaches.* Engaging community change agents in the spirit of collaboration and empowerment serves to facilitate healing within culturally significant settings and institutions. Competent therapists should experience opportunities to collaborate with community-based organizations with which clients have a natural history (e.g., church, schools). In this respect, readily working with nontraditional healers or religious leaders (e.g., *curanderos*, priests, or other clergy) whom Latino clients trust is recommended. These might be especially important community contacts for assisting the new therapist in addressing the symptomology of several culturally specific syndromes currently identified in the *Diagnostic and Statistical Manual of Mental Disorders (4th ed., Text Revision)* (2000). The developing counselors might be made mindful of ways in which they can further understand culturally specific behaviors. Beginning therapists may well explore the origins and

criteria for these culture-bound syndromes as they approach an understanding of how different cultures organize and conceptualize mental
health and mental health services.

- *Culturally competent counselors advocate for the family with other helping
  agencies.* Empirical findings support a multisystemic approach used for
  describing a family's particular context or niche (e.g., Falicov, 1998). The
  counselor's role in such a model of intervention may involve coordinat-
  ing with multiple agencies and assisting the client with basic decision
  making, particularly when conflict arises. Therapists need to be trained in
  basic needs assessment methodology so as to provide them with a more
  complete picture of the different ecocultural constraints that may affect
  their work with clients. The dictates of such a practice are consistent with
  the empirical work on SFT (SFT; Szapocznik & Williams, 2000).
- *Gather information about the immigration experience.* The multiculturally
  competent counselor should invest in a thorough investigation of the
  background of the client. This will prevent the counselor from making
  assumptions that may be centered upon his or her biases or perceptions.
- *Assess level of acculturation.* As suggested by previous sections in this
  volume, acculturation level may serve as the most salient moderator
  of the therapeutic experience with clients. As a tool for self-reflection,
  therapists in training might reflect upon their level of entrenchment
  in society and explore how this entrenchment influences assumptions and beliefs about and, ultimately, interactions with clients in the
  therapeutic setting.
- *Speak the language.* Counseling administrators and trainers should consider the empirical bases for ethnic-matching hypotheses that describe
  the benefits of having homogeneity with respect to counselor/counselee
  dyads, particularly around language (Sue et al., 1991).
- *Consider the cultural significance of within-family dominance hierarchy:
  machismo.* This principle is based on the culturally specific notion
  of machismo, which is the traditional patriarchal structure (Falicov,
  1998). Although research shows that Latino fathers are less involved
  in the daily children-rearing and household chores (Roopnarine &
  Ahmeduzzaman, 1991), they are generally considered the major decision maker for family decisions that might include which or when
  outsiders (i.e., therapists) should be given information about the
  family. Appropriate respect for father's role is accorded when he is
  interviewed first and "rights of entry" are negotiated with him in the
  beginning of therapy. Interview techniques based upon characteristics
  of the family system need to be emphasized in family therapy training
  programs. In some cases, separate interviews within each subsystem
  may allow for more freely expressed and honest communication as
  the therapist joins each subsystem (Falicov, 1988).

- *Provide the family with suggestions that can quickly be implemented and engage the family in the first session with warmth and a personal approach.*

CONCLUSIONS

The overall effects of Latino population growth on the nation are shifting significantly. Latinos have been described as the least educated and least economically successful Americans (Casas et al., 2002). Earlier research has found that Latinos ranked higher in dropout percentages than did other major population groups, thus hindering their advancement toward college (Carter & Wilson, 1991). In 2000, almost half the population of first-generation Latinos lacked high school diplomas, compared to less than a quarter of native-born Latinos (Suro & Passel, 2003). Several reports have indicated that Latino families are four times more likely than their white counterparts to live in poverty.

It has now become obvious that the nation and societies across the world must pay attention to providing human services for Latinos. The field of multicultural counseling, in particular, needs to continue its effort to learn about Latino families and the Latino cultures. Contemporary issues and research needs to involve Latino families. Fortunately, the importance of this significant population, often described as Latino, is beginning to be acknowledged; awareness is considered the first step to change. The increase in the number of articles concerning Latinos found in the professional literature and research is also an indicator suggesting greater inclusion and acknowledgment of Latino families and the Latino cultures.

REFERENCES

Aboud, F. E. (1987). The development of ethnic self-identification and attitudes. In J. S. Phinney & M. J. Rotherman (Eds.), *Children's ethnic socialization* (pp. 32–55). Newbury Park, CA: Sage.

Acuña, R. F. (2003). *U.S. Latino issues*. Westport, CT: Greenwood.

Aguirre, A., Jr., & Martinez, R. O. (1993). *Chicanos in higher education: Issues and dilemmas for the 21st century* (ASHE-ERIC Higher Education Report No. 3, pp. 17–51). Washington, DC: George Washington University, School of Education and Human Development.

American Psychiatric Association. (2000). *Diagnostic and Statistical Manual of Mental Disorders* (4th ed., Text Revision). Washington, D.C.: Author.

Arce, C. H., Murgia, E., & Frisbie, W. (1987). Phenotype and the life chances among Chicanos. *Hispanic Journal of Behavioral Sciences, 9*, 19–32.

Arredondo, P., & Perez, P. (2003). Counseling paradigms and Latina/o Americans: Contemporary considerations. In F. D. Harper & J. McFadden (Eds.), *Culture and counseling: New approaches* (pp. 115–132). Boston: Allyn & Bacon.

Balgopal, P. R. (2000). Social work practice with immigrants and refugees: An overview. In P. R. Balgopal (Ed.), *Social work practice with immigrants and refugees* (pp. 1–29). New York: Columbia University Press.

Baruth, L. G., & Manning, M. L. (1992). Understanding and counseling Hispanic American children. *Elementary School Guidance & Counseling, 27*(2), 113–123.

Bean, R. A., Perry, B. J., & Bedell, T. M. (2001). Developing culturally competent marriage and family therapists: Guidelines for working with Hispanic families. *Journal of Marriage and Family Therapy, 27*, 43–54.

Bergin, A. E., & Garfield, S. L. (1992). *Handbook of psychotherapy and behavior change* (4th ed.). New York: John Wiley & Son.

Bernal, M. E., Knight, G. P., Ocampo, K. A., & Cota, M. K. (1990). The development of ethnic identity in Mexican American children. *Hispanic Journal of Behavioral Sciences, 12*, 3–24.

Bernal, M. E., Knight, G. P., Ocampo, K. A., Garza, C. A., & Cota, M. K. (1993). Development of Mexican American identity. In M. E. Bernal & G. P. Knight (Eds.), *Ethnic identity: Formation and transmission among Hispanics and other minorities* (pp. 31–46). Albany: State University of New York Press.

Bobo, J. K., Gilchrist, L. D., Cvetkovich, G. T., Trimble, J. E., & Schinke, S. P. (1988). Cross-cultural service delivery to minority communities. *Journal of Community Psychology, 16*(3), 263–272.

Carter, D. J., & Wilson, R. (1991). *Minorities in higher education: Ninth annual status report.* Washington: American Council on Education.

Casas, J. M., Vasquez, M., & Ruiz de Esparza, C. A. (2002). Counseling the Latino/a: A guiding framework for a diverse population. In P. B. Pedersen, J. G. Draguns, W. J. Lonner, & J. E Trimble (Eds.), *Counseling across cultures* (5th ed., pp. 133–159). Thousand Oaks, CA: Sage.

Cervantes, J. M., & Sweatt, L. I. (2004). Family therapy with Chicana/os. In R. J. Velásquez, L. M. Arellano, & B. W. McNeill (Eds.), *The handbook of Chicana/o psychology and mental health* (pp. 285–322). Mahwah, NJ: Lawrence Erlbaum.

Coatsworth, J. D., Santisteban, D. A., McBride, C. K., & Szapocznik, J. (2001). Brief strategic family therapy versus community control: Engagement, retention, and an exploration of the moderating role of adolescent's symptom severity. *Family Process, 40*(3), 313–333.

Cortese, M. (1979). Intervention research with Hispanic Americans: A review. *Hispanic Journal of Behavioral Sciences, 1*, 4–20.

Cuellar, I., Arnold, B., & Maldonado, R. (1995). Acculturation rating scale for Mexican Americans-II: A revision of the original ARSMA scale. *Hispanic Journal of Behavioral Sciences, 17*, 275–304.

Cuéllar, I., Siles, R. I., & Bracamontes, E. (2004). Mestiza/o and Chicana/o Psychology: Theory, research, and application. In R. J. Velásquez, L. M. Arellano, & B. W. McNeill (Eds.), *The Handbook of Chicanao Psychology and Mental Health* (pp. 285–322). Mahwah, NJ: Lawrence Erlbaum.

Curtis, P.A. (1990). The consequences of acculturation to service delivery and research with Hispanic families. *Child and Adolescent Social Work, 7*(2), 147–159.

Evenson, M. L., & Evenson, T. L. (1991, April). *Creative family rituals as a way of maintaining wellness.* Paper presented at the annual meeting of the American Association for Counseling & Development, Reno, NV.

Falicov, C. (1988). Learning to think culturally. In H. A. Liddle, D. C. Breulin, & R. C. Schwartz (Eds.), *Handbook of family therapy training and supervision* (pp. 335–357). New York: Guilford.

Falicov, C. (1998). Latino families in therapy: A guide to multicultural practice. New York: Guilford.

Flores, L. Y. & Heppner, M. J. (2002). Muticultural career counseling: 10 essentials for training. *Journal of Career Development, 28,* 181–202.

Fry, R., & Lowell, B. L. (2002). *Work or study: Different fortunes of U.S. Latino generations.* Washington, D.C.: Pew Hispanic Center.

Garcia-Preto, N. (1996). Latino families: An overview. In M. McGoldrick, J. Giordano, & J. K. Pearce (Eds.), *Ethnicity & family therapy* (2nd ed., pp. 141–154). New York: Guilford.

Gibson, M. A. (2002). The new Latino diaspora and educational policy. In S. Wortham, E. G. Murillo, & E. T. Hamann (Eds.), *Education in the new Latino diaspora: Policy and the politics of identity* (pp. 241–252). Westport, CT: Ablex.

Gil, A. G., & Vega, W. A. (1996). Two different worlds: Acculturation stress and adaptation among Cuban and Nicaraguan families. *Journal of Social and Personal Relationships, 13,* 435–456.

Gilbert, M. (1989). Alcohol use among Latino adolescents: What we know and what we need to know. *Drugs & Society, 3*(1–2), 35–53.

Guarnaccia, P. J., and Martinez, I. (2002). *Comprehensive in-depth literature review and analysis of Hispanic mental health issues.* Retrieved April 12, 2005, from http://www.njmhi.org/litreviewpdf.pdf

Guendelman, S., & Perez-Itriago, A. (1987). Migration tradeoffs: Men's experiences with seasonal lifestyles. *International Migration Review, 21,* 709–727.

Hamann, E. T., Wortham, S., & Murillo, E. G. (2002). Education and policy in the new Latino diaspora. In S. Wortham, E. G. Murillo, & E. T. Hamann (Eds.), *Education in the new Latino diaspora: Policy and the politics of identity* (pp. 1–16). Westport, CT: Ablex.

Helms, J. E. (1990). Three perspectives on counseling and psychotherapy with visible racial/ethnic group clients. In F. C. Serafica, A. T. Schwebel, R. K. Russell, P. D. Isaac, & L. B. Myers (Eds.) *Mental health of ethic minorities* (pp. 171–201). New York: Praeger.

Henry, W. P., Strupp, H. H., Schacht, T. E., & Gaston, L. (1994). Psychodynamic approaches. In A. Bergin & S. Garfield (Eds.), *Handbook of psychotherapy and behavior change* (pp. 467–508). New York: Wiley.

Hirschfeld, L. A. (1994). The child's representation of human groups. *The Psychology of Learning and Motivation, 31,* 133–185.

Jenkins, J. H. (1998). Conceptions of schizophrenia as a problem of nerves: A cross-cultural comparison of Mexican Americans and Anglo Americans. *Social Science and Medicine, 26,* 1233–1244.

Kouyoumdjian, H., Zamboanga, B. L., & Hansen, D. J. (2003). Barriers to community mental health services for Latinos: Treatment considerations. *Clinical Psychology: Science and Practice, 10,* 394–422.

Lee, J., Martin, J., & Fogel, S. (2005). *Immigrant stock's share of U.S. population growth: 1970–2004.* Retrieved April 1, 2005, from the Federation for American Immigration Reform [FAIR] Web site: http://www.fairus.org/Files/OpenFile.cfm?id=2634.

Longres, J. F., & Patterson, D. G. (2000). Social work practice with Latino American immigrants. In P. R. Balgopal (Ed.), *Social work practice with immigrants and refugees* (pp. 65–126). New York: Columbia University Press.

Magana, J. R., de la Rocha, O., Amsel, J., & Magana, H. A. (1996). Revisiting the dimensions of acculturation: Cultural theory and psychometric practice. *Hispanic Journal of Behavioral Sciences, 18,* 444–468.

Matute-Bianchi, M. (1986). Ethnic identities and patterns of school success and failure among Mexican descent and Japanese descent students in a California high school: An ethnographic analysis. *American Journal of Education, 95,* 233–255.

McGoldrick, M., & Giordano, J. (1996). Overview: Ethnicity and family therapy. In M. McGoldrick, J. Giordano, & J. K. Pearce (Eds.), *Ethnicity & family therapy* (2nd ed., pp. 1–27). New York: Guilford.

Muir, J. A., Schwartz, S. J., & Szapocznik, K. (2004). A program of research with Hispanic and African American families: Three decades of intervention development and testing influences by the changing cultural context of Miami. *Journal of Marital and Family Therapy, 39*(3), 285.

Navarro, A. M. (1993). Efectividad de las psicoterapias con latinos en los Estados Unidos: Una revision meta-analitica. *Revista Interamericana de Psicología/ Interamerican Journal of Psychology, 27*(2), 131–146.

Ocampo, K. A., Bernal, M. E., & Knight, G. P. (1993). Gender, race, and ethnicity: The sequencing of social constancies. In M. E. Bernal & G. P. Knight (Eds.), *Ethnic identity: Formation and transmission among Hispanics and other minorities* (pp. 11–30). Albany: State University of New York Press.

Ogbu, J. U. (1994). From cultural difference to differences in frame of reference. In P. M. Greenfield & R. R. Cocking (Eds.), *Cross-cultural roots of minority child development* (pp. 365–392). Hillsdale, NJ: Lawrence Erlbaum.

Ogbu, J. (1978). *Minority Education and Caste.* San Diego, CA: Academic Press.

Ortiz, V. (1995). The diversity of Latino families. In R. E. Zambrana (Ed.), *Understanding Latino families: Scholarship, policy, and practice* (pp. 18–39). Thousand Oaks, CA: Sage.

Pescosolido, B. A., Wright, E. R., Alegria, M., & Vera, M. (1998). Social networks and patterns of use among the poor with mental health problems in Puerto Rico. *Medical Care, 36,* 1057–1072.

Pew Hispanic Center/Kaiser Family Foundation. (2002, December). *National survey of Latinos* (report #3300). Washington, D.C.: Pew Research Center.

Pew Hispanic Center/Kaiser Family Foundation. (2004, January). *National survey of Latinos: education* (report #3031). Washington, D.C.: Pew Research Center.

Pew Research Center. (2005). Hispanics: A people in motion. In *Trends: 2005* (pp. 71–89). Washington, D.C.: Pew Research Center.

Phinney, J. S., & Chavira, V. (1995). Parental ethnic socialization and adolescent coping with problems related to ethnicity. *Journal of Research on Adolescence, 5,* 31–53.

Pizarro, M., & Vera, E. M. (2001). Chicana/o ethnic identity research: Lessons for researchers and counselors. *The Counseling Psychologist, 29,* 91–117.

Ponterotto, J. G., Costa, C. I., & Werner-Lin, A. (2002). Research perspectives in cross-cultural counseling. In P. B. Pedersen, J. G. Draguns, W. J. Lonner, & J. E. Trimble (Eds.), *Counseling across cultures* (5th ed., pp. 395–420). Thousand Oaks, CA: Sage.

Portes, A. (1984). The rise of ethnicity: Determinants of ethnic perception among Cuban exiles in Miami. *American Sociological Review, 49,* 383–397.

Quintana, S. M. (1994). A model of ethnic perspective-taking ability applied to Mexican American children and youth. *International Journal of Intercultural Relations, 18,* 419–448.

Quintana, S. M., & Vera, E. M. (1999). Latino children's understanding of ethnic prejudice: Educational implications. In S. Tomlinson (Ed.), *Building multicultural communities: Contributions from counseling psychology and higher education.* Newbury, CA: Sage.

Quintana, S. M., Ybarra, V. C., Gonzalez-Doupe, P., & De Baessa, Y. (2000). Cross-cultural evaluation of ethnic perspective-taking ability: An exploratory investigation with U.S. Latino and Guatemalan Ladino children. *Cultural Diversity and Ethnic Minority Psychology, 6,* 334–351.

Rampton, B. (1995). *Crossing: Language and ethnicity among adolescents.* New York: Longman.

Relethford, J., Stern, M., Gaskill, S., & Hazuda, H. (1983). Social class, admixture, and skin color variation among Mexican Americans and Anglo Americans living in San Antonio, Texas. *American Journal of Physical Anthropology, 62,* 97–102.

Roopnarine, J. L., & Ahmeduzzaman, M. (1991). Puerto Rican fathers' involvement with their preschool-age children. *Hispanic Journal of Behavioral Sciences, 15,* 96–107.

Rosado, J. W. (1980). Important psychosocial factors in the delivery of mental health services to lower-class Puerto Rican clients: A review of recent studies. *Journal of Community Psychology, 8,* 215–226.

Rosenthal, C. (2000). Latino practice outcome research: A review of the literature. *Smith College Studies in Social Work, 70*(2), 217–240.

Rotherman, M. J., & Phinney, J. (1987). Introduction: Definitions and perspectives in the study of children's ethnic socialization. In J. S. Phinney & M. J. Rotherman (Eds.), *Children's ethnic socialization* (pp. 10–28). Newbury Park, CA: Sage.

Ruiz, R. A., & Padilla, A. M. (1977). Counseling Latinos. *Personnel and Guidance Journal, 55,* 401–408.

Sanchez, A. R. (2001). Multicultural family counseling. In J. G. Ponterotto, J. M. Casas, L. A. Suzuki, & C. M. Alexander (Eds.), *Handbook of multicultural counseling* (2nd ed., pp. 672–700). Thousand Oaks, CA: Sage.

Santisteban, D. A., Szapocznik, J., Perez-Vidal, A., Kurtines, W., Murray, E. J., & LaPerriere, A. (1996). Efficacy of intervention for engaging youth and families into treatment and variables that may contribute to differential effectiveness. *Journal of Family Psychology, 10,* 35–44.

Sluzki, C. (1979). Migration and family conflict. *Family Process, 18,* 379–390.

Smith, M. L., & Glass, G. V. (1977). Meta-analysis of psychotherapy outcome studies. *American Psychologist, 32,* 752–760.

Sodowsky, G. R., & Lai, E. W. M., & Plake, B. S. (1991). Moderating effects of sociocultural variables on acculturation attitudes of Hispanics and Asian Americans. *Journal of Counseling and Development, 70,* 194–204

Sue, S., Chun, C., & Gee, K. (1995). Ethnic minority intervention and treatment research. In J. E. Aponte, R.Y. Rivers, & J. Wohl (Eds.) *Psychological interventions and cultural diversity* (pp. 266–282). Boston: Allyn & Bacon.

Sue, S., Fujino, D. C., Hu, L., Takeuchi, D. T., Zane, N. W. S. (1991). Community mental health services for ethnic minority groups: A test of the cultural reponsiveness hypothesis. *Journal of Consulting and Clinical Psychology, 59,* 533–540.

Sue, S., Zane, N., and Young, K. (1994). Research on Psychotherapy with culturally diverse populations. In A. E. Bergin, and S. L. Garfield (Eds.), *Handbook of Psychotherapy and Behavior Change*. New York: John Wiley and Sons, Inc., pp. 783–817, 1994.

Suro, R., & Passel, J. S. (2003). *The rise of the second generation: Changing patterns in Hispanic population growth*. Washington, D.C.: Pew Hispanic Center.

Szapocznik, J., Santisteban, D. A., Kurtines, W. M., Perez-Vidal, A., & Hervis, O. (1984). Bicultural effectiveness training: Treatment intervention for enhancing intercultural adjustment in Cuban American families. *Hispanic Journal of Behavioral Sciences, 6*, 317–344.

Szapocznik, J., Perez-Vidal, A., Brickman, A. L., Foote, F.H., Santisteban, D.A., Hervis, O. E., & Kurtines, W. M. (1988). Engaging adolescent drug abusers and their families into treatment: A Strategic Structural Systems approach. *Journal of Consulting and Clinical Psychology, 56*(4), 552–557.

Szapocznik, J., Kurtines, W., & Santisteban, D. A. (1994). The interplay of advances among theory, research, and application in family interventions for Hispanic behavior-problem youth. In R.G. Malgady & O. Rodriguez (Eds.), *Theoretical and coneptual issues in Hispanic mental health* (pp. 156–180). Malabar, FL: Robert E. Krieger.

Szapocznik, J. & Williams, R. A. (2000). Brief Strategic Family Therapy: Twenty-five years of interplay among theory, research, and practice in adolescent problem behaviors and drug abuse. *Clinical Child and Family Psychology Review, 3*, 117–334.

Steinberg, L., Dornbusch, S. N., & Brown, B. B. (1992) Ethnic differences in adolescent achievement: An ecological perspective. *American Psychologist, 47*, 723–729.

Vega, W. A. (1995). The study of Latino families: A point of departure. In R. E. Zambrana (Ed.), *Understanding Latino families: Scholarship, policy, and practice* (pp. 3–17). Thousand Oaks, CA: Sage.

Vega, W. A., & Alegria, M. (2001). Latino Mental Health and Treatment in the United States. In: M. Aguirre-Molina, C. Molina, & R. Zambrana (Eds.), Health Issues in the Latino Community (pp. 179–208). San Francisco: Jossey-Bass.

Vera, E. M., & Quintana, S. M. (2004). Ethnic identity development in Chicana/o youth. In R. J. Velásquez, L. M. Arellano, & B. W. McNeill (Eds.), *The handbook of Chicana/o psychology and mental health* (pp. 43–59). Mahwah, NJ: Lawrence Erlbaum.

Wampold, B.E., Mondin, G.W., Moody, M., Stich, F., Benson, K., & Ahn, H. (1997). A Meta-analysis of outcome studies comparing bonafide psychotherapies: Empirically, "all must have prizes." *Psychological Bulletin, 122*, 203–215.

Wells, K., Klap, R., Koike, A., Sherboune, C. (2001). Ethnic disparities in unmet need for alcoholism, drug abuse, and mental health care. *American Journal of Psychiatry, 158*: 2027–2032.

Wilson, D. (1995). Women's roles and women's health: The effect of immigration on Latina women. *Women's Health Issues, 5*, 8–14.

Wortham, S. (2002). Gender and school success in the new Latino diaspora. In S. Wortham, E. G. Murillo, & E. T. Hamann (Eds.), *Education in the new Latino diaspora: Policy and the politics of identity* (pp. 117–141). Westport, CT: Ablex.

Wortham, S., Murillo, E. G., & Hamann, E. T. (Eds.). (2002). *Education in the new Latino diaspora: Policy and the politics of identity*. Westport, CT: Ablex.

Glossary

Ability to laugh   A characteristic desired of counselors defined as the capability of seeing the bittersweet in life events and seeing humor in them while maintaining the ability to be genuine. Humor can be an effective intervention tool for counselors if it is developed with planned spontaneity and an understanding of the client's ability to integrate therapeutic humor.

Ability to listen   Desired counselor characteristic defined as the ability to find listening stimulating. Counseling involves the ability to listen and react in a way that will help others solve their problems and attain their potential.

Aborigine   A person indigenous to a particular geographical and cultural region.

Abuelita   Translation: Grandma; a key figure in Latino culture.

Academic and vocational adjustment   The process of becoming accustomed to and being productive in academic and employment situations.

Accommodation   The process of changing one's own understanding to incorporate new knowledge and attitudes toward differences such as social networks, wealth, education, access to power, and group values.

Accommodation   Approach whereby clients modify thought process and/or behavior to promote healthy selves or relationships; defined as the change of existing structures to accommodate to the new; relates to the family or couple identity and is basic to understanding systems functioning.

Accommodation techniques   Examples of accommodation techniques include interviewing, the use of anecdotes, and assimilation.

Acculturation   Process of adopting the cultural traits or social patterns of another group; process by which minorities adjust to a majority culture; refers to integration.

Active Parenting   Active Parenting Publishers, Inc. was founded in 1980 by Dr. Michael H. Popkin; APP delivers quality education programs for parents, children, and teachers to schools, hospitals, social services organizations, churches, and the corporate market. The Active Parenting model is heavily based upon the theories of Alfred Adler and Rudolf Dreikurs.

Adjustment disorder with mixed disturbance of emotions and conduct   *DSM-IV* 309.4; defined as an inability or maladaptive reaction to an identifiable stressful life event or stressor (e.g., divorce, family crises ...). Symptoms must occur within 3 months of the event or stressor and persist for no longer than 6 months.

Age hierarchies   Level of organization based on age.

Alborotados   Translation: wild, roaring.

Alternative transactional patterns   The repeated transactions establishing patterns of how, when, and to whom to relate.

Altruistic in spirit   A desired counselor trait defined as a selfless concern for other people purely for their own sakes; virtue.

Amabilidad   Translation: amiability; also, gentle and civil.

Amerindian family members   Amerindians are the descendants of the indigenous people of Guyana; they are broadly grouped into coastal and interior tribes. Most were interdependent, living and working together toward sustaining the community or tribe.

Apple of discord   In classical mythology, an apple of gold thrown into a banquet of the gods and goddesses by the goddess Discord, who had not been invited. The apple had "for the fairest" written on it; when three goddesses claimed it, the choice among them was referred to the handsome Paris, prince of Troy.

Appreciate the influence of culture   Awareness of how a person's culture affects him or her and sensitivity to diversity.

Arousal phase   The first stage of the human sexual response cycle, also known as the excitement phase; occurs as the result of any erotic physical or mental stimulation, such as kissing, petting, or viewing erotic images, that leads to sexual arousal. During the excitement stage, the body begins becoming prepared for coitus, or sexual intercourse, in the plateau phase.

Assimilation   From Latin *assimilatio* meaning "to render similar"; defined by Jean Piaget as what is perceived in the outside world is incorporated into the internal world.

Attachment theory   A theory (or group of theories) about the psychological concept of attachment: the tendency to seek closeness to another person and feel secure when that person is present; has its origins in observation of and experiments with animals. According to attachment theory, attachment is not just a consequence of the need to satisfy various drives.

Authenticity   The quality of being authentic or of established authority for truth and correctness; genuineness; the quality of being genuine or not corrupted from the original; a characteristic of counselor/family therapist desired by Latinos.

Authoritarianism   A term used to describe an organization or an individual that enforces strong and sometimes oppressive measures against others, generally without attempts at gaining the consent of others.

Autonomy   The condition of something that does not depend on anything else.

Barrio   Translation: neighborhood.

Bien educatos   Translation: well educated; used within Latino culture to define children who are well-mannered and respectful.

Bilingual   Knowledge of two languages; text reference to Spanish/English.

Bilingualism   From *bilingual*; the ability to use two languages. Fluency in a second language requires skills in listening comprehension, speaking, reading, and writing, although in practice some of those skills are often considerably less developed than others.

Birth order   The place of a child's birth in the family; children are "first born" or "later borns." The influence of birth order is still an open issue, but some clear patterns have been established. In the Latino culture, older siblings warrant the most respect and have the most authority over other siblings.

***Bracero* Program**   A joint labor program initiated in August 1942, by the U.S. and Mexican federal governments designed to bring skilled Mexican agriculture laborers to the United States to fill gaps in the agricultural labor market. The program made a large contribution to U.S. agriculture, leading to the advent of mechanized farming. Workers who participated in the Bracero Program have led large fights with the U.S. and Mexican governments to receive pensions legally guaranteed to them but not given until the workers fought the respective governments in court.

Brainstorming   An organized approach for producing ideas by letting the mind think without interruption.

Bulimia nervosa   An eating disorder more commonly known as bulimia; a psychological condition in which the subject engages in recurrent binge eating followed by intentionally doing one or more of the following in order to compensate for the intake of the food and prevent weight gain: vomiting, inappropriate use of laxatives, enemas, diuretics or other medication, excessive exercising, and fasting.

Cada persona es un mundo   Translation: each person is a world in his or her own right.

Capacity for intimacy   One's ability or willingness to engage in emotional or physical closeness.

Capacity for self-denial   The ability or willingness to focus on those other than oneself; a desired counselor characteristic.

Casa chica   Translation: small house; in the Mexican culture, defines the father's "on-the-side" family.

Casa grande   Translation: big house; in the Mexican culture, defines the father's legal family.

Chicanos   A person of Mexican American descent born in the United States. *Chicana* is the female form of the word; it often also has feminist connotations. The term *Chicano* is believed to be offensive by some Mexican Americans, who prefer other terms such as Mexican, Hispanic, Latino, or even Spanish. In Mexico, the term can connote a person of low class and poor morals, but in the United States it carries multiple meanings.

Choteo   Defined as "not taking anything seriously"; the use of humor as a way of ridiculing or making fun of people, situations, or things; may involve exaggerations, jokes, or satire to modify tense situations; positive emotional expression is highly valued in the Latino culture.

Codependence   A psychological condition in which someone exhibits too much, and often inappropriate, caring for other people's struggles.

Cognitive constructivism   Based on the work of Jean Piaget. His theory has two major parts: an "ages and stages" component that predicts what children can and cannot understand at different ages, and a theory of development that describes how children develop cognitive abilities.

Collaborator   The role of the clinician to work with clients toward identified goals.

Collectivism   A worldview and a dimension of culture that emphasizes group needs via harmony and cooperation over individual needs and desires.

Colonialism   Foreign rule that impose culture and custom on people.

Color blind   When a person is not aware of or minimizes racial differences.

Color-blind approach   Promotion of colorblind equal opportunity and racial harmony; one way to deemphasize group membership. Racial or ethnic differences are minimized and emphasis is on the universal or "human" aspects of behavior. This has been the traditional U.S. focus on assimilation, with its melting pot metaphor that this is a nation of immigrants that together make one whole, without a focus on any one individual cultural group.

Color obsession   When a person or group overemphasizes the salience of skin color and race to the point of obscuring related factors such as socioeconomic status.

Comfort with power   Desired counselor characteristic; defined as acceptance of power with a certain degree of detachment.

Comida   Translation: food.

Community-based counseling programs   Programs that keep youth living with their families and out of the more costly correctional institutions, foster homes, residential treatment, and chemical abuse treatment facilities.

Compadrazgo   Pseudokinship tradition that is important in Latin American societies, but perhaps not to the same extent on Galapagos as on the continent; a compromise that attempts to combine the best of friendship with the advantages of kinship. The godparents are to sponsor and provide religious education for their godchild, but the most important link is between the parents and the godparents; parents and godparents are considered ritual kin and are supposed to help each other at all times.

Compadres **and** ***comadres***   Term used for the relationship between parents and godparents; they may act as guardians or sponsors of the godchild and care for him or her in emergencies, and they may be chosen from among members of the extended family or from outside.

Companion traveler   A role of the clinician as one who is joining the family through their counseling journey, rather than as the "only expert."

Conditional homework   Such a technique is consonant with a culture that values chance and spontaneity in interpersonal relationships. Conversely, Mexicans would not be comfortable with the idea of scheduling certain times to be intimate, express affection, or resolve problems.

Congruence   Defined as rapport within oneself or internal and external consistency; perceived as sincerity.

Congruent, genuine, and integrated   Terms coined by Rogers; refer to individuals and families seeking out therapists who are self-aware and therefore congruent, genuine, and integrated.

Constructivism   A theory of clinical practice in which a person actively constructs his or her personal realities and creates his or her own representational models of life and world.

Consultation   A meeting of two or more health professionals to discuss the diagnosis, prognosis, and treatment of a particular case.

Context   A temporal, social, cultural, physical, chemical, biological, and metaphysical environments in which a person live and that his or her everyday existence, adaptation, and interaction.

Controlado   Translation: in control.

Coraje   Translation: anger in her heart.

Core conditions   Defined by Carl Rogers as essential to therapy. Three core conditions necessary for therapeutic change are empathy, congruence, and unconditional positive regard.

Cosmos   The universe regarded as an orderly, harmonious whole.

Cotherapist   A second therapist who helps oversee and participates in the counseling process.

Counselor ethnicity   The counselor's identity with or membership in a particular racial, national, or cultural group and observance of that group's customs, beliefs, and language.

Coup d'etat   Sudden overthrow of a government.

Couple counseling   Counseling with both partners in a relationship to help the couple improve their relationship.

Coyote   A term used for an individual who smuggles people into the United States.

Cross-cultural counseling models   Reference to the work of Tat Tsang et al., who described the incorporation of personal views and counseling experiences into the counseling process.

***Cuento* therapy**   A culturally sensitive modality for Puerto Rican children; emphasizes cultural connections (specific to Puerto Rican children).

Culture   It makes reference to the common lifestyles, languages, behavior patterns, traditions, and beliefs that are learned and passed from one generation to the next.

Cultural assessment   A systematic appraisal of people, groups, and communities as to their cultural beliefs, values, and rituals to determine explicit needs and interventions practices within the cultural context of the people being considered.

Cultural awareness   The deliberate cognitive and emotional process in which clinicians appreciate their own cultural heritage and are sensitive to the cultural values of the client.

Cultural bridges of connectedness   Opens the door for cultural bridges of connectedness between family and therapist.

Cultural engagement   Presenting oneself and one's message to a culture in a way that is sensitive to and effective in that culture.

Cultural identity   The (feeling of) identity of a group or culture, or of an individual as far as he or she is influenced by belonging to a group or culture.

Cultural imperialism   Practice of promoting the culture or language of one nation in another. It is usually the case that the former is a large, economically or militarily powerful nation and the latter is a smaller, less affluent one.

Cultural sensitivity   An understanding and acceptance of individuals of cultures different from one's own; presents the individual with the larger possibilities of life in an inherently diverse world through exposure to other people and their ways.

Culture shedding   Reference to culture and losing a natural growth or covering by natural process.

Cultural stereotypes   A trite expression or idea based on culture.

Culturally concordant treatment   A formal cultural agreement to treatment.

Culturally responsive helpers   Individuals who respond to assist others of the same cultural background.

Culture   Comes from the Latin root *colere* (to inhabit, to cultivate, or to honor); in general, refers to human activity.

Curanderismo   The practice of healing the sick with a traditional folk healer or shaman that is prevalent in Mexico and Chicano communities in the southwestern United States. *Curanderos* (healers) are often respected members of the community because they are highly religious and spiritual. They often use herbs and other natural remedies to cure illnesses, but their primary method of healing is the supernatural because they believe that the cause of many illnesses is evil spirits, the punishment of God, or a curse.

Curiosity and inquisitiveness   Desired counselor characteristics; defined as any naturally inquisitive behavior or interest in people.

Dar por recibir no es dar sino pedir   Translation: to give in order to receive is not to give but to ask.

Delayed ejaculation   An inhibition of ejaculation; the male is unable to ejaculate during sexual intercourse or with manual stimulation in the presence of a partner, in spite of his wish to do so.

Delinquency and substance abuse   Two identified program areas for Latino youth, in most cases intertwined; defined as a pattern of continued commitment of antisocial or criminal acts or continued harmful use of a mood-altering substance that results in adverse social consequences, such as failure to meet work, family, or school obligations; interpersonal conflicts; or legal problems. Demilitarized zone   An area between two or more groups where specific activity is not permitted, usually by treaty or other agreement.

De padres sanos, hijos honrados   Varied translations due to dialect differences among Latino cultures include: from wholesome parents, honorable children, from wholesome parents, honest children, and from healthy parents, decent children.

Department of Homeland Security   Cabinet department of the federal government of the United States that is concerned with protecting America's people from harm and its property from damage; created primarily from a conglomeration of existing federal agencies in response to the terrorist attacks of September 11, 2001.

Dependency   Such a strong need for a person, object, or substance that it becomes necessary to have it just to function properly.

Desire phase disorders   Disorders including hypoactive sexual desire (low sex drive), sexual aversion disorder, including panic disorder and active revulsion from sexual stimulation.

Dichos   Translation: proverbs. A therapist's knowledge and timely use of *dichos* is an invaluable and aesthetic communicational resource for many groups, but Latinos are particularly adept with these metaphorical statements.

Differentiation and union   The act of perceiving or showing the difference in or between things; discrimination and the act of becoming united.

Dignidad   Translation: dignity.

Discrimination   The differential treatment of others based solely on their membership in a socially distinct group or category, such as race, ethnicity, sex, religion, age, or disability.

Disengagement   The act or process of detaching: detachment, disconnection, separation, uncoupling; the act of releasing from an attachment or connection.

Disequilibrium   The absence or loss of balance or stability.

Diversity   A term that speaks of gender, sex, age, culture, ethnicity, disabilities, sexual orientation, among others' differences.

Dominant culture   The culture that has the greatest influence on a given society, usually by comprising the majority of the population or having a disproportionate amount of socioeconomic power.

Dysthymic disorder   Form of the mood disorder of depression characterized by a lack of enjoyment or pleasure in life that continues for at least 6 months; usually does not prevent a person from functioning, but prevents full enjoyment of life.

Ecological niches   Term describing the place or function of a given organism or population within its ecosystem (ecological community together with its environment, functioning as a unit).

Ecological systems theory   A model of human behavior that explicitly considers multiple layers of influence from the micro level (personality, past experiences) to the macro systems level (national economy, social trends).

Egalitarian   Belief that all people have rights to the same privileges, treatment, and opportunities.

Emotional insightfulness   Desired counselor characteristic; showing or having insight into emotions; defined as comfort with dealing with a wide range of feelings.

Emotions bingo   This game can be used in several ways. It can be a simple matching game, allowing the child to match the cards with the faces that appear on the game board or with the playing cards that ask several different questions, including naming a time that he or she or someone else experienced the pictured emotion or a time when he or she made someone else feel that way.

Empathic bond   A connection developed due to an understanding of one another's beliefs, desires, and emotions.

Empathy and understanding   An essential core condition of person-centered theory; defined as the recognition and understanding of the beliefs, desires and, particularly, the emotions of others; often characterized as the ability to put oneself into another's "shoes."

Empowerment   Enabling others by instilling self-confidence, encouraging, supporting, and providing opportunities for them to act more freely.

En casa   Translation: at home.

Encouragement   The final step in the LIBRE process; the expression of approval and support; the act of giving hope or support to someone.

Enculturation   The process of socialization wherein individuals learn and internalize the particular values, conducts, and worldviews of their native culture

Energy   A fundamental quantity that every physical system possesses; defined by Samuel Gladding (2000) as being able to stay active and sustain oneself when working with others.

Engagement   The act of sharing in the activities of a group.

English-only movement   A political movement for establishing the English language as the only official language in the United States. The term *movement* here is a loose collective term because the idea has had incarnations in different political eras.

Enmeshment   The condition of being entangled or implicated: embranglement, embroilment, ensnarement, entanglement, involvement.

Erectile dysfunction   Impotence or, more clinically, the inability to develop or maintain an erection of the penis for satisfactory sexual intercourse regardless of the capability of ejaculation.

Espiritismo   Spanish word for "spiritualism" that refers to religious practices that connect human beings with divine beings through a diversity of rituals that include communication with the spirit of the dead. This belief sustains that good and evil spirits have a direct influence in aspects that affect a person's life.

Estranger   One who is described as hostile, unsympathetic, or indifferent; alienated; from *estrange* meaning to remove from an accustomed place or set of associations.

Ethnic identity   The amalgam of conceptual and behavioral characteristics found in a group of people that set it apart from any other.

Ethnic similarity   Commonalities between individuals of the same ethnic background.

Ethnic-specific counseling   Counseling relating to or being a member of a specific ethnic group.

Ethnicity   One's identity or perception of group membership. Ethnic and ethnicity reflect the process of construction, deconstruction, and reconstructions of identity and life experiences.

Ethnocentrism   The psychological, cultural, theological, and social mindsets that foster belief in the superiority of one's own ethnicity, gender, sexual orientation, faith, socioeconomic status, physical and mental abilities. The belief that one's own culture is the standard against which other cultures can be measured.

Ethnoculturally diverse   Identifies three dimensions (cultural, pedagogical, and sociolinguistic) of ethnocultural knowledge integral to teacher preparation and discusses implementation strategies.

Ethnology   The study of contemporary cultures in an attempt to understand their unique patterns.

Ethos   A dimension of culture that refers to the basic values, assumptions and beliefs held within a cultural group and that guide social relations.

Eurocentric   A worldview that values the ideas, behaviors, traditions, etc. that have their roots in European or European American cultures over those of other cultures.

European American, middle-class culture   A term for Americans of European descent, who are usually referred as White or Caucasian, that are of a social and economic class composed of those more prosperous than the poor, or lower class, and less wealthy than the upper class.

Ex cathedra **manner**   Meaning "from the throne of St. Peter"; also, pretentious or arrogant.

Expanded family   Also extended family. The extended family often includes not only blood relatives but also non-blood relatives such as the best man (*padrino*), maid of honor (*madrina*), and godparents (*compadre* and *comadre*). In societies dominated by the conjugal family, it is used to refer to kindred (an egocentric network of relatives that extends beyond the domestic group) who do not belong to the conjugal family.

Experiential approach   From the perspective of experiential learning, team learning is the process by which teams gain clarity about purpose, develop good working relationships, and effectively accomplish their goals. It involves valuing individual differences, learning how to focus on a common purpose, and sharing responsibility for getting work done.

Familial self   The individualized self and the transcendent self; a basic inner psychological organization that enables women and men to function well within the hierarchical intimacy relationships of the extended family, community, and other groups.

Families and Democracy Project   Launched by family therapist William Doherty (2002); the Families and Democracy Project is a team of faculty, graduate students, and community professionals working on projects and developing the model as they go. The mission is to develop the theory and practice of democratic public work in the family field.

Familismo   Spanish word that refers to importance of family interdependency that serves as the primary social unit and source of social support for its members. This includes the expanded family.

Familocentric   Sentimental or preaching jingoist (advocacy of a policy of aggressive nationalism); "courage" in the face of the enemy.

Family bonds   Ties between family members; regarded as highly important within the Latino culture.

Family empowerment intervention   An innovative service for high-risk youth and their families; designed to help provide better services to these difficult-to-serve clients.

Family identity   Provides a sense of where one came from, one's values, sense of humor, history, and sense of belonging to something comfortable, unique, and bigger than oneself.

Fatalism   A value that underlies the strong Latino identification with members of the extended family; the belief that events are determined by an impersonal fate and cannot be changed by human beings; acceptance of the belief that all events are predetermined and inevitable.

Fatalismo   Spanish word that refers to the belief that some things are meant to happen regardless of a personal intervention.

Faulty beliefs   Untrue or flawed beliefs; in the Latino culture often resulting from misconceptions or misinformation.

Fauna   Goddess of fertility.

Female sexual arousal disorder   Persistent or recurrent inability to reach or sustain the lubrication and swelling reaction in the arousal phase of the sexual response. It is the second most common sexual problem among women, affecting 15 to 20%, and most frequently occurs in postmenopausal women.

Fiesta, siesta y mañana   Latino theme of enjoyment.

Flexibility   The quality of being adaptable or variable; defined by Samuel Gladding as being able to adapt to meet the client's needs.

Flora   Goddess of flowers.

Fourth force in counseling   Multiculturalism has been identified as the "fourth force in counseling."

Fraternal solidarity   Fellowship of responsibilities and interests showing comradeship.

Fuenteovejuna, señor   Translation: Fuenteovejuna [name of town], my lord.

Fuenteovejuna, todos a una   Translation: Fuenteovejuna [name of town], all are one.

Gender socialization   The learning of male versus female roles. In the Latino culture, women learn to be supportive of their husbands and children while forfeiting their own needs and desires.

Generational culture clashes   Differences in views, opinions, or beliefs about culture across generations.

Genograms   Resembles a family tree; however, it includes additional relationships among individuals. The genogram permits the therapist and the patient to quickly identify and understand patterns in family history; the genogram map out relationships and traits that may otherwise be missed on a pedigree chart.

Goodwill   Defined as having the will to do good in a community or simply to try to help people who are in need; will to do good.

Grieving   The process of mourning someone who is deceased.

Gritos   Translation: shouts.

Group counseling   Provides an opportunity for small groups of students to meet and share common concerns, explore personal issues, and learn new skills under the guidance of group leaders. Group members help each other by making suggestions and giving feedback; group members are not forced to reveal more about themselves than they feel comfortable with, but they are expected to maintain confidentiality out of mutual respect for other group members. The counselors are there to make observations from a caring, objective position; group counselors recognize that individuals have different ways of expressing themselves and strive to create an environment that is safe, respectful, and inclusive.

Guidelines on Multicultural Education and Training, Research, Practice and Organizational (Policy) Development   The dissemination of these guidelines and work to ensure the understanding by psychologists who interact with individuals of diverse backgrounds in their professional roles has been limited. These guidelines include: (1) psychologists are encouraged to recognize that, as cultural beings, they may hold attitudes and beliefs that can detrimentally influence their perceptions of and interactions with individuals who are ethnically and racially different from them; (2) psychologists are encouraged to recognize the importance of multicultural sensitivity/responsiveness, knowledge, and understanding about ethnically and racially different individuals; (3) as educators, psychologists are encouraged to use the constructs of multiculturalism and diversity in psychological education; (4) culturally sensitive psychological researchers are encouraged to recognize the importance of conducting culture-centered and ethical psychological research among persons from ethnic, linguistic, and racial minority backgrounds; (5) psychologists strive to apply culturally appropriate skills in clinical and other applied psychological practices; and (6) psychologists are encouraged to use organizational change processes to support culturally informed organizational (policy) development and practices.

Hay de todo en la viña del Señor   Translation: In the Lord's vineyard, there is a little of everything.

Haz mal, espera otro tal   Translation: Do wrong, expect another wrong.

Hermandad   Defined as friendship within the Latino culture.

Heterogeneity   The quality of being made of many different elements, forms, kinds, or individuals; diversification, heterogeneousness, multiplicity, variety.

Hispanic   A term used since 1978 by the U.S. government to designate people of Latin American or Iberian heritage regardless of race or ethnic.

Hispanic alphabet of emotions   The collection of emotions experienced, recognized, and accepted in the Hispanic culture.

Hispanic families   Families from Spain, the Spanish-speaking countries of Latin America, or the original settlers of the traditionally Spanish-held southwestern United States.

Homeostasis   The property of an open system, especially living organisms, to regulate the internal environment so as to maintain a stable condition.

Hospice services   Palliative or medical care or treatment that concentrates on reducing the severity of the symptoms of a disease or slows its progress rather than providing a cure; it aims at improving quality of life—particularly at reducing or eliminating pain.

Human sexual response cycle   Masters and Johnson defined the four stages of this cycle as excitement (initial arousal), plateau (at full arousal, but not yet at orgasm), orgasm, and resolution phases (after orgasm).

Humble expert approach   Approaching the family with curiosity and taking a "not knowing" stance to prevent stereotyping; reflects modesty and genuine respect for the client, the client's family, and the culture in general.

Hypoactive sexual desire   The most common form of female sexual dissatisfaction (FSD), this occurs when there is a persistent lack of desire or absence of sexual fantasies. In other words, one is rarely in the mood, neither initiating sex nor seeking stimulation.

Identity   An inner sense of self that reflects a stable perception of who a person is individually and socially.

Imago relationship therapy   The process of giving couples information and, even more importantly, teaching them tools to help make the unconscious aspects of their relationship conscious, address conflict at its roots rather just trying to solve it in a surface way, be successful in the work of healing and growth, create emotional safety for each other to learn how to better meet each other's needs, transform conflict into opportunities for deeper intimacy and connection, make small changes that make the biggest difference in terms of happiness and fulfillment as individuals and as a couple, learn how to become a source of pleasure instead of pain for the partner, realize how to make a marriage or partnership a fulfilling, alive, passionate, fun, and transforming source of increasing wholeness and sacred transformation.

Immigrant   A person born in a country who decides to live in a different nation.

Inca culture   The Incan Empire was located in South America from 1438 C.E. to 1533 C.E.; over that period, the Inca used conquest and peaceful assimilation to incorporate in their empire a large portion of western South America, centered on the Andean mountain ranges. The Inca empire proved short-lived: by 1533 C.E., Atahualpa, the last Inca, was killed on the orders of the Conquistador Francisco Pizarro, marking the beginning of Spanish hegemony. The Incan Empire is derived from the word *inca*, which means emperor; today Inca still refers to the emperor, but can also refer to the people or the civilization.

Incarnation and idolatry   Incarnation literally means enfleshment and refers to the conception and live birth of a sentient creature (generally human) who is the material manifestation of an entity or force whose original nature is immaterial. Idolatry is a term used by many religions to describe the worship of a false deity, which is an affront to their understanding of divinity.

Indirectas   Used to maintain harmony when the emotion at hand is anger; criticisms often take the form of allusion; diminutives used in a sarcastic way and belittlement. Positive emotional expression is highly valued in the Latino culture.

Individualism   A value that encourages, promotes, and advocates for individual autonomy and for fulfillment of individual needs and desires over the needs of the group.

Individuation   Comprises the processes whereby the undifferentiated becomes or develops individual characteristics, or the opposite process, by which components of an individual are integrated into a more indivisible whole.

Industrial Areas Foundation (IAF)   The leaders and organizers of the IAF build organizations whose primary purpose is power—the ability to act—and whose chief product is social change. They continue to practice what the Founding Fathers preached: the ongoing attempt to make life, liberty, and the pursuit of happiness everyday realities for more and more Americans.

Inequity   Unequal treatment in hiring, education, job pay and promotion usually based on ethnicity, race or gender.

In-groups   A group of people united by common beliefs, attitudes, or interests and characteristically excluding outsiders. People make sense of their social world by creating categories of the individuals around them, which includes separating the categories into in-groups and out-groups. In-groups are more highly valued, more trusted, and engender greater cooperation as opposed to competition.

Inhibited female orgasm   Also anorgasmia; the inability of a woman to have an orgasm. Orgasmic dysfunction may be primary, meaning that the woman has never experienced an orgasm; secondary, meaning that the woman has had orgasms in the past but cannot have them now; or situational, meaning that she has orgasms in some situations but not in others.

Instinctual–indigenous   An instinctual and intrinsic (innate) manner.

Institutional racism   Policies, procedures, or programs at the organizational level that maintain privileges for races in power at the expense of those in less power.

Integration   The process of incorporating aspects of a new culture while maintaining aspects of one's native culture.

Intellectual competence   Being well qualified to learn and reason; capacity for knowledge and understanding; defined by Samuel Gladding (2000) as the ability to learn and think fast and creatively.

Intermittent style of counseling   Counseling at intervals, starting and stopping; a style to which Latinos are not receptive or responsive.

Internalized oppression   The development and maintenance of self-defeating views affecting behavior because of feeling rejected during interactions with others.

Intimacy   Emotional or physical closeness.

Intimidad   Translation: intimacy.

Introspection   Desired counselor characteristic; defined as direct observation or rumination of one's heart, mind, and/or soul and its processes, as opposed to extrospection, which is the observation of things external to oneself.

Kin   Family.

Kith   Friends and acquaintances.

La comida semanal   Translation: the weekly meal; may involve parents and adolescent children in cooking and cleaning.

La familia es el corazón y espíritu de la cultura Latina   Translation: The family is the heart and soul of Latino culture.

La gran familia   Translation: the large family. The Latino culture often consists of three or four generations of relatives and includes horizontal relationships.

La palabra   Translation: the word.

La que este libre de culpa que tire la primera piedra   Translation: He who is free of guilt can throw the first stone.

La raza cosmica   Translation: the cosmic race.

La tia   Translation: the aunt.

Language   Systematic communication by vocal symbols. Many languages use gestures, sounds, pictures, or words, and, as sets of symbols, aim at communicating concepts, ideas, meanings, and thoughts. Because language is a cultural system, individual languages may classify objects and ideas in completely different fashions; for example, the sex or age of the speaker may determine the use of certain grammatical forms or avoidance of taboo words.

Latino-centered needs assessment   Knowledge of the Latino culture and its needs and related presentation in effort to identify area of need appropriately.

Latino culture   Value of collectivism and familism. Cultural norms may also include "hierarchical regard," or respect toward those with power and positions of authority within the home, state, and church. The level of respect paid and the type of relationship developed depend on the person's age, gender, and social class.

Latino families   Latino families have a strong sense of family identification and structure as well as support for extended family. One cultural generalization is that Latinos value the family unity, have a profound loyalty to the family, and place emphasis on cooperation rather than competition among family members and friends. Latino families may give more importance to human interaction rather than to time and its control; being is valued more than doing. Patterns of communication focus more clearly on nonverbal communication, including the social setting and the use of phrasing, gestures, tone of voice, and posture as opposed to direct communication in which words alone carry much of the meaning.

Latino heritage   A person with Latino heritage is a descendant of a family from Mexico, Central America, or South America.

Latino rituals   Include a number of practices specific to the Latino culture such as birthing, grieving, and death rituals, Good Friday, *Las Posadas* rituals, and the like.

Latinos   A Latin American; a person of Hispanic, especially Latin American, descent, often one living in the United States; an American whose first language was Spanish.

LIBRE model   Approach described by Normal Guerra as a problem-solving approach that provides the framework for problem-solving training and practice.

Link therapy   First described by Landau-Stanton in 1990, link therapy mobilizes natural change agents in the service of physical, psychological, and spiritual health across families and communities.

Logical consequences   Logical consequences are situations engineered by the person in authority that are logically connected to the wrong. They are described as logical because they "fit" the offense; this teaches reality to teen-agers. The punishment fits the crime, much as the real world works.

Lord of the Flies   An allegorical novel by the Nobel Prize-winning author William G. Golding; reference to Ralph, the protagonist of *Lord of the Flies*. He is a natural leader and, after discovering the conch shell, he is elected as leader of the boys. Throughout the novel, Ralph tries to establish order and focus on rescue; he also encourages the boys to build huts. He is very much a true human because, although he tries to maintain order, he is often tempted by the indulgences of the other boys. When the numbers in his party begin to diminish, Ralph is left to survive on his own in the forest and is chased by the transformed savage boys.

Lotería   Translation: game of lotto.

Luchan   Translation: fight.

Machismo   A prominently exhibited or excessive masculinity. The word *machismo* (and its derivatives, *machista* and *macho*, "he who espouses *machismo*") comes from the Spanish word *macho*, meaning "male" or "manly". This attitude ranges from a personal sense of virility to a more extreme masculism; most *machistas* believe in conservative gender role ideas. Generally speaking, *machistas* oppose a woman's right to work, participate in sports, or pursue other traditionally male roles in society; *machistas* believe that women were created to stay home and be mothers and wives. Most *machistas* believe firmly in the superiority of men over women.

Macro social systems   Defined as law and politics, economic development, education, social welfare, health, mental health, transportation, housing, and religion.

Manic depressive episodes   Refers to manic depression; also "bipolar mood disorder," which is a disturbance of a person's mood characterized by alternating periods of depression and mania. Switching from one mood to another is referred to as a mood swing; these swings can be mild, moderate, or severe and are accompanied by changes in thinking and behavior. The course of the illness varies from patient to patient; without treatment, the frequency and severity of this recurring illness can increase over the years.

Marginality   Life on the periphery of both native and welcoming culture.

Marginalization   A form of social exclusion wherein those in privilege and power tacitly disregard or fail to recognize others, or to an outcome of accultura-tion where individuals not only lose cultural and psychological contact with their traditional culture but also do not adopt the ways of the new culture.

Mariachi   A type of musical group, originally from Mexico, consisting of at least two violins, two trumpets, one Spanish guitar, one *vihuela* (a high-pitched, five-string guitar) and one *guitarrón* (a small-scaled acoustic bass), but sometimes featuring more than 20 musicians.

Marianismo   The stereotyped gender role of females in Mexican society, *marianismo* is related to *machismo*, which is characterized by hypervirility, the aggressive masculine behavior expected of the Latin American male. *Marianismo*, the female counterpart, is characterized by hyperfeminine behavior; "the roots of *Marianismo* are both deep and widespread, springing apparently from the primitive awe at woman's ability to produce a living human creature from inside her body." The *mariana* is pure; submissive to her father, brothers, and spouse; and lacks sexual desires. The ideal *mariana* is often thought of as someone like the Virgin Mary. *Marianismo* is not a religious practice although the word "Marianism" is sometimes used to describe a movement within the Roman Catholic Church that has as its object the special veneration of the figure of the Virgin Mary.

Masters and Johnson Institute   William Howell Masters and Virginia Eshelman Johnson opened the Masters & Johnson Institute in 1964 to provide sex therapy and counseling based on their findings. The research, books, and media activities of Masters and Johnson profoundly affected American society.

Masters and Johnson model for sex therapy   Many psychiatrists and psychologists were outraged over what they viewed as impossible results; accusations were made in many quarters that the Masters and Johnson therapy could, a priori, only address superficial sexual symptoms rather than deep-seated psychological problems and would thus have no chance of achieving sustained results. Others dismissed their approach as mechanistic, formulaic, and simplistic.

Matriarchal   A family or society in which women hold authority and power.

Matrilineal   The custom of tracing kinship, descent, and inheritance through women.

Maturity   State of being mature; full development.

Mestizo   Person of mixed race, particularly of Indian and White blood.

Mexican American   U.S. citizens of Mexican ancestry (14 million in 2003) and Mexican citizens who reside in the United States (10 million in 2003). According to the Pew Hispanic Center, in mid-2001, 4.5 million Mexicans were residing illegally in the United States. Mexican Americans account for 64% of the Hispanic or Latino population of the United States and may sometimes be referred to as Chicanos.

Monocultural   A worldview informed by a single culture, characteristically the predominant culture in a given society.

Mosaic of people   A composite of people compared to a picture made of overlapping, usually aerial, photographs.

Mother–son symbiosis   An interaction/relationship between mother and son, symbiosis reflects two organisms existing together and mutually dependent.

Moviola technique   Presented by Guidano in 1991, its goals include: to generate a change in the "self"-evaluation with respect to the "I," which enables the production to produce a viable assimilation of the unsettling feelings; that the client begin to differentiate between the "how" ("to experience") of his or her unsettling events and the "why" ("to explain"), being able even to refer the latter to the former; and to reach a significant rearrangement of the client's unsettling experiences, which allows him to recognize as his own a wide range of feeling tonalities as well as the dynamics of his internal coherence.

Mulatto   A person of Black and White heritage. The terms biracial and multiracial are preferred.

Multicolor group of people   A group of people of various ethnic cultures and/or backgrounds.

Multicultural competence   Sufficient awareness, knowledge, skills and attitudes to relate effectively with those who differ in race, sex, age, sexual orientation, ability, language, nationality, faith, socioeconomic status, etc.

Multicultural counseling competencies paradigm   This paradigm was shaped during the past 25 years by professional development committees of the Association of Multicultural Counseling and Development (AMCD), a division of the American Counseling Association (ACA) and Division 17 Society of Counseling Psychology, American Psychological Association (APA).

Multicultural counselors   Counselors that are trained to work with multicultural issues.

Multidimensional Family Prevention Program   Howard Little's program is an intensive, family-based counseling program in which a family-specific prevention agenda is crafted with each family. This collaborative, individualized approach to intervention requires a high degree of engagement on the part of families.

Multidimensional family therapy   Approach developed by Howard Little; a family-based treatment developed for adolescents with drug and behavior problems and for substance abuse prevention with early adolescents.

Multiethnic group   The integration of different ethnic groups, irrespective of differences in culture, race, and history, under a common social identity larger than one "nation" in the conventional sense.

Multiracial   A person whose ancestry includes different races.

Mutuality   A reciprocity of sentiments; reciprocal relation between interdependent entities.

Nationalistic self-identity   Devotion to the interest or culture with which one identifies.

Natural consequences   Natural consequences are situations that are not controlled by anyone; they happen naturally. If one puts a finger into an electrical socket, one gets a shock.

Nice   Characteristic of counselor/family therapist desired by Latinos; someone described as kind, pleasant, and polite.

Not knowing stance   Taking on this stance evokes an attitude of genuine curiosity and breaks down the hierarchical barriers that naturally exist between client and therapist.

Nuclear family   A household consisting of two married, heterosexual parents and their legal children (siblings), as distinct from the extended family.

Nuclear family models   Refers to nuclear family (see preceding glossary item), which is too narrow for application to many Latinos. The modern nuclear family can vary in the degree of their isolation and restrictedness.

Open minded   Having or showing receptiveness to new and different ideas or the opinions of others; ready and willing to receive favorably, such as with new ideas.

Oppositional defiant disorder   Defined as a pattern of negativistic, hostile, and defiant behavior lasting at least 6 months, during which four (or more) of the following are present: often loses temper, often argues with adults, often actively defies or refuses to comply with adults' requests or rules, often deliberately annoys people, often blames others for his or her mistakes or misbehavior, often touchy or easily annoyed by others, often angry and resentful, and often spiteful or vindictive.

Organization of personal meaning (OPM)   The gradual construction of a sense of self in the interaction with the other and also to the interrelated development of the cognitive, emotional, and behavioral domains in a unitary process with characteristics of internal coherence.

Orgasm phase disorders   Also orgasmic disorder; delayed or absent orgasm after a normal excitement phase; may be secondary to chronic illness or side effects of certain medications. Disorders of orgasm can be related to difficulty in "letting go" or facilitating the mental and physical stimulation sufficient to evoke the reflex; individuals who try to have excessive control in their lives may experience problems with orgasm.

Orthogonal cultural self-identity   An assertion that personal identity is multifaceted, complicated by simultaneous group membership and the resulting interactions.

Out-groups   A group of people excluded from or not belonging to one's group, especially when viewed as subordinate or contemptibly different. It is quite common to have automatic biases and stereotypic attitudes about people in the out-group and, for most psychologists, individuals in racial/ethnic minority groups are in an out-group. The stereotype or the traits associated with the category become the predominant aspect of the category, even when disconfirming information is provided.

Overmedicalization   A term used to describe situations in which treatment interventions rely too heavily on highly technological interventions when a less invasive, aggressive approach would be of similar or greater benefit and when the medical approach is applied to situations that are not fundamentally a "treatment" issue. One way in which women's health is overmedicalized occurs when natural processes, such as menstruation, pregnancy, menopause, and ageing, are treated as a disease or medical condition.

Padrinos y ahijados   Translation: godparents and their godchildren.

Paradigm   A set of assumptions and beliefs about how life and the world work that structures a person's perception and understanding of reality.

Paraphilias   A mental health term recently used to indicate sexual arousal in response to sexual objects or situations that may interfere with the capacity for reciprocal affectionate sexual activity.

Parent effectiveness training (PET)   Developed by Thomas Gordon, the first national parent-training program to teach parents how to communicate more effectively with kids and offer step-by-step advice to resolving family conflicts so that everybody wins; presents training to teach parents how to avoid being a permissive parent, to listen so that kids will talk and talk so that kids will listen, to teach their children to "own" their problems and to solve them, and to use the "no-lose" method to resolve conflicts. PET provides immediate results: less fighting, fewer tantrums and lies, no need for punishment. This is described as an effective way to instill responsibility and create a nurturing family environment in which the child will thrive.

Patriarchy   A system or society where authority and power are vested in males.

Patrilineal   The custom of tracing kinship, descent, and inheritance through males.

Personalismo   Spanish word that describes the mindset that values human relationships over formal rules and regulations. Warmth and familiarity in a relationship are central to the establishment and maintaining of it.

Person-centered approach   Originated over 50 years ago by Dr. Carl R. Rogers, the theoretical basis for the person-centered approach (PCA) is that people have within themselves vast resources for and the natural tendency toward personal development and continual improvement. These resources are most quickly and effectively realized when people are facilitated by an expert PCA consultant whose way of being is congruent and empathetic, while maintaining unconditional positive regard.

Pew Hispanic Center   A project of the Pew Research Center, a nonpartisan "fact tank" that provides information on the issues, attitudes, and trends shaping America and the world; it is supported by the Pew Charitable Trusts.

Policulture   Being from or identifying with many cultures.

Policultural family   A family with members from many cultures or who identify with many cultures.

Postmodern   A philosophy that emphasizes the dialectical and narrative aspects of human experience. Postmodernism postulates that there are many beliefs, multiples realities, and a plethora of worldviews.

Power struggles   Struggles for control or power, often between parent and child or between siblings.

Prejudice   Either an antipathy or negative feeling, expressed or not expressed, based upon a faulty and inflexible generalization that places a group of people at some disadvantage.

Primo hermanos   A term used for cousins by Latinos.

Prototype   A standard or typical example; an original, full-scale, and usually working model of a new product or new version of an existing product.

Psychoeducational interventions   Interventions that are a specialized form of education aimed at helping people to learn about a broad range of emotional and behavioral difficulties, their effects, and strategies to deal with them.

Putting Family First   Program launched by Barbara Carlson and William Doherty (2002), based on the belief that "family relationships are the irreplaceable core of a full human life" and that soccer practice, violin lessons, and other extracurricular activities serve to overwhelm children and distance them from their loved ones. Reclaiming the family meal, where parents establish and lead rituals (e.g., discussion, prayer) instead of just eating as quickly as possible, allows everyone to reconnect. This, in turn, eases further reclaiming, for example, vacations and bedtimes.

¿Quién mató al comandante?   Translation: Who killed the commander?

Race   Social categorization of human beings based on geographic ancestry, color, and other physical attributes, as determined by the perceptions of the dominant group.

Racial identity development   The process of acquiring awareness and appreciation of one's own race and acceptance of the racial differences of others.

Racial profiling   The practice of targeting members of a particular racial or ethnic group for investigation or illegal behavior.

Racism   A system whereby a group maintains power and privileges by disadvantaging others or failing to recognize others based on race or ethnicity.

Rapid ejaculation   Usually called "premature ejaculation"; ejaculation that occurs immediately prior to or just after insertion of the penis into the partner, without any sense of voluntary control. It is a common sexual phenomenon, occurring in approximately one third of men under 25, and in about 10% of men older than 25. General causes of premature ejaculation include overstimulation, anxiety over sexual performance, and stress.

Rational emotive behavior therapy (REBT)   Developed by Albert Ellis, REBT is a brief, direct, and solution-oriented therapy that focuses on resolving specific problems facing a troubled individual. REBT is one form of cognitive behavior therapy. Fundamental to this therapy is the concept that emotions result solely from beliefs, not from the events that occur in life. Therefore, it is of utmost importance for beliefs to be healthy and rational because the consequences of these beliefs will be emotional growth and happiness. REBT is an educational process in which the therapist teaches the client how to identify irrational beliefs, dispute them, and replace them with rational ones; once the client is equipped with healthy beliefs, emotional difficulties and problematic behavior are abated.

Reality testing   Involves techniques used to adjust perceptions that do not conform to the realities of the situation.

Relational perspective   A framework for the social sciences that emphasizes the salience of interpersonal relationships for mental health and well-being.

Relationship contracting   Seeking to avoid or limit disputes by recognizing and developing convergent interests among the parties involved. Parties are encouraged to manage and resolve difficulties and conflicts proactively for their mutual success. These models have been very successfully applied in specific projects as well as in longer term strategic relationships; the most recognized examples of relationship contracting are partnering and alliancing.

Religion   Religion has a major influence in Latino families. They believe strongly in the importance of prayer and going to church. Latino families believe that sacrifice leads to salvation. As a result of their religious beliefs, they tend to consider problems or events as something is meant to be that cannot be changed (fate versus personal control over environment).

Resilience   The manifestation of the innate essence enacted through supported relationship and availability of and accessibility to resources that promote an ability to maintain or regain a level of control, intention, and direction before, during, or after an encounter with adversity.

Respect for family structure   A Latino expectation of counselors to understand the role of the elderly in the family and the role of the father; not making comments that make them look inferior to the other members of the family.

Respectful questioning   Inquiry performed in a manner showing or marked by proper respect.

Respeto   A Spanish word for respect.

Risk-taking ability   An important characteristic according to Peterson & Nisenholz (1999), defined as being able to challenge and at times confront.

Roman Catholic   Refers to Roman Catholicism, which is the largest religious denomination of Christianity with over one billion members; it claims that it is organizationally and doctrinally the original Christian Church, founded by Jesus Christ. The Roman Catholic Church is said to be the largest and the oldest continuously operating institution in existence. Latino culture often includes beliefs consistent with Roman Catholicism.

Ropaje   Translation: clothing.

Roundtable   A conference or discussion involving several participants who sit at a round table; consistent with Arthurian legend and the table at which King Arthur and his knights held court.

Safer Choices   Safer Choices is a sexuality education program for high-school students that promotes abstinence and, for sexually experienced teens, condom use. The program is designed to have classroom-level, school-level, family-level, and community-level components; an experimental evaluation found that participation in Safer Choices led to higher rates of condom usage in teens.

Salsa Translation: sauce; style of music of Caribbean origin.

Santeria Traditional syncretic religious practice that combines African, Indian and Roman Catholic religious rituals.

School-based counseling programs Programs designed to service students within schools; described as an effective way to capture the attention of youth that would be challenging to get into counseling.

Self-actualization interest and desire To possess an interest in and seek intrinsic growth.

Self-awareness The ability to perceive one's existence, including one's traits, feelings, and behaviors. In an epistemological sense, self-awareness is a personal understanding of the core of one's identity.

Self-denial and abnegation To deny oneself; text reference to the idealized role of the mother.

Self-disclose The practice of revealing information, often intimate details about oneself or one's life.

Self-in-relation The perspective of considering the individual person in the context of his or her relationships with others and with the environment

Self-instructional training Approach created by Meichenbaum (1977); a type of cognitive behavioral intervention used as an effective means of increasing independent work performance in preschoolers.

Self of the therapist Virginia Satir describes her invitation to therapists to work on their own unresolved issues in their training through various methods, such as family of origin, family reconstruction, ingredients of an interaction, and parts party. Her goal is to increase self-esteem, foster better choice making, increase responsibility, and facilitate personal congruence through a therapeutic process.

Self-possession Great coolness and composure under strain; full command of one's faculties, feelings, and behavior.

Sensate focus A series of specific exercises for couples that encourages each partner to take turns paying increased attention to his or her senses. These exercises were originally developed by Masters and Johnson to assist couples experiencing sexual problems, but can be used for variety and to heighten personal awareness with any couple.

Sex therapy techniques Therapy and related techniques to address the treatment of sexual dysfunction; techniques include Semans' technique, sensate focus therapy, and the squeeze technique.

Sexual aversion Typically classified as a subcategory of hypoactive sexual desire disorder (HSSD) and often confused with a lack of sexual desire.

Sexual compulsion Also *sexual obsession* or *sex/sexual addiction*; an overwhelming need and preoccupation with sex and the procurement of sex in spite of negative consequences.

Sexual desire discrepancy   One of the most common occurrences that lead couples to seek professional help. Sex counselors and therapists as well as marriage counselors frequently encounter couples with one partner less interested in sex than the other.

Sexual dissatisfaction   Also *sexual dysfunction*.

Sexual dysfunction   Also called *sexual problems* or *sexual malfunction*; defined as difficulty during any stage of the sexual act (which includes desire, arousal, orgasm, and resolution) that prevents the individual or couple from enjoying sexual activity.

Sexually transmitted diseases   Diseases that are commonly transmitted between partners through some form of sexual activity, most commonly vaginal intercourse, oral sex, or anal sex. They were commonly known as venereal diseases (VD) until some time around 1990, when public health officials introduced the new term in an effort to improve the clarity of their warnings to the public.

Si Dios quiere   Translation: if it is God's will; suggests a deference to or acceptance of a higher power to determine the outcome of life situations.

Sibling subsystem   Sibling subsystem is that of the children; boundary around the children in a family.

Simpatia   Translation: sympathy; emphasizes the expectation of individuals to avoid interpersonal conflict and to expect high frequencies of positive social behaviors; the importance of polite social relations that shun assertiveness, negative responses, and criticism. Educators need to be aware that Latinos may appear to agree with a message that they may not understand or intend to follow.

Sliding scale fees   Variable costs for services or products based on the buyer's ability to pay and the provider's ability to make a variable profit or have the cost subsidized by other means. The provider may wish to extend a service by reducing the cost to clients who otherwise may not be able to afford it and then charge a higher cost to a wealthy client.

Social bonds   Community or societal ties; considered significantly important in the Latino culture and should be understood, acknowledged, and respected by therapists.

Social constructionism   A school of thought introduced into sociology by Peter L. Berger and Thomas Luckmann with their 1966 book, *The Social Construction of Reality*. The interest of social constructionism is to discover the ways that individuals and groups create their perceived reality. As an approach, it involves looking at the ways in which social phenomena are created, institutionalized, and made into tradition by humans. The focus is on the description of the institutions, the actions, and so on—not on analyzing causes and effects.

Social constructivism   A theory that assumes that reality is a social construction.

Social mobility   The ability of a person or group to move upward or downward in status.

Social stratification systems   The complex social institutions that generate observed inequalities of this sort limit the possibility of discovering the full range of talent available in a society. This results from unequal access to appropriate motivation, channels of recruitment, and training centers.

Socialization   The process of learning and internalizing norms, attitudes, values, and beliefs of a given culture.

Socioeconomic status   An individual's or group's position within a hierarchical social structure. Socioeconomic status depends on a combination of variables, including occupation, education, income, wealth, and place of residence.

Spic Spanish   From *spic*, which is a derogatory term whether used as a noun or as an adjective; refers to the Spanish language.

Spirituality   In a broad sense, a concern with matters of the spirit; a wide term with many available readings. It may include belief in supernatural powers, as in religion, but the emphasis is on personal experience. For many Latinos, the interrelationship between spirituality and/or religion and cultural practices is extraordinarily close.

Stereotype   A generalized belief about a group that is used to distinguish that group from others and to interpret actions of that group's members. A cultural stereotype is the unsubstantiated assumption that all people of a certain group are alike.

Strength-based approach   Intended to enable the identification of the most successful strategies that families use to support children.

Structurally oriented therapist   Approach to therapy that is less active.

Sufrido   Translation: suffering; misery; defined as any unwanted condition and the corresponding negative emotion. It is usually associated with pain and unhappiness, but any condition can be suffering if it is unwanted.

Supervision   Management by overseeing the performance or operation of a person or group.

Support   Act or an instance of helping.

Surnames   Part of a person's name that indicates to what family he or she belongs.

Susto   Translation: soul loss; used by Latinos to describe a lost soul; the imagination of the separation of a person's soul from his body. The Western medical model refers to susto as a folk illness, specifically a "fright sickness" with strong psychological overtones. Those most likely to suffer from *susto* are culturally stressed adults—women more than men, though occasionally children suffer susto as well. Etiology generally includes a sudden frightening experience such as an accident, a fall, witnessing a relative's sudden death, or any other potentially dangerous event. Research will likely show that knowledge of the existence of susto is a major contributing factor in susceptibility to the "disease"; symptoms of susto are thought to include nervousness, anorexia, insomnia, listlessness, despondency, involuntary muscle tics, and diarrhea.

Systemic thinking　Embodies a worldview that implies that the foundation for understanding lies in interpreting interrelationships within systems; a simple technique for gaining deep insights into complex situations and information very quickly.

Systematic training for effective parenting (STEP)　Developed by Don Dinkmeyer, this is described as a democratic, practical parenting style to raise cooperative, responsible children. It is an easy, effective way for a therapist to help parents improve relationships in their families and is available in English and Spanish.

Task-oriented approach　Businesslike, structured; guidelines seek to change behaviors by making statements involving some or all of the following tasks: (1) setting of goals or constraints; (2) making decisions among alternatives; (3) sequencing and synchronization of actions; and (4) interpreting data.

***Tejano* culture**　The culture of people of Mexican heritage born and living in the U.S. state of Texas; Tejanos may variously consider themselves to be Hispanic, Mexican, Mexican American, mestizo, or (more rarely) Latino in ethnicity. Tejanos are often as hostile as or more hostile than Anglo Americans are to indigent Mexican American immigrants. However, in urban areas, Tejanos tend to be well integrated into Hispanic and Anglo American communities.

The Labyrinth of Solitude　A book written by Mexican writer Octavio Paz (1964); provides an examination of Mexico's history and mythology. Paz laments the loss of Mexican identity and sees that as due to the enormous number of influences that have affected the country, particularly its Indian and Spanish past and the pervasive presence of the United States.

Therapeutic alliance　Indicates the unconscious aspects of the cooperation between the patient and the therapist. What is important in establishing the alliance is not the therapist's theory or how empathetic the therapist thinks he is, but rather whether the patient thinks the therapist is present with or understands him.

Therapeutic working alliance　The product of the patient's and the therapist's conscious determination and ability to work together on the troublesome aspects of the patient's internal world, his relationships with others, and other aspects of his life. No successful therapy can take place without a working alliance equivalent to a working relationship in any team effort outside the therapeutic setting. A good working alliance requires the patient, together with the therapist, to be able to look at himself objectively; to do so, he must have sufficient trust in the therapist.

Tolerance of ambiguity　Capacity for or the practice of recognizing and respecting uncertainty.

Tolerance of intimacy　Capacity for or the practice of recognizing and respecting condition of being intimate.

Trabajo duro, lealtad, y fortaleza　Translation: hard work, loyalty, and fortitude.

Transactional analysis A psychoanalytic theory developed by psychiatrist Eric Berne, who identified three "ego states" that coexist in all people: parent, adult, and child states. He then considered how individuals interact with one another, and the ego states that were participating, ostensibly and actually, in each set of transactions.

Transcendence A process by which a person, family, group, or community reaches higher understanding of non-ordinary realities.

Transcultural universality Cultural change induced by introduction of elements of a foreign culture in an effort to become universal; text reference; suggests that certain factors, conditions, and therapist characteristics are important regardless of culture.

Transferential phenomenon How it is related to the client's past; text reference to resistance to therapy.

Transformation A marked change, as in appearance or character, usually for the better.

Transgressing the partner's limits To go beyond or overstep others; text reference to a partner.

Trusting relationship Signs of a trusting relationship include eye contact, facial expressions and body language, not twisting around the words that you say, friends and family members, developed by trust over time, think of you first/they put everything aside for you, respect who you are as a person and does not ignore you, good role models, tone of voice, accepting me for who I am (whether I have a label or not), people who respect my decisions and are positive around me.

Trustworthy Characteristic of counselor/family therapist desired by Latinos; warranting trust; reliable; capable of being depended upon.

Un abrazo Translation: a hug.

Una empleada Translation: an employee; represents another excruciating social injustice toward "service" people in some cultures.

Unconditional positive regard An essential core condition of person-centered theory that means that individuals are nonjudgmentally accepted regardless of their behavior.

Universalism Perspective affirming the fundamental similarities in human perception and experience and minimizing differences between people and groups.

Values A measure of those qualities that determine merit, desirability, usefulness, or importance; account; valuation; worth.

Verguenza Translation: guilt, indebtedness.

Viagra A drug used to treat male erectile dysfunction (impotence) developed by the pharmaceutical company Pfizer. The pills are blue with the words "Pfizer" on one side and "VGR xx" (xx = 25, 50, or 100 mg) on the other.

Victims of pervasive stereotyping Individuals who have been negatively affected by a conventional, formulaic, and oversimplified conception, opinion, or image.

Violence   General term to describe actions, usually deliberate, that cause or intend to cause injury to people, animals, or nonliving objects. Violence is often associated with aggression and is a significant problem among Latino youth.

Virgen de Guadalupe   Translation: Our Lady of Guadalupe (the Virgin Mary); defender of the poor and powerless in Latino culture. La Virgen's image and influence permeate Latin American culture.

Vocational exploration programs   Goals are to expose youth to various careers in order to excite interest; includes obtaining/improving basic skills, pre-employment skills, career direction, and work maturity.

Warmth   Friendliness, kindness, or affection.

Worldview   Conceptual framework from which to interpret and make sense of the world.

Xenophobia   An unreasonable fear or distrust of strangers, foreigners, or anything perceived as being different.

INDEX